AMERICANINDIANS
AMERICANPRESIDENTS

Bogy Johnson B

Falk de Smet

APACHE CHIEF JAMES A. GARFIELD

Father and governor
Neptune

EDITED BY

CLIFFORD E. TRAFZER

HARPER
An Imprint of HarperCollins*Publishers*

IN ASSOCIATION WITH THE NATIONAL MUSEUM
OF THE AMERICAN INDIAN, SMITHSONIAN INSTITUTION

AMERICANINDIANS
AMERICANPRESIDENTS

A HISTORY

Library of Congress Cataloging-in-Publication Data

American Indians/American presidents : a history / edited by Clifford E. Trafzer. — 1st ed.
    p. cm.
"In association with the National Museum of the American Indian, Smithsonian Institution."
Includes bibliographical references and index.
ISBN 978-0-06-146653-3
1. Indians of North America—Government relations. 2. Indian leadership—History. 3. Indians of North America—Politics and government. 4. Self-determination, National—History. 5. Presidents—United States—History. 6. Presidents—United States—Racial attitudes. I. Trafzer, Clifford E. II. National Museum of the American Indian (U.S.) III. Title.

E93.A458 2009
323.1197—dc22   2008046603

---

09 10 11 12 13 ID/QW 10 9 8 7 6 5 4 3 2 1

CONTENTS

INTRODUCTION

CLIFFORD E. TRAFZER

Mount Rushmore National Memorial, Black Hills, South Dakota. *Photo by Ed Menard, 2007. Courtesy National Park Service.*

In the heart of the United States, a great granite mountain stands majestically overlooking the western part of South Dakota and eastern Wyoming. Carved into Mount Rushmore are the faces of Presidents George Washington, Thomas Jefferson, Theodore Roosevelt, and Abraham Lincoln—symbols of the democratic political tradition that binds our nation together. Yet Mount Rushmore has always been more than a monument to great men and high ideals. For Lakota people, the mountain is known as the Six Grandfathers, and the surrounding Black Hills are called *Paha Sapa,* a sacred Native place revered since the beginning of time. Sanctified by stories, songs, and prayers, the Black Hills hold a special place in American Indian histories, connecting the past to the present and the spiritual world to the physical world. For many Native people, the Six Grandfathers are still alive with spirit and power. And the presidents' faces have never erased the understanding that Mount Rushmore lies in Indian Country—*Paha Sapa,* a gift to the Lakota from long ago.[1]

American presidents have loomed large in the lives of Native people since the founding of the United States. Many critical events in American Indian history—including the Lewis and Clark expedition, the Trail of Tears, the rise of Indian reservations, the appropriation of Indian lands, the Indian "New Deal," and increasing support for tribal self-determination since the 1970s—can be linked, in many ways, to the residents of 1600 Pennsylvania Avenue.

This volume reveals what America's presidents and Native people, particularly Indian leaders, have said and felt about one another, from the presidency of George Washington through the administration of George W. Bush and beyond. Books about the presidents' lives, leadership styles, policies, and peccadilloes abound, but far less is understood about Indian leaders, and less still is known about the historical relationship of Native leaders and the presidents. *American Indians/American Presidents* seeks to redress this imbalance. Written by six scholars of Native American history (four of whom are of Indian ancestry), the book shows how American Indians have advanced their own agenda for tribal self-determination for more than two hundred years, often in the face of adversity from the Oval Office.

The story of American presidents and Indian leaders sheds light on an important subject in Native American history, culture, and politics: sovereignty. That word means many things to many Native people, but at bottom, American Indian sovereignty encompasses a system and philosophy of self-rule, in which each Native nation is preeminent in its own affairs, maintaining its own rules, laws, boundaries, and responsibilities, just like any other independent, self-governing nation.[2]

Tribal sovereignty has been a source of contention between presidents and Native leaders throughout American history. But things did not start out that way. As the authors show, early American presidents viewed Native leaders as the rulers of sovereign nations, and established a tradition of nation-to-nation relations between the United States and powerful Indian tribes. In the nineteenth century, Native leaders continued to proclaim the sovereign status of their tribes, but as Native populations declined through war and disease, and the Supreme Court and Congress limited Indian power, American presidents increasingly downplayed, ignored, or undermined tribal governments and appropriated Indian homelands, eroding the bedrock of Indian sovereignty. By the 1970s, American presidents would come full circle, again recognizing Indian self-determination and championing the nation-to-nation relationship of the U.S. and tribal governments. The presidents' ever-changing attitudes toward Native sovereignty, as well as Indian leaders' steadfast defense of self-governance, is the main focus of this book.

NATIVE SOVEREIGNTY AND TRIBAL LEADERS

Tribal sovereignty emerged at the beginning of time, when natural forces set the world in motion. Those forces infused the earth and its

---

MOUNT RUSHMORE AND THE SIX GRANDFATHERS

Lakotas refer to it as the Six Grandfathers, a sacred place where their ancestors sought visions and held ceremonies. In 1885, non-Indians renamed it Mount Rushmore, after a New York attorney who was visiting the Black Hills of South Dakota on business. In 1923, local boosters promoted the idea of creating a tourist attraction, and a year later, the artist Gutzon Borglum was invited to consider sculpting a monument. The idea caught on, and in 1925, Congress created the Mount Rushmore National Memorial Commission.

President Calvin Coolidge liked the idea of sculpting the face of President George Washington, but he also wanted two Republicans and one Democrat included in the monument—Presidents Thomas Jefferson, Theodore Roosevelt, and Abraham Lincoln. Between 1927 and 1941, Borglum and four hundred workers blasted and removed 450,000 tons of rock, carving four gigantic heads measuring twenty-one feet from head to chin. (The nose on the face of George Washington is longer than the head of the Great Sphinx at Giza, Egypt!) Behind the carved faces is the Hall of Records, a little-known vault containing sixteen panels inscribed with the texts of the Declaration of Independence, the United States Constitution, and biographical sketches of the four presidents.

In 1991, President George H. W. Bush dedicated the Mount Rushmore National Memorial, a world-renowned symbol of American freedom, which hosts almost three million visitors a year. For many Native Americans, however, Mount Rushmore holds negative associations. "A lot of Indian people look at Mt. Rushmore as a symbol of what white people did to this country when they arrived—took the land from the Indians and desecrated it," observed Mount Rushmore Park Superintendent Gerard Baker (Mandan-Hidatsa). Baker, who was appointed park superintendent in 1994, contends that "there's a huge need for Anglo-Americans to understand the Black Hills before the arrival of the white men."

If bigger is better in the world of monuments, then Native Americans may yet claim title to the most monumental. Just fifteen miles from Mount Rushmore, workers are carving the Crazy Horse Memorial, a 563-foot-tall sculpture of the Native leader who defeated Lieutenant Colonel George A. Custer at the Battle of the Little Bighorn. The idea for the granite sculpture was conceived in the late 1930s by Chief Henry Standing Bear, who invited the Boston sculptor Korczak Ziolkowski to design it. When finished, the monument will dwarf Mount Rushmore: the heads of all four presidents will fit inside Crazy Horse's eighty-seven-foot-tall head.[3]

original people with an aboriginal sovereignty—a spirit, philosophy, law, and guiding principle that continues to live within the people and their lands.

This ancient, aboriginal sovereignty is known to contemporary Native people through stories, songs, ceremonies, and rituals, which tribal elders have always shared with children through oral traditions. The sacred narratives establish the place of human beings in relation to the universe. They explain the sovereign being, laws, and duties of Native people, tribes, leaders, and nations.[4] Native American leaders know tribal sovereignty because they carry the blood memory of their people and sacred lands. It is a sovereignty that connects contemporary leaders to their past, that charges Indian leaders—both past and present—with responsibility for caring for their people, protecting their lands, and looking to the future for the benefit of unborn generations.

Sovereignty resonated deeply among tribal leaders, who represented their people in relations with other tribes, European colonial powers, and, after the American Revolution, the United States. Americans know these leaders as "chiefs," a word that tends to homogenize a remarkably diverse group of men and women who received their leadership positions in many ways. Some tribes had leadership families, from which people emerged into positions of influence based on familial connections. Hinmatoweyalaket (Chief Joseph, 1841–1904) originally became a civilian leader because his father had led the Wallowa Band of Nimipu (Nez Perce). Chief Joseph retained his position because he proved himself a strong, competent, and able leader who spoke forcefully on behalf of his people. His brother, Ollokot, became a noted war chief because of his exploits on the battlefield. Other Native leaders, such as Tecumseh, Black Hawk, Cochise, and Crazy Horse, came to prominence in the same way.

Many leaders emerged as a result of experience or personal ability.[5] Medicine people frequently became leaders because of their ability to access power and use it for healing. Kenneth Coosewoon (Comanche), Jim Henson (Cherokee), Sam Fisher (Palouse), Andrew George (Nez Perce/Palouse), Ruby Modesto (Cahuilla), Pedro Chino (Cahuilla), Croslin Smith (Cherokee), Beverly Patchell (Cherokee/Creek), and Joe Patencio (Cahuilla) all earned their positions as medicine people through their ability to heal.[6]

In the eighteenth century, Native American leaders such as the Mahican-Mohawk chief Tee-Yee-Neen-Ho-Ga-Row, or Hendrick (ca. 1680–1755), traveled to the heart of the British Empire to conduct diplomatic relations with the Crown. In 1710, Hendrick led a four-man delegation to London to appeal for arms and supplies, which would bolster the Indians' power to defend Britain's North American colonies from French Canada. Enmeshed in a constant war for North America, Britain hoped to ensure the allegiance of its Native allies, and welcomed the "Four Indian Kings" in grand fashion. During their five-week stay in London, the visitors met with Queen Anne; dined with William Penn, founder and proprietor of Pennsylvania; and held talks with representatives of the British Board of Trade, the Hudson's Bay Company, and the Society for the Propagation of the Gospel. Before long, they had become celebrities. Their speech to the queen was widely circulated, inspiring a bevy of ballads, books, and broadsides. The Dutch artist John Verelst painted their portraits, including one of Hendrick, shown here, dressed as a European nobleman holding a wampum belt. The four were wined and dined at the estate of the Duke of Ormond, rode aboard the royal yacht, watched a production of *Macbeth*, and toured Hampton Court, Windsor Castle, and the Woolwich dockyards. When they boarded the HMS *Dragon* for their return voyage, the delegates lugged a treasure trove of British goods,

Tee-Yee-Neen-Ho-Ga-Row, or Hendrick, by John Verelst (ca. 1648–1734). Oil on canvas, 1710. *Courtesy Library and Archives of Canada/C-092415.*

including clothing, necklaces, looking glasses, tobacco boxes, pistols, swords, and other gifts befitting the leaders of eighteenth-century sovereign nations.[7] ◄

Other Native American leaders held dual positions as medicine leaders and civilian leaders, or as war leaders and civilian leaders. Main Poc, the Potawatomi *wabeno* (fire handler, or medicine man), was a noted war chief who fought beside Tecumseh during the War of 1812, but he also had medicine power. In the early twentieth century, William Mike, a Chemehuevi leader from Southern California, served as a village chief and Indian doctor. And Pakuma, or Santos Manuel, led the Serrano people of Southern California as a village leader and Native healer in the late nineteenth and early twentieth centuries.

During the twentieth century, Martha Manuel Chacon, a direct descendant of Santos Manuel, rose to prominence as a leader of the Serranos. Chacon became a spokesperson of her people and protector of the ceremonial house on her reservation. Still other Native American leaders, such as Smohalla, the Wanapum *yanchta*

CHIEFLY DECISIONS: THE BURDEN OF LEADERSHIP

American Indian leaders have always faced difficult decisions. The American Revolution, westward expansion, the rise of Indian reservations, the division of tribal lands, assimilation, and efforts to "terminate" the government's trust relationship with Native tribes in the 1950s and early 1960s—these and many other issues and events required Native leaders to make decisions that affected the fate of their people.

American Indian leaders made decisions in a number of ways. Like all leaders, chiefs were sometimes required to act immediately, drawing on their experience and knowledge to make spur-of-the-moment decisions. Typically, leaders had more time to consider tribal problems, and asked for help to solve them. Among some tribes, leaders could draw on the knowledge of elders or on the expertise of people who had special experience in war, negotiations, and healing. By listening to these prominent individuals, chiefs gathered knowledge, gauged tribal opinion, and then made decisions that could influence an individual, a family, a clan, a village, a band, or an entire tribe.

Chiefs often conferred with other leaders, both inter- and intratribally, especially those with particular expertise, in order to make wise decisions. Among the Haudenosaunee (Iroquois Six Nations), leaders of one nation could call a council of the other leaders of the Iroquois nations to help determine a course of action. Among the Serrano Indians of Southern California, a *kika* could ask men and women to gather in the Big House to discuss a particular issue, solicit advice, or come to a consensus about a problem facing the tribe. Women often had a say in policy decisions, although non-Native recorders of events often ignored these important consultations.

Native Americans sometimes took a democratic approach to issues and decisions, drawing on the voices of many before following a certain path. But many American Indian leaders would have agreed with President Harry Truman that, in the end, the president had to make the final decision. And so it was among the tribes. Leaders had to make the final decision. They did their best, determining what was in the interest of the people, choosing paths for the good of the whole, not just the few.

(preacher), combined the position of village and spiritual leader. Smohalla lived on the Columbia Plateau during the mid-nineteenth century and led his people in a religious revitalization movement of the Washani faith, an ancient religion that became formalized in the 1850s with divine teachings and ritualistic worship.[8]

Men typically led in the realms of politics, war, and hunting, but tribal leadership, as Martha Manuel Chacon's experience suggests, was by no means a male-only sphere. In many Native American communities before European contact, women held influential positions as clan leaders, scientists, doctors, artists, musicians, educators, historians, farmers, healers, and heads of families. They cared for their communities in numerous ways, keeping family histories, serving as birthing doctors, tending family gardens, teaching languages, leading expeditions to gathering areas, providing plant medicines, and caring for the infirm. Generally, women played important roles within families and often had a say in the decisions that affected families, tribes, bands, and villages.[9]

They still do. Among Iroquoian people, women lead the clans and select the chiefs. Contemporary Onondaga chief Oren Lyons often tells audiences that he holds a "temporary" position of leadership as a spokesman of his people. He serves at the will of women, and he is on a temporary appointment as long as the clan mothers approve of his leadership.[10] Within their communities, American Indians well knew women leaders of singular ability—women who would be discounted by, or invisible to, non-Natives, including presidents of the United States.

Face-to-face meetings with the president were often short and unsatisfying for Native leaders who visited the White House, and this was particularly true for Native women. American presidents, like most non-Natives, were typically unaware of the status of women in Native communities and often failed to extend diplomatic protocols to women. During the Civil War, for example, President Abraham Lincoln entertained delegations from Indian Territory (modern-day Oklahoma), including leaders representing the Arapaho, Caddo, Kiowa, Comanche, and Kiowa-Apache peoples. Although Lincoln's assistants introduced each of the male leaders to the president, they failed to introduce two Kiowa women who accompanied the delega-

Ruth Muskrat (Cherokee) presenting President Calvin Coolidge with a copy of *The Red Man in the United States,* with Reverend Sherman Coolidge (Arapaho) looking on, 1923. A graduate of Mount Holyoke College, Muskrat (1897–1982) was a lifelong Indian activist who embraced education as a way of training a new generation of Indian leaders. Rejecting calls for Indians to choose between Native identity and American citizenship, she became active in the newly formed National Congress of American Indians (NCAI), serving as executive secretary from 1946 to 1949. *Courtesy Library of Congress, LC-USZ62-107775.*

tion. When Lincoln finally noticed them, he shook their hands and said a few words, but made no effort to use an interpreter to engage them in conversation. "Those girls will go home highly elated by the honor thus unexpectedly conferred upon them," one observer noted, "and will probably boast all their days that they shook hands with the great chief of the palefaces."[11] It is more likely that the two discussed the day's events with other Kiowa attending the meeting, wondering if the delegation had accomplished anything positive for the benefit of their people.

PRESIDENTS AND NATIVE DIPLOMACY

When Europeans began to colonize North America, they found a continent populated by sovereign Indian tribes and governed by leaders who practiced distinct protocols of diplomacy. To acquire lands and establish peace, representatives of England, France, and

Spain entered into treaties with tribal leaders and governments. After the American Revolution, the new U.S. government adopted the tradition of government-to-government relations with sovereign Native nations. Under the Constitution, Congress—rather than the states—was given the power to conduct Indian affairs, and the president was given authority to make treaties, with the advice and consent of the Senate. Since the new nation conducted Indian affairs through treaties, American presidents would play an important role in dealing with Native nations.

Early American presidents often dealt directly with Indian leaders. The small size of the United States, the power of Native tribes, and the prominence of Indians in the everyday lives of early Americans made this possible. As the new government sought to acquire Indian lands and resources through treaties, executive orders, and war, presidents negotiated directly with Native American leaders or sent their representatives to negotiate on their behalf. Agents of the presidents—including William Henry Harrison, Andrew Jackson, and Ulysses S. Grant, each of whom would later occupy the White House—engaged Indian leaders through negotiation and war in Indian Country.

George Washington set many precedents that established the principles and protocols of diplomacy between the United States and Indian nations. The first president invited and entertained American Indian leaders in Philadelphia, New York, and Mount Vernon, including Seneca chief Cornplanter and Mohawk chief Joseph Brant, who visited the president without appointments or ceremony. In so doing, Washington hoped to repair relations between the United States and the Iroquois tribes that had supported Britain during the American Revolution. In an address to the "sachems and Warriors of the Five Nations," Washington said he wished to "remove all causes of discontent" and "cement the peace between the United States and you" so the two peoples could be "brothers."[12] He asked Indian leaders to "forget the misunderstandings of past times. Let us now look forward, and devise measures to render our friendship perpetual." Declaring that the United States would "require no lands but those obtained by treaties, which we consider as fairly made," Washington assured the Iroquois that the Indians of the Ohio Country were

WAMPUM AND TREATIES: SYMBOLS OF ACCORD

Before Europeans arrived in the Western Hemisphere, American Indians made agreements with other tribes, marking the event on wampum belts, hides, wood, and other materials. After Contact, Native Americans made treaties with European nations, which colonial representatives recorded in writing. In 1765, Sir William Johnson, Great Britain's Superintendent for Indian Affairs in the Northern Department of North America, signed the treaty shown here with the Delaware, Shawnee, and Mingo (Ohio Valley Iroquois). The signatures of the Delaware chiefs Agassqua, Weeweenoagh-wah, and Tedabaghsika appear in the first row. (Note the pictographs next to each name.) The signatures of the Shawnee and Mingo chiefs appear in the middle and bottom row, respectively. [13]

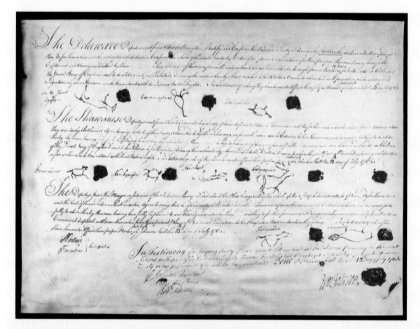

Treaty of Peace of the Delaware Nation. *National Museum of the American Indian, P11421.*

Western Chippewa wampum belt, 1807. Shells were used to make the wampum belt shown here, said to have commemorated the visit of an Ojibwe chief to Great Britain's King George III. [13] *Photo by Walter Larrimore. National Museum of the American Indian, 1/4004.*

"misinformed" about American intentions "to wrest their lands from them." To demonstrate his sincerity, Washington gave the chiefs a white wampum belt.[14]

Seneca leader Red Jacket responded to Washington, saying that the president had correctly addressed the chiefs as "free men" who "might speak with freedom." He told the Americans the only way "two brothers speak freely" was if the brothers "are upon equal ground."[15] After six weeks of discussion, Washington gave Red Jacket a large silver medal, depicting the general presenting a pipe to a chief. In the background, a white man appeared, plowing his fields with a yoke of oxen. On the other side was an eagle's image, with the words "E Pluribus Unum." For years, Red Jacket wore the medal with pride.[16]

While Red Jacket, Cornplanter, Muskogee chief Alexander Mc-Gillivray, Mohican chief Hendrick, and others crafted a positive relationship with Washington, Joseph Brant found little to trust in the president. In 1792, Brant told the Lenape (Delaware) of Ohio that he had seen Washington's "heart and bowels," and if the Delawares believed the president, "you will be greatly deceived."[17] Washington had asked Chief Hendrick to take a four-foot-long wampum belt with fifteen square symbols to the Delaware as an act of friendship. Brant countered by sending a messenger to the Delaware. Do not trust Washington, Brant warned them. The president might proclaim peace, Brant declared, but he coveted the Ohio Country, home to the Delaware, Wyandot, Shawnee, Ojibwe, and Miami Indians.[18]

Brant was correct. Though Washington desired a "firm peace" with Native nations, based "upon the principles of justice and humanity, as upon an immovable rock," the president also desired lands for the new nation and its burgeoning population.[19] Rather than take Indian lands by force—a problematic proposition for the cash-strapped and war-weary new nation—Washington advocated a peaceful, pragmatic, and cost-effective solution. By negotiating treaties with Indian tribes, the United States could liquidate Indian title to land, open new territories to white settlement, and keep the peace with sovereign Indian nations. Written treaties became the foundation of United States Indian policy. Between 1778 and 1868, the United States ratified some three hundred and seventy-seven

INDIN PEACE MEDALS

Every presidential administration from George Washington's to Benjamin Harrison's presented peace medals to Indian leaders, often during visits to Washington, D.C., and at treaty-signing ceremonies in Indian Country. Engraved on the front with the likeness of the president, early U.S. peace medals featured the image of two clasped hands, a symbol of unity and accord. Peace medals were worn proudly by Native leaders, who viewed them as emblems of the nation-to-nation relationship that existed between their tribe and the United States. The value Native leaders attached to peace medals is reflected in the words of the Potawatomi chief New Corn: "I hope, after our treaty [the Treaty of Greenville, 1795], you will exchange our old medals, and supply us with General Washington's. My young men will no longer listen to the former; they wish for the latter. They have thrown off the British, and henceforth will view the Americans as their only true friends."

The presentation of peace medals waned during the Gilded Age, reflecting the diminished population and status of Indian tribes and the end, in 1871, of treaty-making with Indians entirely. By the 1880s, peace medals had lost much of their original meaning, and the practice of distributing them to Indians fell into further decline.[20] ◣

George Washington peace medal. Silver, with engraved decoration, 1793. *Courtesy National Portrait Gallery, Smithsonian Institution; gift of Betty A. and Lloyd G. Schermer; NPG.99.107.*

treaties with Indian tribes.[21] The government intended the documents, which today can be found stored in tribal offices and the National Archives, to establish peace, acquire Indian resources, ensure Indian allegiance to the United States and to "no other sovereign," and achieve other outcomes.[22] But the government primarily used treaties to acquire Indian lands for American expansion.

Some suggest that George Washington and other early presidents believed that treaties granted Indians the right to occupy, but not to own, their lands. Perhaps so. But Native leaders never conceived of land in this way. Indian leaders understood that treaties confirmed their sovereignty and recognized Native ownership of specific lands. They well understood the concept of land ownership, defined within the languages of the people in many ways, but the idea of tribal "ownership" and "control" of land and resources also existed among the tribes. Many leaders agreed to treaties to secure for themselves a small portion of their traditional lands and to preserve their people and sovereignty. And many Indian leaders, past and present, have spent enormous amounts of time, energy, and blood fighting wars, lobbying Congress, filing lawsuits, and meeting with the presidents to defend their homelands and treaty rights.[23]

Tse-wa-án-ye (Antonio al Churleta), governor of San Juan Pueblo, holding a cane given by President Abraham Lincoln, 1877. Thirteen years before this photo was taken, Lincoln had sent silver-headed canes to each of the nineteen governors of the Rio Grande Pueblos. Each stick was inscribed with the name of the pueblo, the year, and the words "A. Lincoln." Canes were traditional emblems of Spanish colonial justice, and the tradition of presenting to the governors was continued when the United States extended jurisdiction over the Pueblos after the war with Mexico. The Lincoln canes were passed down from governor to governor, and remain cherished emblems of Pueblo sovereignty to this day.

Early presidents not only viewed Native nations as sovereign bodies, but also acknowledged the stature of Native American leaders. Gifts given by presidents to Native leaders, and vice versa, became a staple of United States–Indian relations. Rooted in Native tradition and colonial practice, the giving of gifts provided symbolic acts of respect and friendship, no matter how short-lived the friendship. Government officials gave Indian leaders medals, flags, wampum belts, canes, and guns—many of which are extant today within American Indian communities.[24]

Native American leaders gave presidents items that were valued in Indian communities, including tobacco, weapons, moccasins, feathered headdresses, animal skins, textiles, baskets, pottery, and prayer sticks.[25] During the gift giving, leaders also shared speeches. Historical speeches often cast Native Americans and their leaders as "children" and presidents as the "Great Father," but there is no question that American Indian leaders negotiated as men, just as did the presidents. Native American leaders may have even allowed Americans to cast them as children because it proved beneficial to Indian people, creating relationships and attracting infusions of foreign aid to Native communities.[26] Whatever their reasons for accommodating—and even appropriating—the language of paternalism, Native American leaders perceived themselves as equals of the presidents, worthy of being treated in an elevated and dignified manner.

PRESIDENTS AND INDIAN LANDS

Throughout the nineteenth century, American presidents pressured Indian tribes to surrender land and assimilate into white society. President Thomas Jefferson believed Native Americans had the capacity to move from "savagery to civilization" if only they would abandon hunting and adopt farming. As independent farmers cultivating their own property, American Indians, Jefferson believed, would enjoy fuller and richer lives, using less labor and less land.[27] Jefferson also believed that assimilation was for their "greatest good." Although he admired American Indian character, language, and artifacts, he viewed American Indians as noble but doomed savages who could not survive the juggernaut of white civilization. For Jefferson, Indians had two choices: They could either assimilate into white society as yeoman farmers or remove themselves to the "Great American Desert" west of the Mississippi River.[28]

Jefferson's understanding of Native life was flawed, and his motives, as the historian Reginald Horsman has observed, "were not entirely altruistic."[29] The nation's third president conveniently neglected to acknowledge that Indians had been farming their homelands, from Virginia to Mississippi and from Florida to Michigan, for generations. Instead, he typecast Native people as hunters who should adopt agriculture or quit their eastern homelands and move beyond the Mississippi.

Jefferson also neglected to mention that whites would be the principal beneficiaries of Native assimilation—that the Indians' former hunting grounds would almost certainly fall into white hands, once Natives abandoned the chase. And by raising the specter of removal,

Pipe tomahawk, ca. 1812.
This pipe tomahawk was given to the Shawnee leader Tecumseh by British Colonel Henry Proctor, commander of Fort Malden on the east bank of the Detroit River, headquarters of British land forces during the War of 1812. *Photo by R. A. Whiteside. National Museum of the American Indian, 17/6249.*

by making the issue fit for public discussion, Jefferson set the United States on a path that led to the forced eviction of Indians from the East during the administration of President Andrew Jackson. In the end, according to the noted anthropologist Anthony F. C. Wallace, Thomas Jefferson should properly be remembered as a "planner of cultural genocide, the architect of [Indian] removal policy, and the surveyor of the Trail of Tears."[30]

By the administrations of James Monroe and John Quincy Adams, the United States had established policies that would lead to the dispossession of nearly all American Indian lands east of the Mississippi River. As Donna Akers (Choctaw) demonstrates in chapter two, Native American men, women, and children fought removal using many strategies, including moving themselves away from settlers, negotiating, acculturating into white society, establishing formal governments, and engaging in warfare. Some Native American leaders, including Tecumseh (Shawnee) and Black Hawk (Sac and Fox), fought the United States. Other leaders, such as Pushmataha (Choctaw), John Ross (Cherokee), and William Walker (Wyandot), chose paths of peace. Each leader believed their strategy to be the best means of dealing with the American presidents while protecting their people and their sovereignty.

In the early nineteenth century, Native American leaders in the eastern part of the United States complained of encroachment, theft, and exploitation of their lands, either directly to Presidents James Monroe, John Quincy Adams, and Andrew Jackson, or to their representatives. By the 1820s, it was no secret that the United States hoped to remove the eastern tribes beyond the Mississippi River. To hasten the process, state and federal officials did little to keep settlers from trespassing on Cherokee, Choctaw, Seminole, Muscogee, Chickasaw, Delaware, Potawatomi, Wyandot, and Ojibwe lands. Presidents could have committed the United States Army to protect Indian lands and sovereignty, but they typically turned a blind eye and failed to honor treaties, which obligated the United States to keep trespassers off Indian lands. By failing to honor past treaties and prevent settlers from taking Indian lands, presidents enabled settlers to violate treaties, steal lands, ignite conflicts, and effectuate the forced removal of thousands of Native Americans.[31]

The election of Andrew Jackson in 1828 spelled doom for the eastern tribes. Jackson had favored Indian removal for years and had tried to coerce tribes to surrender their lands and move west to Indian Territory. Removal was in the Indians' best interest, Jackson opined, because white settlers had destroyed "the resources of the savage" and thereby doomed the tribes "to weakness and decay, the fate of the Mohegan, the Narragansett, and the Delaware." This trend, he argued, was "fast overtaking the Choctaw, the Cherokee, and the Creeks." As a result, he said, "Humanity and national honor demand that every effort should be made to avert so great a calamity."

To "avert calamity," Jackson opted for Indian removal rather than treaty enforcement.[32] In a letter to the Muscogee (Creek) people of Alabama, Jackson urged the tribe to move west where they could escape their troubles with land-hungry white settlers and coercive state laws. In the West, Jackson said, the Creeks would enjoy "peace and plenty" on their own lands for "as long as the grass grows or the water runs."[33] This phrase has become a hallmark of American history, repeated in many forms for nearly two hundred years.

Jackson did not deceive the astute Muscogee leaders Opothleyoholo, Jim Boy, and others who pointed to the 1826 Treaty of Washington, which "guaranteed to the Creek Nation forever all the lands we now hold. . . . All we want, we expect, and all we desire is the complete fulfillment of that Treaty." Creek leaders reminded the president, "Our country has and is still annoyed by the appearance of white men under the garb and character of agents, sub-agents, etc., persuading, bribing, and by all the arts of deception endeavor[ing] to get our people to go to that unhospitable [sic] clime, near the borders of the Rocky Mountains." Like many other tribes, the Muscogees took their case to Congress—knowing that President Jackson would not support their cause. Creek leaders pointed out the "unprecedented attack upon liberties" of the Creek Nation "in gross violation" of treaties. They asked "to be left, where your treaties have left us, in enjoyment of rights as a separate people, and to be treated as unoffending, peaceable inhabitants of our own, and not a borrowed country."[34]

Native American leaders from all Indian nations in the eastern part of the United States made similar pleas. But, in the end,

Congress passed the Removal Act of 1830 and began the process of forced removal, despite a Supreme Court decision (*Worcester v. Georgia*) that recognized the relationship of the United States with Indian Nations.[35] Indian removal proved devastating for thousands of Indian people and their leaders. Removal uprooted Native Americans from their homes, killed thousands, and resulted in disease, death, and violence within the new nations west of the Mississippi River.

Removal significantly split Indian leaders among many eastern tribes: Some Native American leaders refused to sign removal agreements, while others acquiesced to pressure, violence, and bribes. Some Native American leaders agreed to removal because they felt it was the only way to save their nations, protect their people, and survive to fight again. Other Indian leaders took families and friends into hiding, or moved nearby in the hope that they could someday return to a portion of their traditional homeland. The decision to sign removal treaties cost some Native American leaders their lives, and the splits that occurred among Indian leaders during the 1830s and 1840s survive today. More important, decisions made by President Andrew Jackson, congressmen, Supreme Court justices, and tribal leaders still affect the lives of contemporary citizens of Indian nations.

Native American leaders worked diligently to reestablish new nations in Indian Territory, but the Civil War stymied their efforts. Some members of Native nations in Indian Territory sided with the Union, while others sided with the Confederacy. In 1862, the Cherokee Nation elected Stand Watie as principal chief. A pro-Southern leader, Watie served as a Confederate general during the Civil War. Concerned for the fate of his nation, Cherokee principal chief John Ross met with President Lincoln to assure the president that most Cherokees remained loyal to the United States and had only sided with the Confederacy "under duress." Ross met with Lincoln several times, but to no avail. At war's end, the United States punished the Cherokees and other Indian nations by having them sign Reconstruction treaties that greatly reduced Indian lands and forced Indians from Kansas into Indian Territory. President Andrew Johnson believed that the tribes had forfeited their rights under past treaties

A Southern Plains delegation posing in the White House Conservatory, March 27, 1863. The delegation of Comanches, Kiowas, Cheyennes, Arapahos, Caddos, and Apaches included (front row from left), War Bonnet, Standing in the Water, Lean Bear (Cheyenne), and Yellow Knife (Kiowa). Standing, at left, is William Simpson Smith, an interpreter, and Samuel G. Colley, an Indian agent. The identities of the white women and the Native delegates in the second row are unknown. Eighteen months later, the four men in the front row were dead: Yellow Wolf died of pneumonia, War Bonnet and Standing in the Water were killed in the Sand Creek Massacre, and Lean Bear was killed by soldiers. *Courtesy Library of Congress, LC-USZ62-11880.*

and had to be punished. He was "willing to grant them peace, but wants land for other Indians, and a civil government for the whole Territory."[36] Thus, during the Civil War and Reconstruction, the United States took more Indian lands and relocated Indians onto an ever-shrinking land base.

Despite the erosion of the Native estate, Presidents Abraham Lincoln and Andrew Johnson could not diminish the innate tribal sovereignty that was and is the foundation of all Native nations.

During Lincoln's presidency, American Indian leaders continued to remind the president that they did not view themselves as subordinates. When Cheyenne chief Lean Bear met President Lincoln in 1863, he recognized Lincoln as "the Great Chief of the White People," but also reminded him, "I am the Great Chief of the Indians." He told Lincoln that the Cheyenne wished to live in peace with white people, but he worried that this could not be, because white people had invaded Cheyenne Country and threatened the security of his people.[37] Like so many Native leaders, Lean Bear knew the United States sought to claim hegemony over Indian tribes, force them onto a smaller land base, and dictate policies related to them.

Lean Bear had only to look to Minnesota to see the bitter fruit of American Indian policy. In 1862, the Dakota chief Little Crow led his people in a violent protest against the starvation they were suffering at the hands of corrupt Indian agents. The people of Minnesota asked the Army to "exterminate the wild beasts," and a military court condemned 303 Dakota Indians to death by hanging. After reviewing the cases, Lincoln allowed the Army to hang thirty-eight of these convicted warriors in the largest mass execution in the history of the United States.[38]

The Dakota uprising was an extraordinary event that focused Lincoln's attention on the problems of Native America. The president's preoccupation with the Civil War, however, offered him little time to focus on American Indian affairs. That was not the case for one of his generals, Ulysses S. Grant, who, as president, took pleasure

A THANK-YOU CARD, INDIAN-STYLE

In 1873, President Grant and his wife, Julia, sent gifts of pipes and shawls to Crow delegates visiting the nation's capital. When the gifts arrived, Blackfoot, a Crow delegate, showed his appreciation by dictating a thank-you note: "I can't smoke Larb in the Pipe you sent me but its nice and I will keep it all the same. Tell your squaw that our squaws are pleased with the shawls and their little girls will wear them in the first dance, they are nice and warm."[39]

in serving as the "Great Father" to several Indian groups that visited Washington, D.C. Talking, smoking, and sharing gifts with tribal leaders, Grant sought to establish a new day in American Indian affairs. In an effort to lessen the violence between Native Americans and frontier settlers, President Grant inaugurated a "peace policy" that favored the establishment of reservations administered by Christian ministers as Indian agents. This approach, Grant believed, would save lives and money and provide greater success in dealing with Indian leaders.

AMERICAN PRESIDENTS AND INDIAN POLICY, 1870–1970

Throughout the nineteenth century, hundreds of Native leaders came to Washington, D.C., to meet with presidents and other government officials. During these visits, officials wined and dined their visitors at the White House and arranged tours of the nation's capital to impress tribal leaders with the power of the United States and the benefits of "civilized" life. Some Native leaders had their portraits painted, and many delegates sat for group photographs, some of which are reproduced in this volume.

After Grant's administration, American presidents took less interest in playing the "Great Father." Native nations had grown smaller and less powerful than they had been during George Washington's time, and during the Gilded Age, American Indian policy competed for the president's time and attention with immigration, labor unrest, civil-service reform, tariff reform, and other pressing national issues. In addition, presidents viewed Indians as a vanishing people who would soon be only a memory. During his administration, President Rutherford B. Hayes began to limit the number of Native delegations visiting the White House, and his attention to Indian problems diminished greatly.[40]

After the 1880s, most presidents encouraged their secretary of the interior or commissioner of Indian affairs to deal directly with Native American leaders. This was the diplomatic state of affairs that Chief Harlish Washomake (Wolf Necklace), a Palouse Indian from the Columbia Plateau, encountered when he visited Washington in 1893.[41] After the Palouse fought the United States during the Plateau Indian War of 1855–58 and the Nez Perce War of 1877, Wolf's

family refused to move to the Yakima or Umatilla Indian reservations. Instead, Wolf's people lived free on their former homelands, raising thousands of horses of high quality. As white settlers moved into the area, they claimed the chief's grazing areas and demanded that Wolf control his horses. Some settlers wanted Wolf to move to a reservation in the Northwest, but Wolf remained free. Realizing he needed more land than his quarter section from an Indian homestead, Wolf decided to buy more land for his horse ranch. To do this, he needed the support of the Indian Office, because he was not a citizen of the United States.[42]

In 1893, Wolf and his interpreter, Charley Ike, traveled by railroad to meet President Grover Cleveland at the White House. Being

A Yankton Sioux delegation outside the United States Capitol, Washington, 1905.
Indian passengers include (from left), Yellow Thunder, Black Thunder, Charging Bear,
Hollow Horn, Eagle Track, and Shooting Hawk. *Photo by Karl H. Claudy. Courtesy
Smithsonian Institution.*

a practical man, Wolf felt this was the most efficient way to resolve his issues. Much to his chagrin, however, neither the president nor the commissioner of Indian affairs would meet with him. The commissioner left Wolf a note that his case would be "held in status quo until the department could perfect a necessary inquiry into the case." This never happened, and Wolf returned home to face additional problems from the tax assessor of Franklin County, who ordered the sheriff to round up and sell Wolf's livestock in payment for back taxes—even though Wolf was not a citizen. In frustration, the Indian leader sold nearly two thousand horses and moved to the Umatilla Indian Reservation, where his descendants live today.[43]

Wolf's experience was not unusual. For more than two hundred years, presidents of the United States met few American Indian leaders face-to-face. Yet, as Matthew Sakiestewa Gilbert (Hopi) shows in chapter three, Native American leaders from 1880 to 1930 continued to view themselves as equal to the leaders of the United States, traveling great distances to the nation's capital to visit presidents, commissioners, and congressmen. In Washington, they addressed long-standing Indian grievances, including removal, resources, reservations, land theft, and government assimilation policies. After 1887, tribal leaders would face a new problem.

ALLOTMENT

Under the Dawes Act of 1887, Congress demanded the division of reservation lands into individual allotments, or small parcels, for distribution to individual tribal members. The government opened "excess" lands, which were not allotted to Indians, to white settlement. The plan found support among a wide variety of Americans, including presidents, Indian reformers, oilmen, land speculators, and white farmers. By dividing tribal reservation lands into small parcels for individual Indians, reformers believed that allotment would imbue Native people with respect for private—rather than tribal—property, and help Indians assimilate into mainstream American culture. For white homesteaders, the breakup of the tribal estate opened new lands for settlement and exploitation. For presidents and policymakers, allotment struck at the roots of

Hinmatoweyalaket, or Chief Joseph (Nez Perce), with Fanny Ward and Major Shore, Washington, 1889. *National Museum of the American Indian, P13200.*

Native sovereignty by undermining the material and spiritual foundation of tribal power.[44]

Some Native people embraced allotment, welcoming the opportunity to own and till their own land. Others resisted, claiming that the policy was nothing but a land grab that benefited whites and violated treaty-guaranteed land rights. Still others sought spiritual answers, joining religious revitalization movements like that of Paiute leader Wovoka, the originator of the Ghost Dance.

A staunch supporter of allotment, President Theodore Roosevelt viewed the Dawes Act as "a mighty pulverizing engine to break up the tribal mass."[45] Apart from allotment, Roosevelt showed minimal interest in American Indian affairs or in holding official meetings with Native people during his years in the White House. Chief Joseph (Nez Perce) became one exception. In 1903, the president paid Joseph's expenses to visit Washington, maintaining that the Nez Perce leader "had some genuine ground of serious complaint against our Government and people."[46]

But Roosevelt had no interest in Joseph's wish to return his people to the Wallowa Valley of Oregon, land the United States had taken from the Nez Perce in the "Thief Treaty" of 1863. At the turn of the twentieth century, Roosevelt was more interested in his romantic image of Indians and the West than he was in addressing the real issues facing Native Americans. Like many turn-of-the-century Americans, Roosevelt believed white civilization was superior to that of Native societies, and viewed assimilation as the only way of ensuring Indian survival. It was this fundamental idea that fueled Roosevelt's support for on- and off-reservation boarding schools.

The contours of late nineteenth- and early twentieth-century United States Indian policy—allotment, assimilation, and education—were largely carried forward by Roosevelt's successors, Presidents William Howard Taft, Woodrow Wilson, Warren G. Harding, and Calvin Coolidge. But business as usual in Native American affairs was about to change.

In 1928, a team of social scientists led by Lewis M. Meriam released a report that blasted American Indian policy. *The Problem of Indian Administration*, known as the Meriam Report, revealed that Native Americans were neither disappearing nor assimilating, but rather living in jeopardy and hardship. The authors revealed that Indian communities throughout the United States were wracked by poverty, unemployment, poor housing, disease, lack of sanitation, and substandard education. They concluded that government policies, including allotment, were responsible for the woeful state of Native America. The Meriam Report led to reforms recommended under the administrations of Herbert Hoover and Franklin D. Roosevelt—presidents who occupied the White House during the Great Depression, the New Deal, and World War II. This transitional era in

American history also saw the rise of new Indian leaders who helped promote greater self-determination for Native nations. As Duane Champagne (Turtle Mountain Chippewa) shows in chapter four, the social, economic, and political challenges of this era encouraged American presidents to become more active in American Indian affairs both by challenging the status quo of the Office of Indian Affairs and listening to the voices of Native American leaders.

President Hoover had lived part of his childhood among the Osage and had a genuine interest in American Indian people. In 1928, he selected as his running mate Kansas senator Charles Curtis—a man of Kaw, and Osage ancestry. By respecting tribal traditions and favoring Indian self-respect and political self-determination, Hoover and Curtis took small steps toward establishing the modern agenda of United States Indian policy.

These steps led to more changes under President Franklin D. Roosevelt, who felt that the United States government had been too heavy-handed in American Indian affairs and unsupportive of Native nations. Roosevelt selected John Collier, a reformer and activist, to serve as commissioner of Indian affairs. A severe critic of past Indian policy, Collier initiated a New Deal for American Indians, ending the disastrous allotment program that had placed thousands of acres of tribal lands into white hands. Collier launched new programs that improved American Indian social, economic, political, and cultural life. But Collier's occasional heavy-handed dealings with tribal leaders alienated many in Indian Country who sought greater tribal self-determination.

After World War II, Presidents Harry S. Truman and Dwight D. Eisenhower favored full citizenship for American Indians, including citizenship within their home states. Both presidents, however, pursued a policy of termination, which aimed at destroying the tribes' legal relationship with the United States and divesting Indians of their lands. Many tribal leaders, including Ada Deer (Menominee) and Lucy Covington (Colville), opposed the policy, as did leaders of the National Congress of American Indians, such as Joe Garry (Coeur d'Alene), D'Arcy McNickle (Flathead), and Vine Deloria, Jr. (Sioux). Many postwar Native leaders also opposed the federal relo-

cation program, which moved American Indians from rural reservations to urban areas where they were to find jobs and assimilate into mainstream America.

When John F. Kennedy took office in 1961, the United States as a whole seemed poised for change. Young, handsome, and energetic, the new president seemed to embody a new day in American life—a spirit reflected in the moniker chosen for his idealistic political platform, the New Frontier. The civil rights movement was in full swing, and throughout the nation, African Americans mobilized in support of equality, voting rights, integration, jobs, and better housing. In 1961, Native American leaders from across the country met to create their own statement about American Indian affairs. Helen Scheirbeck (Lumbee), D'Arcy McNickle, Vine Deloria, Jr., Jack Forbes (Powhatan-Delaware), Ada Deer, Helen Peterson (Oglala), William Paul (Tlingit), and many others attended the Chicago Conference, producing a Declaration of Indian Purpose, which they read to President Kennedy at the White House. The document had a long-term effect on American history, encouraging presidents to listen more often and more intently to the voices of Native American leaders.

During the 1960s, new leaders such as Wendell Chino (Mescalero) and Mel Thom (Paiute) pressured President Lyndon Johnson to join them in supporting greater sovereignty and self-determination for Native nations. Their efforts bore fruit in 1968, when President Johnson delivered his "Special Message to Congress on the Problems of American Indians," which criticized the policy of tribal ter-

Participants in the Constitutional Convention of the National Congress of American Indians, 1944. Indians from fifty tribes, hailing from twenty-seven states, converged on Denver, Colorado, in November 1944, to form the National Congress of American Indians (NCAI), the first nationwide organization for Native American rights founded and run by Indians. The delegates hoped "to bring all Indians together for the purpose of enlightening the public, preserving Indian cultural values, seeking an equitable adjustment of tribal affairs, securing and preserving their rights under treaties with the United States, and streamlining the administration of Indian affairs." *Courtesy National Anthropological Archives, Smithsonian Institution.*

mination and supported greater Indian self-determination.[47] Johnson asked Congress for funds to encourage economic development and greater Native involvement in their own affairs, including Indian advisory boards at government schools.

SELF-DETERMINATION: 1970 TO THE PRESENT

Presidents who followed Lyndon Johnson have increasingly embraced tribal self-determination. President Richard Nixon added his influence to the fuller recognition of tribal sovereignty, strongly supporting the self-determination of Native nations. As chapter four suggests, "Chief" Wallace Newman, a Luiseño Indian and Nixon's football coach at Whittier College, influenced Nixon's enlightened Indian agenda. Though later tarnished by the Watergate affair, Nixon is remembered in Indian Country as the president who set the agenda for contemporary United States Indian policy, which rests on the recognition of Native American political, economic, intellectual, and social sovereignty.

The 1970s witnessed a mass upsurge in Native American activism, consciousness, and pride. Influenced by the civil rights movement, many Native people banded together in the red power movement to claim Native rights and reject the arbitrary Indian policies of the Bureau of Indian Affairs. The red power movement emerged in urban areas and spread to reservations, where Indian activists of all ages demanded greater voice in all affairs affecting Native Americans, including land, water, resources, politics, health, and education. Activist leaders demanded more from federal and tribal officials for the benefit of all Native people. The modern red power movement began with the widely publicized takeover of Alcatraz Island in 1969, the occupation of the Bureau of Indian Affairs in Washington, D.C., in 1972, and the occupation of the village of Wounded Knee on the Pine Ridge Reservation in South Dakota in 1973. Red power fixed American attention on a panoply of Indian grievances and galvanized non-Native support for reform. At the same time, Native nations insisted on greater control of tribal resources and community decisions, rather than allowing the Bureau of Indian Affairs to determine measures significant to tribal nations.

The White House sensed the winds of political change in Native

America, and presidents made efforts to involve Indian leaders directly in decisions that affect tribal people. Presidents Ronald Reagan, George H. W. Bush, Bill Clinton, and George W. Bush all publicly recognized tribal sovereignty and encouraged Native American leaders to have a greater voice in Indian affairs. Indeed, as Professor Troy Johnson shows in chapter five, President Clinton never forgot the unique relationship of the United States and Native nations, and may have accomplished more in American Indian affairs than any president since Richard Nixon. President George W. Bush continued to recognize tribal sovereignty and took part in honoring Native Americans who bravely served in the armed forces during World War II and the Korean War. But, for the most part, the forty-third president did not engage directly in Indian affairs or evince interest in the growth and development of modern Native nations.

Over the years, Native nations have exercised sovereignty on many fronts, challenging federal, state, and local authority in a time-honored effort to uphold treaty rights and benefit their people. Tribal leaders are actively engaged in solving a range of problems and issues that swirl around Indian Country. In every part of the United States, American Indian leaders are helping to build tribal businesses, invest in new ventures, establish judicial systems, develop tribally administered health care programs, and send Native children to universities. None of these leaders has forgotten the past, when presidents spoke of the well-being of the tribes only to pursue policies detrimental to the people. Native leaders know the history of their people and their relationship with individual presidents. But they neither dwell on past injustices nor fixate on past policies that were designed to destroy their nations. Instead, they look toward tomorrow, knowing that the future rests in the hands of their people, rather than in the hands of presidents or the Bureau of Indian Affairs. Perhaps most important, they treasure, preserve, and protect their unique sovereignty—a gift of creation that can never be denied them.

Today, the National Park Service oversees Mount Rushmore, which lures thousands of visitors worldwide to view the carved faces of four famous presidents. The path leading from the visitor's center is officially called the Presidential Trail, but for Native Americans, the path leads to a sacred center, a seat of tribal sovereignty. Native people still know and honor these special tribal places. And American Indian leaders will always draw strength and inspiration from the lands that hold this abiding sovereign spirit, the bones of their ancestors, and the future of Native nations.

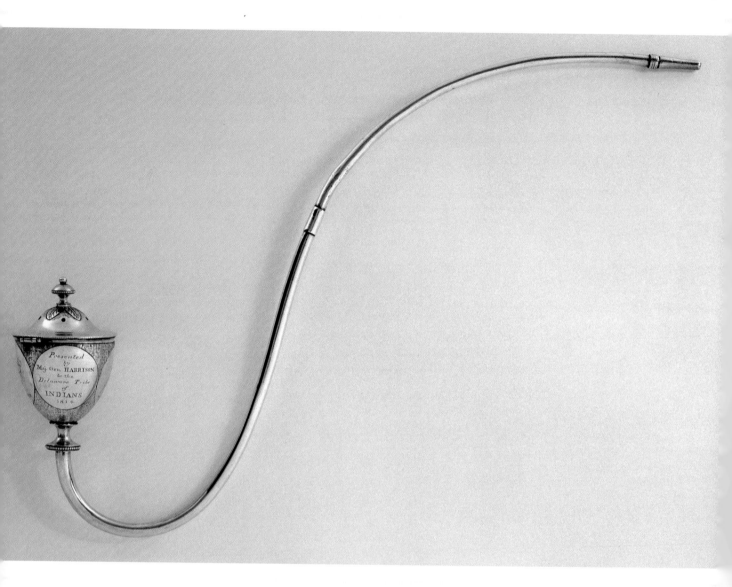

Silver pipe with curved handle, 1814. This pipe was a gift from Major General (and future president) William Henry Harrison to the Delaware Nation. The four sides of the bowl are engraved with images of an American officer and a Native man shaking hands, the American eagle, clasped hands with the words "Peace and Friendship," and an inscription: "Presented by Maj. Gen. Harrison to the Delaware Tribe of Indians, 1814." The giving of pipes and other symbolic gifts to North American Indians had a nearly two-hundred-year history when President Washington took the oath of office on April 30, 1789. During the colonial era, British, French, and Spanish officials presented medals, tomahawks, flags, guns, and other items to maintain peace with—and win the allegiance of—powerful Indian nations. The new United States government adopted and continued the custom of giving gifts to prominent chiefs in recognition of their loyalty. *Courtesy Department of Anthropology, Smithsonian National Museum of Natural History, E362061.*

CHAPTER I

NATIVE NATIONS AND THE NEW NATION, 1776–1820

ROBERT W. VENABLES

When the American colonies defeated Britain during the War of Independence, Native American leaders began to establish diplomatic relations with the new nation, continuing a tradition of government-to-government relations that had flourished between Indian tribes and European nations during the colonial era. In their dealings with the United States, Indians preferred to hold negotiations, or councils, that would lead to treaties of mutual respect. War was always the last option. But war was an Indian nation's ultimate assertion of sovereignty. When Native lands were engulfed by invasions of settlers in the 1780s and 1790s, treaties of mutual respect became irrelevant, and Indian people were forced to defend their homelands.

Early American presidents were committed to preventing war with Indians. After the drafting and ratification of the Constitution, President George Washington and his representatives met Native leaders face-to-face, negotiating treaties of good faith that recognized the sovereignty of Native nations. Washington's good faith, however, was not shared by all.

Showing blatant disregard for Native rights, white settlers continually encroached on Indian lands, violating the new nation's treaties with Indians. The settlers' actions raised a host of thorny questions for the presidents. Should the United States evict the squatters and honor its treaty commitments with Indian nations? Or should the president cast a blind eye and allow the new nation to expand at the expense of Native sovereignty? The ultimate question was: Who did the president represent? The land-hungry citizens of the United States or the sovereign Indian nations that lived on the frontiers, north to south? The answer to these questions often led to war.

AMERICAN VISIONS OF INDIANS

Relations between Indians and the nascent United States were shaped—and strained—by broad spiritual and philosophical differences between Euro-Americans and indigenous peoples. In 1791, the Mohawk leader Thayendanegea (Joseph Brant) summarized these differences, noting that Indians "believe the same supreme power created both them and the whites, but perhaps for different purposes."[2] While some colonists, including Quakers and Moravians, held that a supreme being had endowed Indians with their own set of spiritual beliefs, most whites contended that there could be just one single spiritual/ethical path, with clear and limited philosophical signposts.[3]

Some Americans also felt that whites were superior to Indians—a widely held belief that enabled white settlers to violate Indian rights by invading lands set aside by treaty. Even American leaders, including some of the presidents covered in this chapter, believed that Indians held an inferior position on a continuum that ran from barbarism to civilization. In the 1720s, Cadwallader Colden, a member of the Governor's Council of New York, declared that "the Greeks & Romans . . . [were] once as much Barbarians as our Indians now are. . . . We are fond of searching into Remote Antiquity to know the Manners of our Earliest Progenitors: if I be not mistaken, the Indians are living images of them."[4]

[T]he basis of our proceedings with the Indian Nations has been, and shall be justice, during the period in which I may have anything to do in the administration of this government.

—PRESIDENT GEORGE
WASHINGTON, 1790 [1]

George Washington, and other leaders during the era of the American Revolution were influenced by the Enlightenment, a European philosophical movement that allowed the colonists to recognize the common humanity of Native peoples while at the same time viewing Indian cultures as inferior, unequal, and under-developed.[5] While this complex viewpoint was inherently contradictory, it was not hypocritical. George Washington's generation could argue that Indian nations were inferior and at the same time advocate the transformation of American Indian culture along Euro-American lines.

Such a philosophical outlook could lead to contradictions in the behavior of even the most ethical colonists. Consider the early military career of George Washington.[6] In the 1750s, Washington was an officer in the Virginia militia. He served on the Virginia frontier with Indian leaders such as Alliquippa (Seneca), a female diplomat in the area of what is now Pittsburgh, Pennsylvania.[7] During the French and Indian War (1754–63), Washington also worked with Indian warriors who acted as his scouts. One of those who closely interacted with Washington was Tanacharisson (Seneca), who served as a diplomat for the Iroquois on the Ohio Valley frontier. Called the "Half King" by the English—to indicate his influence as a representative of the Iroquois Confederacy in Ohio and western Pennsylvania—Tanacharisson viewed Washington as a "good natured" but inexperienced military leader who would "Command the Indians as his Slaves," and who "would by no Means take Advice from the Indians."[8]

When Washington became America's first president in 1789, he did his best to establish honorable diplomatic relations with Indian nations.[9] But Washington's original attitude continued to shape his dealings with Indians. He was not prone to listen to Indians because he, like most whites of his era, believed that Euro-American culture was more advanced. Americans believed that Indians would assimilate into American culture, give up their citizenship in Indian nations, and join the American experiment after prolonged exposure to white civilization.

The Founding Fathers were convinced that Indians would become more civilized because their own ancestors had evolved over time through contact with invaders. Before the Roman conquest, Thomas Jefferson observed, Europeans were not yet civilized. They were transformed only "when the Roman arms and arts first crossed the Alps."[10] These historical lessons were clear to Jefferson. By exposing Native Americans to Euro-American culture, Indians would gradually assimilate into American life. "Before we condemn the Indians of this continent as wanting genius," he noted in 1782, "we must consider that letters [European knowledge] have not yet been introduced among them."[11]

Two issues complicated the Enlightenment ideal of reshaping Indian societies. First, Native leaders possessed their own ideas about whether or to what extent their nations should follow the ways of whites. Second, American greed for Indian land created a relentless impulse that led whites, including presidents, in the exact opposite direction of Enlightenment-inspired policies—and almost always into war.[12]

THE AMERICAN REVOLUTION

Colonial protests over British policies erupted in revolution at Lexington, Massachusetts, on April 19, 1775. The presidents discussed in this chapter, including George Washington, John Adams, Thomas Jefferson, James Madison, and James Monroe, were all involved, in one way or another, with the American Revolution. As president, each dealt with Indian leaders whose nations had either allied with the colonies during the War for Independence or had fought for Great Britain. A survey of the Revolutionary frontier, from the north to the south, helps explain the attitudes and actions of Indians and whites after the Revolution.

When the American Revolution began, most Indians on the colonial frontier intended to remain neutral.[13] Certainly the Indians owed the British no debt of gratitude. After 1763, Native lands were whittled away through various schemes hatched by colonists and British officials, and British imperial laws were not enforced, enabling white settlers to encroach on Indian lands and kill Native men, women, and children with impunity. From north to south, all along the frontier, squatters and settlers loyal to King George III antagonized Indians. Land speculators, such as Dr. John Connolly on the Virginia-

George Washington at Princeton, by Charles Willson Peale (1741–1827). Oil on canvas, 1779. In this portrait, General George Washington is depicted as a victorious commander of American forces, leaning confidently on the barrel of a captured cannon after the Battle of Princeton (1777). American victory in the War of Independence gave the United States approximately 541 million acres of land within the borders of the former colonies, as well as 230 million acres between the Appalachian Mountains and the Mississippi River. After the Revolution, Americans claimed dominion over these territories and pressured Native nations to cede their homelands. When war resulted, American leaders eventually rejected coercion and adopted treaty negotiations as a means for acquiring Indian lands. President George Washington played a key role in developing the new policy, which recognized Indian tribes as sovereign nations. *Courtesy U.S. Senate Collection.*

Pennsylvania frontier, were often Loyalists as well.[14] Clearly, being a Loyalist did not imply adherence to imperial laws, from an Indian point of view. Nor did being a patriot necessarily alienate Native people. Independence was favored by many highly regarded traders, such as George Galphin, who dealt with the Creeks.[15] Thus, neutrality was a logical strategy for Indian nations at the beginning of the American Revolution.[16]

Indian desire for neutrality was exemplified by Tese [Jesse] Mico, chief of the Creek Confederacy, which stretched from what is now eastern Georgia through Alabama. On September 7, 1775, Mico defined the Creek position on the War of Independence and sent it to the British as well as the patriots, saying, "We are determined to lye quiet and not meddle with the Quarrel. . . . We wish all the white People well . . . as you are all one Mother's Children we hope that the great man above will soon make Peace between you."[17]

The American Indian quest for neutrality soon foundered due to the colonists' lust for land. The Declaration of Independence, written primarily by Thomas Jefferson in 1776, condemns King George III for preventing the colonists from appropriating western lands that belonged to Native nations, and for endeavoring "to bring on the inhabitants of our frontiers, the merciless Indian Savages, whose known rule of warfare, is an undistinguished destruction of all ages, sexes and conditions."[18] The words were unmistakable. If the patriots prevailed, Indian nations would have to defend their homelands against an invasion of settlers.

Most Indian nations east of the Mississippi River eventually were forced to side with the British, viewed as a bulwark against American expansion. Indians who favored neutrality or supported the patriots found themselves at odds with their countrymen. In New York during the summer of 1777, factions within the Iroquois Confederacy began their own civil war. On August 6, Mohawk and Seneca warriors fought alongside British soldiers, Hessian mercenaries, and Americans loyal to King George III in a bloody stalemate with patriot militia at the Battle of Oriskany, at the western end of the Mohawk Valley. At Oriskany, pro-British Iroquois warriors under Thayendanegea (Joseph Brant) and Théwonyas (Chainbreaker), a Seneca, fought pro-patriot Iroquois warriors from the Oneida and Tuscarora nations under Honyery Tewahangaraghkan (Honyery Doxtader), an Oneida.[19]

Pro-British Iroquois warriors fought furious battles with the patriots, especially in western and northern Pennsylvania and in New

York's Mohawk Valley. In April 1779, a patriot army destroyed the towns of the Onondagas.[20] The towns of the Cayuga and Seneca nations were next. In May, General George Washington, the patriots' commander in chief, ordered John Sullivan, his commander in the field, to lay waste to "Iroquoia":

> The immediate objects are the total distruction [sic] and devastation of their settlements and the capture of as many prisoners of every age and sex as possible. It will be essential to ruin their crops now in the ground & prevent their planting more . . . parties should be detached to lay waste all the settlements around, with instructions to do it in the most effectual manner, that the country may not be merely overrun but destroyed. [21]

Sullivan's army marched into Cayuga and Seneca territories as another army moved northward from Pittsburgh. More than forty Iroquois towns, as well as all apple and peach orchards and all cornfields, were destroyed.[22] Since Washington issued the orders for this scorched-earth policy, the Iroquois dubbed him "Hanadahguyus"—Town Destroyer—a title the Iroquois have used to identify every subsequent American president to the present day.[23]

AFTER THE REVOLUTION

After the American Revolution, Indian nations throughout eastern North America discovered that the 1783 Treaty of Paris transferred British jurisdiction of Indian lands south of the Great Lakes and east of the Mississippi to the United States.[24] Not one Native American leader participated in the negotiations that led to the treaty. Indian nations, such as the Iroquois in the north and the Cherokees and the Creeks in the south, did not forget what had befallen them. Nor did the patriots forget the ferocity of frontier warfare. Indian nations and the new United States remained fearful of each other, because each side had seen what the other could do.

Indian nations that had been neutral or had sided with the patriots, such as the Oneidas and Tuscaroras of New York, found that their territories were no safer from white expansion than the lands of Indians who had fought for the Crown. The lands of the Oneidas were especially coveted because they encompassed a series of major waterways that would become part of the Erie Canal, completed in 1825. George Washington understood this. On October 12, 1783, just ten months after the end of the Revolution, Washington described how he had

> . . . made a tour . . . up the Mohawk river to Fort Schuyler (formerly Fort Stanwix), and crossed over to the Wood Creek which empties into the Oneida Lake, and affords the water communication with Ontario. I then traversed the country to the head of the Eastern Branch of the Susquehanna and viewed the Lake Otsego [Cooperstown, New York], and the portage between that lake and the Mohawk river at Canajoharie. Prompted by these actual observations, I could not help taking a more contemplative and extensive view of the vast inland navigation of these United States. . . . Would to God we may have wisdom enough to improve them.[25]

Ultimately, the Oneida Nation would be betrayed by their former allies, New York State and the United States. The Oneidas lost lands in a succession of treaties with New York beginning in 1785, two years after the end of the Revolution. In all, some twenty-seven treaties were made between 1788 and 1846.[26] In 1822, the Oneidas began a two-decade period of removal to lands near Green Bay, Wisconsin. In 1855, about one thousand Oneidas were living in Wisconsin; only 161 Oneidas were left in New York State.[27]

The net beneficiaries of the Revolution were the "Brothers of the Thirteen Fires," as the Indians called the thirteen fiercely individualistic American states. Loosely governed by the Articles of Confederation, the states cast covetous eyes on Native lands. No one knew this better than Joseph Brant (1743–1807), the Mohawk statesman and soldier who had supported the Crown during the War for Independence. After the war, Brant's pro-British Mohawks had taken refuge in Canada, having lost their New York homes to the patriots. But Brant was convinced that other Indian nations could resist American expansion, if only they could stand together. In 1786, Indian na-

Joseph Brant/Thayendanegea
by Charles Willson Peale,
from life, 1797. *Independence*
National Historical Park.

tions north of the Ohio River gathered at Hurontown, near Detroit, to listen to Brant describe his vision of a new confederacy, which would replace all the old Indian alliances—including his own, the Iroquois Confederacy.[28] "It is certain," Brant asserted, "that before Christian Nations Visited this Continent we were the Sole Lords of the Soil!"[29]

Internal dissent among the Indian nations and suspicion of Brant's ego delayed delivery of the "Hurontown Letter," a communication from the "United Indian Nations" to the Continental Congress, which implied that peace with Indian nations was still possible if Americans steered clear of lands north of the Ohio River.[30] By the time the letter was delivered in June 1787, however, the thirteen states were moving toward a greater unity of their own, having already convened a constitutional convention in Philadelphia.

The price of independence was high for the new nation. The national government, under both the Articles of Confederation and the Constitution, owed money to soldiers who had served in the Continental Army, as well as to creditors whose businesses or capital had provided much-needed war supplies. These debts would be paid with Indian lands. The Continental Congress's Committee on Indian Affairs stated the issue bluntly in 1783: "Although motives of policy as well as clemency ought to incline Congress to listen to the prayers of the hostile Indians for peace, yet . . . the faith of the United States stands pledged to grant portions of the uncultivated lands [i.e., Indian lands] as a bounty to their army, and in reward of their courage and fidelity. . . ." The committee also noted that "the public creditors have been led to believe and have a right to expect that those territories will be speedily improved into a fund towards the security and payment of the national debt."[31]

In 1789, as the administration of President George Washington began under the new Constitution, the Shawnees, Miamis, and Wabash Confederacy Indians were at war with Americans in the Ohio Valley.[32] The Indians were convinced that whites would never cease illegal trade practices or incursions onto their lands. In truth, fault lay on both sides of the frontier. Unruly individuals among whites and Indians continued to steal and murder, provoking both sides to respond with force. The worst elements of each society ultimately involved both societies in war.[33]

As violence flared on the northern frontier, President Washington and Congress demonstrated their intention of dealing honorably with Indian nations through the support and passage of the Trade and Intercourse Act of 1790.[35] The act guaranteed fair trading practices with Indians, through licensing of all traders by the United States, and established the integrity of Indian lands by declaring invalid all land acquisitions not sanctioned by the federal government. Unfortunately, the new federal government was unable to enforce the Trade and Intercourse Act, even when the law was strengthened in 1793. State governments, such as Georgia, held firm to the principle of states' rights, and continued their determination to acquire

[T]he protection of the Indians, from the violences of the lawless part of our frontier inhabitants are insufficient. . . . Unless the murdering of Indians can be restrained, . . . all the exertions of the government to prevent destructive retaliations, by the Indians, will prove fruitless; and all our present agreeable prospects illusory.[34]

—PRESIDENT
GEORGE WASHINGTON,
DECEMBER 8, 1795

Indian lands.[36] That determination would lead to war with another group of Indians: the Creeks.

The Creek Confederacy was guided by Alexander McGillivray, once a brave war leader, but now a sickly man in his late twenties or early thirties. Three-quarters white, McGillivray was the son of a Scottish plantation owner and trader and popular with the Creeks. Realizing that force was the only way to halt American land grabbers, the Creek Council declared war on Georgia on April 2, 1786. Creek warriors were authorized to attack only those white settlements that had been established illegally on Creek land, a strategy McGillivray hoped would leave the door open for a peaceful, final settlement. In the end, President George Washington invited McGillivray to come to New York City, the capital of the new nation, to negotiate. There, on August 7, 1790, McGillivray and twenty-three other Creeks—a full representation of the Creek Nation—made peace with the United States in the Treaty of New York. Under the treaty, the Creeks gave up a small section of their lands in exchange for recognition by the United States and protection of Creek lands outside the jurisdiction of Spanish Florida.[37]

Washington's diplomatic efforts brought peace to the South, but the winds of war continued to blow heavily on the Ohio frontier. As whites continued to trespass on their homelands, Native nations in the western woodlands mobilized for war. In 1790, Washington dispatched an army under General Josiah Harmar to attack the towns of the Miami Nation. But on October 19 and again on October 22, Miami chief Mishikinakwa (Little Turtle) and his warriors thoroughly defeated the American troops, forcing the entire army to retreat. Little Turtle's fame as a great war chief quickly spread through the Indian towns.[38]

For President Washington, it was imperative to keep the Iroquois Confederacy neutral in the war on the Ohio frontier. In the midst of the crisis, three Seneca leaders—Cornplanter, Half-Town, and Big Tree (also known as the Great Tree)—visited Philadelphia, the new American capital. There, on December 1, 1790, the three Native diplomats wrote a speech that was presented to President Washington:

KI-ON-TWOG-KY or CORN PLANT
A SENECA CHIEF.

PUBLISHED BY E. C. BIDDLE, PHILADELPHIA;

FATHER The voice of the Seneca nation speaks to you, the
great councillor, in whose heart the wise men of all the Thirteen Fires have placed their wisdom. . . . When your army entered the country of the Six Nations, we called you the town
destroyer [Hanadahguyus]; and to this day, when that name is
heard, our women look behind them and turn pale, and our
children cling close to the necks of their mothers.[39]

The Senecas contested that the lands secured to the Iroquois in
the 1784 Treaty of Fort Stanwix (now Rome, New York) were being

taken by individuals and by the State of New York. Referring to the 1784 treaty, the diplomats asked, "Does this promise bind you?" They also noted how whites had changed the environment. "The game which the Great Spirit sent into our country for us to eat, is going from among us. We thought he [the Great Spirit] intended that we should till the ground with the plough, as the white people do . . . we must know from you whether you mean to leave us and our children any land to till."[40]

Washington replied on December 29, 1790: "[Y]ou want to know whether the Union mean to leave you any land to till. . . . all the lands secured to you, by the treaty of fort [sic] Stanwix, excepting such parts as you may since have fairly sold, are yours, and that only your own acts can convey them away."[41] Washington further asked the Iroquois to remain neutral during the Ohio conflict.

The Senecas did what President Washington asked, and the United States continued to pursue the war in Ohio, knowing the Iroquois Confederacy would not interfere. On September 7, 1791, a new army, authorized by Washington and under the command of Arthur St. Clair, marched north from Fort Washington (Cincinnati) to strike the Miami Indian towns. St. Clair's army included Chickasaws who, under Chief Piomingo, saw the American expedition as an opportunity to defeat their ancient enemies, the northern Indians. On November 4, 1791, about fifteen miles before St. Clair's army reached the first Miami towns, warriors under Little Turtle engaged and defeated the American army. Of the 1,400 American soldiers, there were 630 casualties, 68 of them officers. St. Clair lost nearly three times the number of soldiers who were killed under Lieutenant Colonel George A. Custer at the 1876 Battle of the Little Bighorn.

President Washington realized the enormity of the crisis. Bold Indian leadership successfully challenged the new government and threatened to confine America to almost the same western boundaries that the colonies possessed prior to the Revolution.[42]

Worse, if the United States failed to protect its frontier population, the areas beyond the Allegheny Mountains might secede. Disgruntled settlers on the frontier could declare themselves independent and ally with the British, who occupied Canada. They could also align themselves with Spain, which held Florida as well as the vast

LITTLE TURTLE: WAR CHIEF AND SOCIAL LION

When the Miami war chief Little Turtle (ca. 1747–1812) met President George Washington in 1797, he was one of the most famous Indians in the United States. Six years earlier, Little Turtle had led a combined Indian force against the army of General Arthur St. Clair, governor of the Northwest Territory, killing 630 United States soldiers and wounding 283 more. The engagement, fought to resist the American invasion of the Old Northwest, was the greatest Indian military victory in American history.

By the mid-1790s, Little Turtle had pledged to support peace with the United States and embraced government efforts to encourage Indians to take up farming. In 1797 he visited Philadelphia, where President Washington presented him with a ceremonial sword. The artist Gilbert Stuart painted his portrait, and, at the suggestion of Vice President Thomas Jefferson, the Indian leader was vaccinated against smallpox by Dr. Benjamin Rush. During his stay in the capital, Little Turtle met with Thaddeus Kosciusko, the Polish patriot and hero of the American Revolution, who presented him with a set of pistols and advised him to use them against "the first man who ever comes to subjugate you." He also met the French philosopher and historian Constantin Volney, who related the theory that Indians had arrived in America by crossing the Bering Strait from Asia. Unconvinced, Little

Mishikinakwa (Little Turtle). Copy of lost portrait by Gilbert Stuart (1755–1828), ca. 1797. *Courtesy National Anthropological Archives, Smithsonian Institution.*

Turtle ventured that Asians descended from Indians who had migrated westward across the strait. Little Turtle died in 1812 and was buried with his most valued possessions, including the sword given to him by President George Washington.[43]

Louisiana Territory—which included almost all of the Mississippi Valley to the west of the Mississippi River, as well as New Orleans, located near the river's mouth. These possibilities were not new. Several years earlier, Washington had noted that, with the Spanish to the south and the British to the north, "The Western Settlers—from my own observation—stand as it were on a pivet [sic]—the touch of a feather would almost incline them any way."[44]

On March 5, 1792, Washington pushed reluctant congressmen to authorize the third federal army of his administration.[45] The previous two federally funded armies sent to the Ohio frontier consisted of militiamen; the new army would be primarily composed of professionals.[46]

The new force, numbering some five thousand men, was called the "Legion"—a name that conjured images of the glories of ancient Rome and reflected late eighteenth-century admiration for the classical world.[47] As early as October 1783, George Washington foresaw the United States as "a New Empire," an empire of liberty that was about to be born if not by justice, then by force.[48]

As the Legion formed, an epidemic of yellow fever struck Philadelphia in 1793, rendering it impossible for Indian leaders to visit the president at the capital.[49] Soon the functions of the still-new government ground to a halt. In the midst of the epidemic, secretary of state and future president Thomas Jefferson, who lived just outside Philadelphia, wrote James Madison, "Everybody who can, is flying from the city."[50] More than four thousand people—about one-tenth of the city's population—died between August and November 1793. Another twenty-five thousand fled, including President Washington, who found safe haven in Germantown at what has been called "the first summer White House."[51] The epidemic continued in 1794, and was one of the reasons the Washington administration held negotiations with the Haudenosaunee (Iroquois Confederacy) at Canandaigua, in western New York State, where Indian people would not be exposed to the disease.[52]

Farther west, Indians in the Ohio Valley stood ready for battle. Emboldened by their rout of American soldiers in 1791, Native warriors were confident that the new American commander appointed by President Washington, Anthony Wayne, could be defeated just as Harmar and St. Clair had been. But in June, a raid against the Americans' supply base ended in defeat. And by July, Little Turtle had grown uncertain about British support for war against the Americans. When the war chief journeyed to Detroit to learn how many soldiers he could count on, the British commander evaded the issue.[53]

The new American general, Anthony Wayne, was nicknamed Mad Anthony for his reckless courage during the American Revolution.[54] Wayne set in motion his elite army and headed toward the source of the Indians' supplies: Fort Miami, the British post on the Maumee River, near present-day Toledo, Ohio. Wayne also deployed Chickasaw and Choctaw scouts who were allied with the United States to avoid ambush. Little Turtle compared the crafty and intrepid Wayne to a black snake that never sleeps, as day and night were the same to him.[55]

Faced with a formidable foe, Little Turtle began to voice his opinion that the Indians should negotiate rather than fight the Americans. Sensing that the British were unreliable for support, he feared the outcome of war with Wayne and his army. But Little Turtle was overruled by leaders such as Shawnee chief Weyapiersenwaw (Blue Jacket), who became the coordinator of the upcoming battle.

The Indians had already selected the place where they would make their stand. Earlier, about five miles from the British post of Fort Miami, close to the Maumee River's northern banks, a tornado had cut a swath through the forest, uprooting and breaking trees into a natural maze. On the frontier, such a phenomenon was known as "fallen timbers." There, fifteen hundred warriors, including Miamis, Wyandots (Hurons), Potawatomis, Delawares, Shawnees, Chippewas, Ottawas, and Seneca Iroquois (from the Iroquois settlement at Sandusky, Ohio) gathered to face the soldiers.[56]

On August 20, 1794, the Indian and American armies fought what became known as the Battle of Fallen Timbers. Heavy musket fire from the warriors cut down many of the infantrymen. But the Americans closed ranks and kept coming. The warriors fell back to a second and then third line of defense, but the soldiers kept marching, bayonets forward. The Indian warriors retreated to Fort Miami.[57]

The warriors expected to make their final stand inside the British installation, forcing Wayne to face the fort's withering artillery. But the gates of Fort Miami were closed. The British commander, Major William Campbell, knew that Great Britain would soon turn over his fort to the United States under the provisions of the Jay Treaty, negotiated far away in England. Bereft of British support and facing three to one odds, the Indians' only choice was to flee.[58]

The Native nations of the Ohio Valley paid dearly for the war. During the summer of 1795, more than one thousand Indians representing a host of Indian nations—including Wyandots, Shawnees, Ottawas, Chippewas (Anishinaabe), Potawatomis, Miamis, Eel River Miamis, Piankashaws, Kickapoos, Kaskaskias, Delawares, and the Ohio settlements of the Iroquois Confederacy—attended a treaty council at Fort Greenville, Ohio. On August 3, 1795, ninety-six Indian leaders, including Little Turtle and Blue Jacket, agreed to

---

"A PRIOR RIGHT": MERCY OTIS WARREN
AND AMERICA'S WARS WITH INDIAN NATIONS, 1805

Not all Americans supported President George Washington's wars with Indians on the Ohio frontier. A prominent critic was Mercy Otis Warren (1728–1814), one of the most important women writers in eighteenth-century America. A poet, dramatist, and historian, Warren was the sister of James Otis and the wife of James Warren, vocal opponents of British colonial rule. The Warren home became a magnet for revolutionaries, offering Mercy Otis Warren a unique window into the causes, conduct, and resolution of America's War of Independence.

After the Revolution, Warren opposed efforts to create a strong central government for the new nation. Arguing that local and state governments were the best assurances of liberty, Warren opposed the newly drafted Constitution, claiming that the new frame of government would undermine the democratic ideals of the American Revolution. In 1805, she published her three-volume *History of the Rise, Progress, and Termination of the American Revolution, Interspersed with Biographical, Political, and Moral Observations,* in which she bluntly reviewed President Washington's Indian wars with a remarkable analogy:

It might have been happy for the United States . . . if, instead of extending their views over the boundless desert [meaning wilderness], a Chinese wall had been stretched along the Appalachian ridges, that might have kept the nations within the boundaries of nature. . . . The lives of our young heroes were too rich a price for the purchase of the acres of the savages, even could the [Indian] nations be extinguished, who certainly have a prior right to the inheritance: this is a theme on which some future historians may more copiously descant.

As readers contemplated Warren's regret that "a Chinese wall" had not been erected across the Appalachians, another woman, Sacajawea (Shoshone), was guiding the Lewis and Clark expedition as far from Warren's Boston as it was possible to travel by land. Later, white settlers would occupy lands west of the Mississippi River, and Warren's vision of a contained republic disappeared into the mists.[59] ◄

the Treaty of Greenville, ceding the entire lower half of what became Ohio as well as a sliver of eastern Indiana. Ironically, one of the Wyandots who signed the treaty with his mark was listed on the treaty as "Queshawksey, or George Washington."[60]

Two factors account for President Washington's military success against the Indian nations on the Ohio frontier. One was the Jay Treaty of 1794, in which Great Britain promised the United States that it would abandon its military posts, such as Fort Miami, Fort Niagara, and Fort Oswego—a promise that the British fulfilled in 1796.[61] The second factor was Washington's effort to keep the Iroquois Confederacy out of the Ohio war. During 1794, Washington's envoy, Timothy Pickering, spent months negotiating in Iroquois Country. The resulting Treaty of Canandaigua, signed on November 11, 1794, was a mutual recognition by the Iroquois and the United States that both entities would negotiate as equals.[62] American recognition of Iroquois sovereignty is clearly stated in Article Two, which declared that "the United States will never . . . disturb them or either of the Six Nations, nor their Indian friends residing thereon and united with them, in the free use and enjoyment thereof: but the said reservations shall remain theirs, until they choose to sell the same to the people of the United States."[63] Among the fifty-nine Native leaders who signed the treaty were Cornplanter, Red Jacket, and the future spiritual leader Handsome Lake.[64] Joseph Brant, for his part, refused to participate in the negotiations. Suspicious of American sincerity at Canandaigua, he was in Detroit encouraging Little Turtle's and Blue Jacket's warriors to contain American expansion.[65]

As if to symbolize the end of George Washington's administration as well as this phase of Indian history, Joseph Brant came to Philadelphia in 1797. Upset over the Jay Treaty of 1794 as well as the failure of the Great Lakes Indians to repel American expansion, the Mohawk leader declined to meet with the outgoing president but found time to have his portrait painted by the noted American artist Charles Willson Peale.[66] Leaving Philadelphia on February 28, just before the inauguration of the next president, John Adams, Brant traveled to New York City and then on to Albany, New York, where he and another Mohawk, John Deserontyon, signed a treaty with the United States that surrendered all Mohawk claims to lands within

New York State.[67] Brant had been at war with the United States since 1775, first on the New York frontier and then, as a supporter of the Great Lakes Indian nations, on the Ohio frontier. Now, at the beginning of John Adams's administration, Brant conceded that his part in the Revolutionary War was finally over.

NATIVE LANDS IN THE AGE OF ADAMS AND JEFFERSON

When President John Adams took office on March 4, 1797, he expressed concern over Great Britain's continued effort to foment Indian resistance to the United States.[68] His greatest concern, however, revolved around the possibility of war with revolutionary France or even Great Britain. Locked in a titanic struggle in Europe, the two superpowers continued to occupy lands in North America and could easily enmesh the United States and Native nations in the conflict. Allying with either France or England had serious consequences for the new nation. If America engaged in a war with France, Indian nations hostile to the United States would almost certainly receive aid from the French in New Orleans. If America fought against Britain, Indians could count on aid from British Canada.

Land-hungry frontiersmen and wayward state governments were also vexing the new president as well as inflaming tensions between the United States and Native people. Keen to acquire Cherokee lands, the Tennessee legislature informed Adams that the Indians occupied their territories as "tenants at will"—that is, at the forbearance of whites.[69] In 1798, the president sent an address to "his beloved chiefs, warriors, and children, of the Cherokee nation," explaining that squatters had pushed beyond a boundary line established in a 1791 treaty and that the settlers had protested when the United States removed them. Diverting attention from the terms of the treaty, Adams claimed that it was the Cherokees who had "long permitted them [the settlers] to occupy" these lands, and managed to define America's faithlessness as good faith. Said Adams:

> You cannot be ignorant how earnestly I have desired to secure peace to your frontier, nor, of my unwearied endeavors and the great expense incurred, to prevent a certain Zachariah Cox, and others, from carrying an armed force into your country,

to take possession of a part of it. . . . I hope you place a just value upon what has been done, as calculated to defend your country from invasion, and make you a happier people; and that you are therefore convinced of the sincere friendship of the United States to the Cherokee people. . . . I think it now proper to observe that, as I have looked upon it as a part of my duty to attend to your interests, I am also under the strongest obligations to hear the complaints, and relieve, as far as in my power, the distresses of my white children, citizens of the United States.[70]

The result was the Treaty of Tellico (1798), in which Cherokees ceded more of their homelands to America.[71] In the north, the Indians of the Great Lakes believed that John Adams and the United States government would uphold the boundary set at the Treaty of Greenville (1795). Settlers crossed the line, however, and in 1800 Adams ignored the treaty and established the Indiana Territory. In 1801, Adams appointed twenty-seven-year-old William Henry Harrison as its territorial governor. An army man who had fought at the Battle of Fallen Timbers, Harrison worked closely with speculators of Indian land, and would go on to serve as governor of the Indiana Territory during the administration of the next president, Thomas Jefferson.[72]

The principal author of the Declaration of Independence, Thomas Jefferson, took office in 1801. Two years later he acquired the immense Louisiana Territory, which extended from the Mississippi to the Rocky Mountains, and fired dreams of American expansion. As president, Jefferson proposed a particularly subversive policy for acquiring Indian lands east of the Mississippi.[73] Government-owned trading posts, called factories, had been established in 1795 to encourage Indians to adopt white-manufactured products and develop small farms. In the process, Indians might be expected to give up hunting and thus require less land—which would, in turn, be ceded to the United States.

Jefferson increased the likelihood of Indian land cessions with a plan he outlined in a letter to William Henry Harrison. "To promote this disposition to exchange lands, which they have to spare and we

President Thomas Jefferson pointing to the Declaration of Independence. Engraving after painting by Rembrandt Peale (1778–1860), ca. 1801. Thomas Jefferson, the nation's third president, was not above condoning chicanery to acquire Native homelands. His Indian policy produced some thirty treaties with a dozen tribal groups, who ceded nearly two hundred thousand square miles of land in nine states. *Courtesy Library of Congress, LC-DIG-ppmsca-15715.*

THOMAS JEFFERSON
President of the United States.

want . . . we shall push our trading uses [familiar trading customs], and be glad to see the good and influential individuals among them run in debt, because we observe that when these debts get beyond what the individuals can pay, they become willing to lop them off by a cession of lands."[74] The consequence of the plan was clear: As more Indians sold their homelands to pay off debts, white settlers would acquire their territories and "gradually circumscribe and approach the Indians." Surrounded and outnumbered, Native people, Jefferson predicted, would "either incorporate with us as citizens of the United States, or remove beyond the Mississippi."[75]

AMERICAN INDIANS OR "INDIAN AMERICANS"

Whether before or after contact with Europeans, Native nations always adapted to changing circumstances. But to what extent would continued adaptation assist Indians to survive as sovereign people? To what degree would adaptation of American ideas and technologies transform "American Indians" into "Indian Americans"—exactly as Jefferson had envisioned?

Native leaders east of the Mississippi pondered these and other questions in the early nineteenth century, and many came up with answers that continue to guide Native people today.[76] In 1799, the Iroquois (in present-day western New York State) were fortunate to be given spiritual guidance from Ganeodiyo (Handsome Lake), a Seneca religious leader. Handsome Lake related a series of visions he experienced in which spiritual messengers brought teachings from the Creator, collectively called the *Gai wiio*, or "Good Word." The teachings warned of the abuse of alcohol, which Europeans introduced as a trade item and used to lubricate land negotiations with Indians. Above all, the messages encouraged the Iroquois to adapt to white agricultural methods, to continue traditional Native ceremonies, and to treat their domesticated animals better than did their white neighbors. The latter message reinforced the importance of humility and of respect for all the world's beings, concepts long central to Iroquois religious beliefs. Thus, the *Gai wiio* was, in comparative terms, more a religious reformation than a brand-new religion.[77]

One of the spiritual messages received by Handsome Lake references George Washington, who was provided by the Creator with a special place in the afterlife—a reward for the good faith the United States had shown the Iroquois during negotiations for the Treaty of Canandaigua in 1794. One English translation of this spiritual message notes that Washington had asserted that the Iroquois were "an

THE HAND OF FRIENDSHIP:
AMERICAN INDIANS AND THE LEWIS AND CLARK EXPEDITION

The Louisiana Purchase of 1803 doubled the size of the United States, adding eight hundred thousand square miles of uncharted land from the Mississippi River to the Rocky Mountains. President Thomas Jefferson soon dispatched his private secretary and Virginia neighbor, Meriwether Lewis, and William Clark, an experienced frontiersman and Indian fighter, on an expedition to explore the new lands, home to many Indian nations. With about forty men and a Shoshone woman named Sacajawea as their interpreter, Lewis and Clark started up the Missouri River in the spring of 1804, crossed the Rocky Mountains, and finally reached the Pacific Coast in the late autumn of 1805.

As they moved up the Missouri, the party distributed to the Indians they met peace medals such as the one shown here, as well as flags. "When you accept [the president's] flag and medal," they told the tribes, "you accept therewith his hand of friendship, which will never be withdrawn from your nation as long as you continue to follow the councils which he may command his chiefs to give you, and shut your ears to the councils of Bad birds."

After covering 7,679 miles of uncharted territory in two and a half years, Lewis and Clark returned to the East amid celebration and fanfare. Soon President Jefferson would promote the idea of moving eastern Indian nations to new lands west of the Mississippi, an idea that

Thomas Jefferson peace medal. Bronze, embellished with porcupine quillwork. *Photo by Walter Larrimore, National Museum of the American Indian, 24/1965.*

reached final fruition in the 1830s, when the Cherokees, Chickasaws, Seminoles, Creeks, and Choctaws were removed from their eastern homelands to Indian Territory (modern-day Oklahoma).[78] 〰

independent people," and "ordered things that we may enjoy ourselves, as long as the sun shines and the waters run."[79]

In 1801, Handsome Lake visited President Jefferson, who wrote the following year to praise the Iroquois for following the Seneca religious leader's guidance about "the ruinous effects which the abuse of spirituous liquors have produced upon them." Then, Jefferson turned to a different issue: land.

> You remind me, brother, of what I have said to you when you visited me the last winter, that the land you then held would remain yours. . . . The right to sell is one of the rights of property. To forbid you the exercise of that right would be a wrong to your nation. Nor do I think, brother, that the sale of lands is, under all circumstances, injurious to your people; while they depended on hunting, the more extensive forests around them, the more game they would yield. But going into a state of agriculture it may be as advantageous to a society as it is to an individual who has more land than he can improve, to sell a part and lay out the money in stocks and implements of agriculture.[80]

In the years that followed, land was taken from the Iroquois, but the Six Nations held on to their reservations, due in part to the influence of the *Gai wiio*, the Good Word.[81]

As Handsome Lake shared the *Gai wiio* with the Iroquois, the Shawnee leader Tecumseh was building a powerful movement in the Great Lakes area based on spiritual ties to the land and a continuation of traditional Native beliefs. A veteran of the wars of the 1790s, Tecumseh built his appeal upon a call for pan-Indian unity to resist American expansion.[82] He also inspired Indian people through the aid of his brother, Lalawéthika (the Noisemaker), a spiritual leader who was influenced by the teachings of Handsome Lake, as well as itinerant Shaker preachers. Lalawéthika's own spiritual insights changed his life and inspired many followers. He soon took the name Tenskwatawa (the Open Door), and was also known as the Prophet.[83]

Toward the close of Thomas Jefferson's administration, Native leaders attracted to Tecumseh's message were invited to Washington, D.C. On January 10, 1809, the president addressed diplomats from the Wyandot, Ottawa, Chippewa (Anishinaabe), Potawatomi, and Shawnee nations, declaring that the United States wished "to befriend you in every possible way." But, Jefferson warned:

the tribe which shall begin an unprovoked war against us, we will extirpate from the Earth or drive to such a distance, as that they shall never again be able to strike us. . . . We wish you to live in peace. . . . In time you will be as we are, you will become one people with us; your blood will mix with ours, and will spread with ours over this great island.[84]

Ultimately, Jefferson held out only two options to Indian people: Be absorbed into the United States and face cultural obliteration, or fight for Indian homelands and face military obliteration.

President James Madison continued Jefferson's policy of pressuring Native nations to cede more of their homelands. The nation's fourth president extended Jefferson's appointment of William Hull as the governor of Michigan territory. In 1809, Governor Hull was addressed by Wyandot chiefs including Schow-Han-Wret (Black Chief) and Maera (Walk-in-the-Water): "We love the land that covers the bones of our fathers. . . . It surprises us, your children, that Our Great Father, the President of the United States [James Madison], should take as much upon himself as the Great Spirit above, as he wants all the land on this island."[85]

Like his predecessor, Madison would also have to deal with Tecumseh, who in 1811 was touring the South to recruit allies among the Creeks, Seminoles, Cherokees, Chickasaws, and Choctaws. Seeking to take advantage of Tecumseh's absence, Governor William Henry Harrison—now reappointed by President Madison—marched one thousand soldiers against Prophetstown, the center of Tecumseh's alliance, at the mouth of the Tippecanoe River, near present-day Lafayette, Indiana. With Harrison's army camped about a mile northwest, the Prophet inspired some five hundred

The Battle of Tippecanoe, **1811, by Kurtz and Allison.** Chromolithograph, ca. 1889. *Courtesy Library of Congress, LC-DIG-pga-01891.*

"WHY NOT SELL THE AIR?":
TECUMSEH CONFRONTS A FUTURE PRESIDENT, 1810

In a bid to halt American expansion, Tecumseh (1769–1813) attempted to forge a powerful pan-Indian confederacy to unite tribes from the Great Lakes to the Gulf of Mexico. In August of 1810, the war chief confronted William Henry Harrison, then governor of Indiana Territory, in a council near the governor's mansion at Grouseland. Proclaiming that he was the "acknowledged head of all the Indians," Tecumseh criticized the Treaty of Fort Wayne (1809)—in which Delaware, Potawatomi, and Miami tribal leaders ceded more than three million acres of land in Illinois and Indiana in exchange for $5,250 in goods and annual subsidies—and blasted the United States for dividing and dispossessing Indian tribes:

> You endeavor to prevent the Indians from doing what we, their leaders, wish them to do—unite and consider their land the common property. . . . Sell a country! Why not sell the air, the clouds and the great sea, as well as the earth? Did not the Great Spirit make them all for the use of his children? . . . The states have set the example of forming a union among all the fires [state capitals]—why should they censure the Indians for following it?

Harrison replied that the United States treated Indians with justice, and that all Indian lands had been purchased through treaties, fair and square. Tense moments followed, and at one point Tecumseh called Harrison a liar, causing soldiers to grab their arms and warriors to heft tomahawks. Eventually calm was restored, and the council adjourned. When subsequent meetings failed to resolve matters, Harrison invited Tecumseh to visit President James Madison in Washington, but Tecumseh refused, saying that he hoped the Great Spirit would "put some sense" into the president and encourage him to restore the Indians' land. If not, Tecumseh declared prophetically, "He may sit still in his town, and drink his wine, while you and I will have to fight it out."[86]

President William Henry Harrison, 1841. As governor of Indian Territory, from 1801–13, Harrison made treaties that ceded millions of acres of Indian land to the United States, earning him the enmity of the Shawnee Chief Tecumseh and his followers. Still, Harrison could not help but admire his adversary, calling him "one of those uncommon geniuses [who] spring up occasionally to produce revolutions and overturn the existing order of things. If it were not for the . . . United States," Harrison asserted, Tecumseh "would be the founder of an empire that would rival in glory Mexico or Peru." *Drawn on stone by Charles Fenderich, from a painting by Mr. Franquinet. Courtesy Library of Congress, LC-USZ62-13009.*

allied warriors, including Kickapoos, Winnebagos, Potawatomis, Shawnees, Piankeshaws, Wyandots, Ohio Iroquois, Ottawas, and Ojibwes, to mount a predawn surprise attack on November 7, 1811. Outnumbered two to one, the allied Indian force was routed. Harrison torched Prophetstown and became a national hero for his victory at the Battle of Tippecanoe. In 1840, he would be elected the ninth president of the United States.[87]

The Battle of Tippecanoe did not destroy Tecumseh's effort to stem the tide of American aggression. When the War of 1812 broke out between the United States and Great Britain, the pan-tribal political leader quickly raised an army of warriors to fight alongside the British. Once again President Madison depended on William Henry Harrison to quash the Indians, and once again Harrison delivered. On October 5, 1813, along the Thames River in what is now Ontario, Canada, Harrison's army defeated Tecumseh, his warriors, and a British contingent. Tecumseh was killed during the battle and was buried in a mass grave.[88]

ANDREW JACKSON AND THE RED STICKS

The majority of Indian people in the South rejected Tecumseh's vision of the United States as an oppressor that should be resisted through force of arms. But Tecumseh had convinced a minority of the Creek Nation to join his movement. They became known as the Red Sticks, a red stick being a Creek symbol of war.

In January 1814, President Madison appointed future president General Andrew Jackson to lead American soldiers in battle against the Red Sticks. Some seven hundred Cherokees and two hundred anti–Red Stick Creeks also joined Jackson's forces to demonstrate their nations' commitment to living in peace with the United States.[89] On March 27, 1814, Jackson attacked the fortified Red Stick town of Tohopeka at Horseshoe Bend, on the Tallapoosa River in Alabama. Approximately one thousand Red Sticks under Menewa (Great Warrior) faced Jackson's army of about three thousand regulars and militia, as well as numerous Chickasaws, Choctaws, Creeks, and Cherokees. Jackson's frontal assault across the neck of Tohopeka's peninsula faltered and suddenly pandemonium broke loose inside the town. Jackson's Cherokee allies, led by Junuluska, decided to swim across the river and attack the town from the rear. Soon pro-American Cherokees were fighting Red Sticks within the town's walls. Jackson ordered his own soldiers to charge. No mercy was shown by either side. In the end, the Red Sticks were defeated. Some 557 Red Stick warriors lay dead on the battlefield; nearly 300 drowned or were shot while trying to escape. About 70 Red Stick warriors escaped, joining 300 women and children who had been sent to safety downstream before the battle began. Thus did Red Stick power come to an end.[90]

After his victory at the Battle of Horseshoe Bend, Jackson marched south and built Fort Jackson at the junction of the Alabama and Tallapoosa River. He then ordered all Creek chiefs, including

Andrew Jackson, by Ralph Eleaser Whiteside Earl (ca. 1785–1838). Oil on canvas, ca. 1817. *Courtesy National Portrait Gallery, Smithsonian Institution; gift of the A. W. Mellon Educational and Charitable Trust; NPG.65.78.*

Red Sticks and pro-American Creek leaders, to accept peace terms he dictated. The Creeks would surrender half of their lands, cease trade with Spanish Florida, and permit the United States to build forts and military roads throughout their country. The Creeks protested, but Jackson refused to differentiate between pro– and anti–Red Stick factions, and refused to acknowledge the assistance his army had received from Creek warriors. On August 9, the Creeks signed the Treaty of Fort Jackson, which claimed, falsely, that "more than two-thirds of the whole number of chiefs and warriors of the Creek nation" opposed the United States during the war.[91] The 1814 treaty was a prelude to the 1830s, when southern Indians, including the Creeks, discovered that Andrew Jackson intended to dispossess them, no matter how loyal they had been to the United States.

The War of 1812 ended with the Treaty of Ghent, which was signed on December 24, 1814, in Ghent, Belgium, and sent to the United States for ratification. Early in 1815, the United States Senate debated the treaty's provisions, which included an article pertaining to the future of Native nations. A significant legal statement emerged during the debate. In February 1815, New York senator Rufus King, a staunch Federalist and a signer of the Constitution, addressed his Senate colleagues about the history of legal relations between Indians and whites in the United States. Using only 1,146 words, King carefully defined the right of preemption, which, under the Treaty of Paris (1783), gave the United States the right to purchase Indian lands within the boundaries set by the treaty. He also carefully separated "preemption" from "sovereignty," concluding with words that were significant for Native nations then and now: "The sovereignty of the UNITED STATES is therefore limited not absolute."[92]

The Senate ratified the Treaty of Ghent, which restored "to such tribes or nations, respectively, all the possessions, rights, and privileges which they may have enjoyed or been entitled to in one thousand eight hundred and eleven, previous to such hostilities."[93] The United States, however, had no intention of respecting Indian rights as they existed before 1811. Under the Treaty of Ghent, for example, Andrew Jackson's 1814 treaty with the Creeks should have been nullified and their ceded lands returned to them. But the Treaty of Ghent was ignored—and continued to be ignored in subsequent treaties with Indian peoples.[94] Far from respecting Indian land rights, settlers in the early nineteenth century pressured Indian nations for more land, and began to demand that Indian nations be removed to lands west of the Mississippi.

In 1816, Rufus King, the New York senator who had so recently declared that the United States did not have "absolute" sovereignty over Indian lands, reluctantly agreed to be the Federalist party's candidate for president. The Federalists did not mount a vigorous campaign against the Republican candidate, James Monroe, who scored an overwhelming victory in the 1816 election.[95] King's position, that the United States had limited sovereignty regarding Indian nations, was ignored by James Monroe and other nineteenth-century presidents, such as Andrew Jackson. For most Americans, individual liberty and opportunity rested on unlimited territorial expansion, and Indians were in the way.

RED JACKET AND PRESIDENT JAMES MONROE

When James Monroe took office in 1817, his administration increased pressure for Indian removal. The new president was so eager to please congressmen that he pushed to remove Cherokees from their lands in the South even before Congress passed an appropriation to pay for it.[96] On July 8, 1817, the Cherokees signed yet another treaty with the United States. The lead American negotiator at the treaty conference was Major General Andrew Jackson, whose military appointment by Madison had been continued by Monroe. In exchange for this cession of Cherokee lands, the United States promised land in Arkansas to encourage the voluntary removal of Cherokee people.[97]

Two years later, President Monroe brought pressure to seize land belonging to the Senecas of western New York, the largest nation of the Iroquois Six Nations Confederacy. Behind all the maneuvering loomed the largest construction project yet undertaken in America: the Erie Canal.[98] To build the canal, Monroe wanted all the Senecas—who lived on eleven reservations of various sizes in western New York[99]—to move onto one: the Senecas' Allegany Reservation. The most important land the Senecas were expected to surrender was the Buffalo Creek Reservation, the capital of the Iroquois Confederacy after the patriots destroyed the traditional capital at Onondaga during the Revolution.[100] Adjacent to the Buffalo Creek Reservation was a small white community called

View on the Erie Canal, by John William Hill (1812–1879). Watercolor on paper, 1829. *Courtesy New York Public Library, 54577.*

Buffalo, a town that would become extremely valuable when the Erie Canal was completed in 1825. On July 9, 1819, at a meeting with United States negotiators at the Buffalo Creek Reservation, the Seneca leader Red Jacket protested President Monroe's effort to pressure the Iroquois into giving up their lands. Wearing a silver peace medal given to him by President George Washington, Red Jacket expressed his people's disappointment with Washington's successors: "We had thought that all the promises made by one President were handed down to the next. . . . Now the tree of friendship is decaying; its limbs are fast falling off, and you are at fault."[101]

Red Jacket and the Senecas successfully blocked President Monroe's attempt to seize their lands, and remained where they were, at least for the moment. But Monroe was reelected in 1820, and the pressures on Indian nations to give up more of their homelands remained relentless, despite treaties that guaranteed their lands. For the Cherokees in the south and the Iroquois Confederacy in the north, the tree of friendship

Red Jacket. Seneca War Chief, from *History of the Indian Tribes of North America,* by McKenney and Hall. Copy after Charles Bird King. The silver medal Segoyewatha (Red Jacket) wore for this portrait was a gift from President George Washington, given in 1792 to represent peace and friendship between the United States and the Iroquois. One side was engraved with the image of Washington offering a pipe to a Native man, who has dropped his tomahawk as a gesture of peace. In the distance, a farmer tills the soil with a team of oxen, reflecting the conviction, expressed by Washington and subsequent presidents and reformers, that Indians would perish unless they adopted the ways of the white man. *Smithsonian American Art Museum, 1985.66.153,293.*

RED JACKET.
SENECA WAR CHIEF.

was indeed decaying. The reason was clear to Red Jacket and other Native leaders: the United States and its presidents were "at fault."[102]

America's first five presidents—George Washington, John Adams, Thomas Jefferson, James Madison, and James Monroe—all involved the new nation in wars with American Indians. War, for the United States as well as for Native nations, asserted a concept central to all nations: sovereignty. Native nations had gone to war to protect their homelands—a bedrock of national sovereignty—against an invasion of white settlers. In the years to come, Native leaders would continue to grapple with these and other challenges, as Americans pushed farther into the west.

Westward the Course of Empire Takes Its Way **(mural study, U.S. Capitol), by Emanuel Gottlieb Leutze (1816–68).** Completed in 1861, Emanuel Leutze's mural study is a quintessential expression of America's "Manifest Destiny"—the idea, popular in the 1840s and 1850s, that the United States was destined, by God and history, to expand its boundaries throughout North America. A triumphant vision of American expansionism, Leutze's picture portrays the West as a land of hope and opportunity—for whites only. *Smithsonian American Art Museum, Bequest of Sara Carr Upton, 1931.6.1.*

CHAPTER II

NATIVE NATIONS IN AN AGE OF WESTERN EXPANSION, 1820–80

DONNA AKERS

From the administration of President James Monroe (1817–25) through the election of President Rutherford B. Hayes in 1877, a tidal wave of white settlers pushed west, invading Native homelands and challenging traditional lifeways. As more homesteaders arrived, the United States pressured Indian nations to cede the lands that held the bones of their ancestors. Embracing the principle that America had a God-given right to expand across the continent, presidents often dispossessed Native people through fraudulent treaties and military conquest, opening Indian homelands to settlers, land speculators, and railroad companies. Some presidents achieved the same ends through inaction, turning a blind eye when state governments, local citizens, and trespassers violated Native sovereignty. Confined to tiny remnants of their once vast estates or exiled to lands in the far West, Native people increasingly faced hunger, death, and wrenching social and cultural dislocation during the age of western expansion.

American Indian leaders responded by invoking a range of strategies to protect their lands and their tribal way of life. Some negotiated treaties with the government, hoping to save as much of the tribal estate as possible for the sake of their people and future generations. Others were forced into war. And many visited the nation's capital to speak directly with the president and other government officials—discussions that, for Indian leaders, reflected the unique nation-to-nation relationship between the United States and Native peoples. That Native nations managed to preserve their sovereignty in these years is, in part, a testament to Indian leaders who helped their people confront, resist, or adapt to the challenges of western expansion.

THE RHETORIC OF AMERICAN INDIAN POLICY

Nineteenth-century American Indian policy was cast in terms of "helping" Native people. American presidents, beginning with George Washington, believed that Indians would be better off if they adopted farming, embraced Christianity, and internalized the values of mainstream American society, including industry, private property, thrift, and sobriety. In many Indian treaties, the United States promised to send teachers, missionaries, blacksmiths, and farm implements to Native communities to help Indians become farmers and Bible-reading Christians. The offers of assistance were sincere, but assimilation was not the primary goal of American Indian policy. In reality, the United States government set Indian policy with one goal in mind: to obtain Indian lands and wealth.[1]

These twin ideals—assistance and dispossession—were mutually exclusive, and led to a confused, aberrant, and pathological system that produced incredible legal contortions and vain attempts to reconcile the irreconcilable. As a result, American presidents invoked a range of actions—from peaceful, sincere diplomacy and friendship to outright genocide—to acquire the Native estate. But whatever tactics they chose, the presidents never wavered from the idea that Americans had a God-given right to acquire Native territories.

This sense of entitlement reflected elements of a world view,

"IF YOU WILL KEEP YOUR PEOPLE OFF IT": SHARITARISH AND PRESIDENT JAMES MONROE AT THE WHITE HOUSE

Far left: **Sharitarish, a Pawnee Chief,** from *History of the Indian Tribes of North America,* **by McKenney and Hall. Copy after Charles Bird King (1785–1862).** *Courtesy White House Historical Association.*

Left: **President James Monroe, by John Vanderlyn (1775–1852).** Oil on canvas, 1816. *Courtesy National Portrait Gallery, Smithsonian Institution. NPG.70.59.*

In 1821, a delegation of sixteen Pawnee, Omaha, Oto, Missouri, and Kansa Indians visited President James Monroe at the White House. The delegates were given new clothes—military uniforms complete with hats, silver epaulets, and black boots—and were greeted by the president in the Red Room. Monroe thanked them for coming, spoke of the benefits of white civilization, and offered to send missionaries to teach the Indians agriculture and Christianity. When Monroe finished, Chief Sharitarish (Pawnee) rose to reply:

> My Great Father, the Great Spirit made us all—He made my skin red, and yours white. He placed us on this earth, and intended that we should live differently from each other. He made the whites to cultivate the earth, and feed on domestic animals; but he made us red skins to rove through the uncultivated woods and plains, to feed on wild animals, and to dress in their skins. . . . I love my country; I love my people, I love the manner in which we live . . . spare me then, my Father, let me enjoy my country, and pursue the buffaloe, and the beaver, and the other wild animals of our wilderness. . . . I have grown up and lived thus long without work; I am in hopes you will suffer me to die without it. We have plenty of buffaloe, beaver, deer, and other wild animals; we have also an abundance of horses; We have everything we want. We have plenty of land, if you will keep your people off it. . . .
>
> It is too soon, my Great Father, to send these good men among us. We are not starving yet. We wish you to permit us to enjoy the chase, until the game of our country is exhausted; until the wild animals become extinct. Let us exhaust our present resources, before you make us toil, and interrupt our happiness. Let me continue to live as I have done, and after I have passed to the Good or Evil Spirit from the wilderness of my present life, the subsistence of my children may become so precarious, as to need and embrace the offered assistance of these good people.[2] ◤

created over centuries by Europeans, that justified the conquest of Native peoples. Fundamental to this belief was the idea that European civilizations were more advanced than those of indigenous peoples, and that this superiority endowed the colonial powers with the right to claim tribal lands and diminish Native sovereignty.[3]

Under the "law of discovery," Native people retained the right of occupancy on their land, but not the right of ownership, which meant that Indian territories could be acquired by the colonial empire that claimed discovery.[4] The law of discovery proved remarkably resilient. When the United States defeated Britain in the American Revolution, the new nation declared that it had inherited all discovery claims of Britain as well as hegemony over the Indian nations.

The widespread conviction that indigenous peoples were savages also legitimized the appropriation of Native lands.[5] Yet when Americans encountered these "wild and barbaric sons of nature," some were surprised to discover that the Indians were both civilized and civil. "The manners and deportment of these men have in no respect differed from those of well-bred country gentlemen," John Quincy Adams remarked when he met a delegation of Cherokee leaders in 1824. A scion of an old aristocratic family and the son of a president,

*At the establishment of the Federal Government . . .
the principle was adopted of considering them as foreign
and independent powers and also as proprietors of lands.
They were, moreover, considered as savages, whom it was
our policy and our duty to use our influence in converting to
Christianity and in bringing within the pale of civilization. . . .
We have been far more successful in the acquisition of
their lands than in imparting to them the principles or
inspiring them with the spirit of civilization.*

—PRESIDENT JOHN QUINCY ADAMS, DECEMBER 2, 1828[6]

President John Quincy Adams, by George Caleb Bingham (1811–79). Oil on canvas, ca. 1850, from an 1850 original. *Courtesy National Portrait Gallery, Smithsonian Institution, NPG.69.20.*

Adams knew civility when he saw it. The Cherokees, he said, "have frequented all the societies, where they have been invited at evening parties, attended several drawing-rooms, and most of Mrs. Adams's Tuesday evenings." These men included Kooweskoowe (John Ross), who served as principal chief of the Cherokees from 1828 until the Civil War, and Elijah Hicks, son of a Cherokee elder statesman. Ross and Hicks were of mixed heritage—white and Cherokee. They were also educated in white-run schools, and were knowledgeable about American law. Hicks was extremely well read; his father owned one of the largest libraries in North America, private or public.

The Cherokees had chosen to adopt many aspects of white civilization—a strategy that many hoped would ensure their survival on their homelands in the Southeast. At first, it seemed to work. In a meeting with President James Monroe and Secretary of State John

Quincy Adams, Secretary of War John C. Calhoun observed that the great difficulty in satisfying white demands for Cherokee lands in Georgia rose from the progress of the Cherokees in "civilization." The Cherokees, Calhoun noted, enjoyed "a representative government, judicial courts, Lancaster schools, and permanent property."

SEQUOYAH AND THE "TALKING LEAVES"

During the administrations of Presidents James Madison and James Monroe, a Cherokee intellectual named Sequoyah (ca. 1770–1843) invented a system for transforming spoken Cherokee into written form. A contemporary of the Seneca spiritual leader Handsome Lake, Sequoyah believed that reading and writing were necessary for the survival of the Cherokee people. Around 1809, he began work on his syllabary—a system that reduced the Cherokee language to eighty-six sounds, each with a corresponding written symbol. Completed in 1821, the syllabary revolutionized communication within the Cherokee Nation. With each passing year, more and more Cherokees acquired the skill of reading and writing—an explosion of literacy that fueled the founding of a tribal newspaper, the *Cherokee Phoenix*. Traditional beliefs and practices were also committed to paper via the syllabary, enabling Cherokees to preserve their culture.

Mindful of the relentless advance of white settlement, Sequoyah believed Cherokees should give up their lands in the East and move west of the Mississippi River. In 1818, he went to Arkansas, following earlier Cherokee migrations that had begun as early as 1794. Most Cherokees stayed in their eastern homelands, however, believing that they could live side by side with Americans, on their own terms, thanks in no small part to the efforts of Sequoyah. But

Se-quo-yah, from History of the Indian Tribes of North America, by McKenney and Hall. Copy after Charles Bird King. *Smithsonian American Art Museum, museum purchase; 1985.66.153,296.*

neither assimilation nor Sequoyah's syllabary could alter the Cherokee Nation's fate under the administration of America's seventh president, Andrew Jackson.[7]

Calhoun also praised the Cherokees for their farming abilities and for their propensity to "write their own State papers, and reason as logically as most white diplomatists."

President Monroe asserted that "the Indians cannot, with justice, be removed from their lands within the State of Georgia by force."[8] Soon, however, another president would do just that.

PRESIDENT ANDREW JACKSON AND INDIAN REMOVAL

The American population was growing rapidly in the second quarter of the nineteenth century. In 1820, the population had reached ten million; by 1830, nearly thirteen million. By 1840, the United States boasted seventeen million people, many of them moving to the western frontier or to lands occupied by Native nations east of the Mississippi River.[9] Population pressure on Native lands—and political pressure to acquire them—was strongest in the Southeast, where sixty thousand Cherokees, Creeks (Muscogees), Choctaws, and Chickasaws occupied a twenty-five-million-acre domain encompassing parts of northeastern Georgia, western North Carolina, southern Tennessee, eastern Alabama, and northern Mississippi. In 1824, government negotiators obtained a treaty from individuals who had no authority to represent the Muscogee Nation. After his inauguration, President John Quincy Adams (1825–29) listened to the arguments of the authentic Muscogee representatives and set aside the treaty. Even though Adams later sent negotiators to obtain a similar agreement with the Muscogees, he listened to Native leaders and attempted to deal fairly with Native nations. Adams's successor would not be so inclined.[10]

Andrew Jackson succeeded John Quincy Adams as president in 1829. America's first "frontier president," Jackson came to office with enormous popular support. His name had become something of a household word during the War of 1812, when, as a major general, he led American troops against the Red Sticks, a pro-British faction of the Muscogee Nation, and defeated the British at New Orleans. Now a national hero, Jackson forced his Muscogee opponents—as well as those who supported the Americans—to make extensive land cessions to the United States. When pro-American Muscogees protested, Jackson replied that they should have done more to stop their disloyal brothers.[11] After this, Native people clearly understood Jackson's nature and were wary of his motives.

As president, Jackson advocated for the passage of the Indian Removal Act, which authorized him to make treaties to remove Indian nations from the Southeast to Indian Territory.[12] For Jackson, Indians were savage nomads who had no permanent home. Devoted to hunting and resistant to assimilating American values, Native people, he argued, would be better off in the West, where they could roam at

Andrew Jackson as "The Great Father," ca. 1830. As president, Jackson advocated moving Indians to the West, where they could live free of white interference. Removal opponents mocked "Old Hickory's" professed compassion for the tribes in cartoons that depicted Jackson as a paternal figure comforting tiny, helpless Indian children. *Courtesy Clements Library, University of Michigan.*

will and live as they saw fit. If the tribes surrendered their eastern homelands, Jackson reasoned, white settlers could move onto and develop their lands.

Jackson's depiction of the southern Indians as nomads conflicted with the reality of life for the "Five Civilized Tribes," as they were known—the Choctaws, Muscogees, Chickasaws, Seminoles, and especially the Cherokees—who lived in permanent homes, grew market crops, and were literate in their native languages as well as English.[13] Never one to let the facts stand in the way, Jackson twisted the truth and exploited an enduring stereotype to push the Indian Removal Act through Congress. In an address to lawmakers, Jackson asked, "What good man would prefer a country covered with forests and ranged by a few thousand savages to our extensive Republic, studded with cities, towns, and prosperous farms, embellished with all the improvements which art can devise or industry execute, occupied by more than 12,000,000 happy people, and filled with all the blessings of liberty, civilization, and religion?"[14]

The Indian Removal Act passed by a slim margin in 1830, in part because Jackson promised that the process would be voluntary. But when few Native nations volunteered to leave their homelands, Jackson resorted to force and chicanery to drive the tribes west. In addition to using troops, the president instructed United States officials to negotiate removal treaties with non-authorized tribal representatives.

John Ross, principal chief of the Cherokees, repudiated the agreement, arguing for his people's right to remain on their homelands and waging a tireless diplomatic and legal campaign against removal. The son of a Scottish father who had married a Cherokee woman of mixed white and Native heritage, Ross had been reared among the Cherokees but operated comfortably in the white world. Highly educated, eloquent, and a natural-born leader, Ross emerged as the Moses of his people, leading the Cherokees during a time of trouble and finally guiding them on their exile into the wilderness: Indian Territory.

Through it all, Ross never wavered in his absolute belief that indigenous people—like whites—had an inalienable right to life, liberty, and property, and that Indian tribes were sovereign nations

DAVY CROCKETT: DEFENDER OF INDIAN RIGHTS

In 1830, Congress began debate on a plan to remove all eastern Indians to lands west of the Mississippi River. The measure, President Andrew Jackson's top legislative priority, ignited a firestorm of controversy that focused national attention on the rights of Native nations. Despite opposition from Indians as well as religious and reform groups, Congress passed the Indian Removal Act, setting the stage for the eviction of thousands of Native people along the Trail of Tears.

Among the lawmakers who voted against the measure was Representative David Crockett of Tennessee. Best remembered as the coonskin-cap-wearing, gun- and axe-toting frontiersman who died heroically at the Alamo, Crockett (1786–1836) was also a champion of Indian rights during one of the darkest hours in Native American history.

Little in Crockett's early life foretold his emergence as a friend of Indians. His father, a poor farmer and tavern keeper, was part of a wave of white settlers who flooded into Tennessee in the 1700s, resulting in the loss of Cherokee and Chickasaw lands. Creek Indians killed Crockett's grandparents, and during the War of 1812 Crockett enlisted to fight the Red Sticks—the pro-British faction of the Creek Nation.

Crockett later began a career in public life, serving as a justice of the peace, town commissioner, and state legislator. In 1827, Tennessee voters sent him to Washington to serve the first of three terms in the House of Representatives. As a lawmaker, Crockett cultivated the image of a humble frontiersman who had risen to prominence through luck and pluck and promoted the interests of his backwoods constituents. "The rich require but little legislation," he declared during debate on a land bill. "[W]e should, at least occasionally, legislate for the poor." Crockett's support for the land bill precipitated a break with his fellow Tennessee Democrats and put him on a collision course with President Andrew Jackson. The rift widened in 1830, when the Indian Removal Act came to the House floor.

Strongly supported by President Jackson, the Indian Removal Act sparked an energetic debate in Congress. No speech by Davy Crockett was printed in the congressional *Register of Debates*, but an address purportedly given by Crockett, as well as his autobiography, *A Narrative of the Life of David Crockett of the State of Tennessee* (1834), indicates that Crockett had become an implacable foe of Indian removal. In his speech to lawmakers, Crockett claimed that he had no desire to see "the poor remnants of a once powerful people" forced from their homelands. He reminded his colleagues that he represented four counties bordering Chickasaw Country and that he would never drive away his Indian neighbors, including the Cherokees, who would prefer "death at [their] homes" to life in the West. The United States had viewed Indian tribes as sovereign nations "since the foundation of this government," he declared, and the government was "bound by treaty" to protect them. Compelling Indians to forsake their lands represented "oppression with a vengeance"—a prospect Crockett could never countenance. Claiming that he "would sooner be honestly and politically d—nd, than hypocritically immortalized" by supporting "a wicked, unjust measure," Crockett recalled, "I gave a good, honest vote, one that I believe will not make me ashamed in the day of judgment."

As payback for opposing Indian removal, Jackson's allies rallied to unseat Crockett in 1831. Reelected in 1833, Crockett again lost his seat in 1835. Weary of politics and hounded by creditors, Davy Crockett left Tennessee and traveled west, where he died fighting for Texas's independence. But Crockett's bold stance in defense of Native rights was hailed and remembered in Indian Country. "To those Gentlemen who have so honorably and ably vindicated the rights of the poor Indians in Congress," Cherokee principal chief John Ross wrote Crockett, "this Nation owes a debt of gratitude, which the pages of history will bear record of until time shall be no more. . . ."[15]

whose claim to the soil was endowed by the highest authority. Said Ross: "Our ancestors from time immemorial possessed this country, not by a 'charter' from the hand of a mortal king, who had no right to grant it, but by the will of the king of kings."[16]

Under John Ross, the Cherokee Nation twice brought cases before the federal courts to defend their sovereignty. In the first case, *Cherokee Nation v. Georgia,* the United States Supreme Court ruled that the Cherokees could not file suit in a federal court because they were *not* an independent nation, but a "domestic dependent nation." The Cherokees sued again with the help of missionary Samuel Worcester and finally won a decision, *Worcester v. Georgia,* which ruled that the Cherokees should be allowed to stay in their homelands in Georgia, unmolested by the state and local governments.[17]

Cherokees and their friends exulted when the Supreme Court announced its decision—the first time a Native nation had used the judicial system of the United States successfully. The president, it seemed, would be forced to comply with the court's decision, signaling a great victory for the Cherokees and for the democratic principle of equality before the law.[18]

Unfortunately, it did not turn out that way. Jackson, intent on evicting the Cherokees, ignored the court's ruling and sent negotiators to make a treaty with a small faction of Cherokees who believed that resistance to removal was futile. Though unauthorized by the Cherokee Nation, the group signed the Treaty of New Echota on December 29, 1835, giving up all Cherokee lands east of the Mississippi in exchange for $5 million and a large tract in Indian Territory. The Senate ratified the treaty, and in 1838, the United States Army forcibly removed most Cherokees from their homelands to Indian Territory, along the Trail of Tears. Although three men who signed the treaty were killed by Cherokees as punishment for selling tribal lands, the damage was done. Jackson had used his power to uproot and relocate a Native nation—a breathtaking violation of Indian sovereignty that would influence American Indian policy for years to come.[19]

The burden of physically removing the Cherokees fell to Jackson's successor, Martin Van Buren, who ordered the United States

"WE HAVE NEITHER LAND, NOR HOME, NOR RESTING PLACE": JOHN ROSS PROTESTS CHEROKEE REMOVAL, 1836

As principal chief of the Cherokee Nation, John Ross (1790–1866) fought tirelessly to keep his people from being removed from their homelands in the Southeast. When a small group of Cherokees signed a treaty transferring to the United States all tribal lands east of the Mississippi River in exchange for $5 million, thousands of Cherokees signed petitions urging Congress to rescind the agreement. One of the most forceful arguments for repeal was issued by Ross, who blasted the Treaty of New Echota (1835) as a violation of Cherokee sovereignty. The treaty, he declared,

> is not the act of our Nation; we are not par-
> ties to its covenants; it has not received
> the sanction of our people. The makers of
> it sustain no office nor appointment in our
> Nation, under the designation of Chiefs,
> Head men, or any other title, by which they
> hold, or could acquire, authority to assume
> the reins of Government, and to make bar-
> gain and sale of our rights, our posses-
> sions, and our common country. And we
> are constrained solemnly to declare, that
> we cannot but contemplate the enforce-
> ment of the stipulations of this instrument
> on us, against our consent, as an act of in-
> justice and oppression, which, we are well

John Ross. A Cherokee Chief, **from** *History of the Indian Tribes of North America,* **by McKenney and Hall. Copy after Charles Bird King.** *Smithsonian American Art Museum, Museum purchase; 1985.66.153,295.*

> persuaded, can never knowingly be coun-
> tenanced by the Government and people
> of the United States. . . .[20] ➤

Army to round up the Cherokees at bayonet point, incarcerate them in pens, and force them to walk five hundred miles west to the "American Desert." The march, which Cherokees remember as the *Nunahi-duna-slo-hilu-I* ("The Trail Where They Cried"), resulted in the deaths of at least four thousand Cherokee men,

Family Removal, by Jerome Tiger (Creek-Seminole, 1941–67). Tempera on paperboard, 1965. *National Museum of the American Indian, 23/6112.*

women, and children, not including the four thousand more who succumbed to disease and starvation during their first year in Indian Territory.[21] John Ross's beloved wife, Quatie, died of pneumonia just before she reached the fledgling village of Little Rock, Arkansas. Ross continued to lead the Cherokee Nation in the West, where he worked tirelessly to reconstitute Cherokee society far from the lands that held the bones of his ancestors.[22]

INDIAN REMOVAL: NORTH AND SOUTH

Indian Removal was not limited to the East. Native nations in the North also faced unprecedented challenges during the Jacksonian era, forcing Native leaders to make difficult choices in their attempts to preserve their people and homelands. Leaders tried peaceful compromise whenever possible, but the American appetite for Native lands was insatiable, and treaties often failed to stem the tide of white settlers. As a result, many Native leaders were forced to choose a path of violent resistance. One of them was the Sac leader Makataimeshekiakiak, or Black Hawk.

Born at Saukenuk, near the mouth of the Rock River in northwestern Illinois, Black Hawk was thirty-seven years old in 1804, the year William Henry Harrison, governor of Indiana Territory, persuaded a small unauthorized delegation of Sac and Fox leaders to cede all tribal lands east of the Mississippi River. The majority of Sac and Fox people refused to accept the treaty and ignored American attempts to force them to comply with its provisions.[23] Led by Black Hawk, many Sac and Fox people continued to live in Illinois, following their routine of farming in the spring and summer and moving onto the plains for their winter hunt. In 1828, the local Indian agent, Thomas Forsyth, informed Black Hawk and his band that they should abandon their farms and villages as instructed in the 1804 and other treaties, but many tribal leaders denied ever ceding the disputed lands at Rock River. When they returned to Illinois in the spring of 1829, Black Hawk and his band discovered that white newcomers had taken their houses and fields. Hoping to prevent a confrontation, Black Hawk and his people retired to the periphery of their old village, sowing corn on the edges of their fields and sheltering themselves as best they could.

Seasonal migration continued in the face of mounting white unease until the spring of 1831, when Illinois militiamen drove Black Hawk's band back across the river into Iowa. When the Indians returned to Illinois nine months later, the frontiersman panicked and persuaded Governor John Reynolds to call for soldiers to protect their villages from "eminent danger." Some seventeen-hundred volunteers responded to the call, including a lanky, twenty-three-year-old store clerk from New Salem named Abraham Lincoln.

The future president saw no action in what became known as the Black Hawk War, but state militia companies and federal army troops did, hunting down Black Hawk's people and killing even those who had raised white flags of surrender. With troops in pursuit, Black Hawk's followers tried to escape by swimming across the Mississippi River to Iowa. Behind them, on the Illinois side, soldiers laid down continuous fire, while the steamer *Warrior*, armed with an artillery gun, cut men, women, and children to ribbons. Those still on the Illinois side were attacked in what newspapers described as an "eight-hour frenzy of clubbing, stabbing, shooting, and . . . scalping."[24] Of the 400 who tried to cross the Mississippi, only about 150 made it to the west bank, where Sioux warriors killed and scalped 68 of the men and took the rest prisoner.[25]

Afterward, Americans dictated a new treaty to the surviving Sac and Fox, taking six million acres of tribal lands in Iowa, in addition to fifty million acres previously seized in Illinois. Black Hawk survived the war that bore his name and was imprisoned at Fortress Monroe in Virginia. After several weeks, he was released on orders from President Andrew Jackson, who agreed to return him to the West. Before leaving, Black Hawk met with President Jackson, whom he greeted with the words, "I am a man and you are another." Those words may sound unremarkable to modern ears, but in 1833, Black Hawk's

BLACK HAWK'S EASTERN TOUR, 1832

When the Sac war leader Black Hawk (1767–1838) was released from prison after the war that bore his name, he was taken on a sightseeing tour of Washington, Baltimore, Philadelphia, New York, Buffalo, and Detroit before rejoining his people in the West. Along the way, he visited government arsenals, buildings, and navy yards and was invited to receptions in his honor. Civic leaders wined and dined him and urban crowds besieged him, eager to catch a glimpse of a famous frontier Indian. In New York, he watched a man pilot a hot-air balloon and declared, "That man is brave—don't think he will ever get back." Later, in 1833, Black Hawk dictated and published an autobiography, which provided a more balanced account of what was known as the Black Hawk War. Edged from power by Keokuk, the moderate, white-appointed head chief of his people, Black Hawk increasingly resembled a "poor dethroned monarch," according to the artist George Catlin, who called him "an object of pity." Even death in 1838 held no mercy for Black Hawk. Grave robbers snatched his body, and his bones were put on display at a museum in Burlington, Iowa.[26]

Múk-a-tah-mish-o-káh-kaik, Black Hawk, Prominent Sac Chief, **by George Catlin (1796–1872).** *Smithsonian American Art Museum, gift of Mrs. Joseph Harrison, Jr.; 1985.66.2.*

claim of equality challenged a central tenet of American national identity—that whites were superior to Indians. By declaring himself "a man," just as was Jackson, Black Hawk pinpointed the pathology of nineteenth-century perceptions of American Indians and exposed the racial bigotry that supported Manifest Destiny.[27]

During the administrations of Presidents Van Buren, Harrison, and Tyler, the United States fought a long and bitter war to evict the Seminole Nation from Florida.[28] Led by Osceola (1803–38), a young warrior from the Tallassee band, and other leaders, the Seminoles refused to leave their homelands, coveted by white settlers. Instead of submitting meekly, Osceola and a group of Seminoles withdrew into the Everglades and waged a guerrilla war against a numerically supe-

Os-ce-o-lá, The Black Drink, a Warrior of Distinction, by George Catlin (1796–1872). During the 1830s, Osceola led the Seminoles in their long struggle to remain in Florida. In 1838, he was imprisoned at Fort Moultrie, South Carolina, where he died shortly after sitting for this portrait. *Smithsonian American Art Museum; Gift of Mrs. Joseph Harrison, Jr; 1985.66.301.*

rior force for two years. Finally, in 1837, a weak and ill Osceola visited General T. S. Jessup under a flag of truce. Instead of honoring this internationally recognized cessation of hostilities, Jessup ordered his soldiers to imprison Osceola, an action that unsettled some Americans, who denounced the move as a "violation of all that is noble and generous in war."[29] The artist George Catlin was so outraged that he immediately went to Fort Moultrie, South Carolina, where Osceola was incarcerated. There, Catlin befriended Osceola and painted his portrait. "This gallant fellow," wrote Catlin, "is grieving with a broken spirit, and ready to die, cursing the white man, no doubt to the end of his breath." After Osceola's death, the attending physician at the fort disinterred his body and removed his head and heart, which he embalmed for display in his home.[30] The Seminoles continued their fight until 1842, by which time most had been removed to—or voluntarily resettled in—Indian Territory. A small group remained in Florida, where their descendants continue to live today.

MANIFEST DESTINY

In 1839, a New York newspaper man, John L. O'Sullivan, asserted that it was America's "manifest destiny to overspread the continent allotted by Providence for the free development of our yearly multiplying millions."[31] Throughout the 1840s and 1850s, the subjugation of indigenous peoples and the abrogation of their human rights would be justified by positing westward expansion as a religious mission ordained by God.

William Henry Harrison, the architect of multiple Indian treaties as governor of Indiana Territory, became president of the United States in 1841. After less than a month in office, Harrison caught a cold that developed into pneumonia. He died on April 4, becoming the first president to die in office. John Tyler, called "His Accidency" by political wags, succeeded "Old Tippecanoe" and continued the basic contours of American Indian policy. Under Tyler's administration, Congress passed the Pre-Emption Act of 1841, which allowed settlers to claim 160 acres of "public" lands, prior to their being surveyed—lands claimed by Indian nations. Since many believed the government would eventually acquire almost all valuable Indian lands, settlers claimed the parcels they wanted and refused to leave.

The case of the Seminoles constitutes at present the only exception to the successful efforts of the Government to remove the Indians to the homes assigned them west of the Mississippi. . . . The continued treacherous conduct of these people . . . leave the Government no alternative but to continue the military operations against them until they are totally expelled from Florida.

—PRESIDENT MARTIN VAN BUREN, DECEMBER 3, 1838.[32]

President James K. Polk. Reproduction of a daguerreotype, ca. 1845–49. President Polk extended the boundaries of the United States to the shores of the Pacific Ocean. By the time he left office in 1849, America encompassed almost all of the territory that constitutes the present-day United States, with the exception of Alaska and Hawai'i. *Courtesy Library of Congress, LC-USZ62-13011.*

American presidents during the 1840s and 1850s were committed to fostering America's westward expansion, and none more so than James K. Polk. Taciturn, humorless, and hardworking, Polk took office in 1845. During the next four years, he masterminded the acquisition of more territory than any other president in American history, expanding by two-thirds the size of the United States through the annexation of Texas and the acquisition of California, New Mexico, and lands in Oregon.[33] The last strong president before the Civil War, Polk reasserted the Monroe Doctrine, warning European powers not to interfere in America's plans to expand across the continent. When word of Polk's pronouncement reached Philadelphia, a joyful crowd shouted, "Hurrah! Jackson is alive again!"[34]

President Polk extended the nation's boundaries to the shores of the Pacific, but the acquisition of the new lands sparked a bitter national dispute over the expansion of slavery into the West—a contest that laid the foundation for the Civil War. It also put white settlers and prospectors on a collision course with Native people.

HUNTING INDIANS IN FLORIDA WITH BLOOD HOUNDS.

***Hunting Indians in Florida with Blood Hounds,* by James Baillie.** Lithograph, 1848. Zachary Taylor came to the White House in 1849 with forty years of experience as a career soldier, during which he fought for Indian removal in the Black Hawk War (1832) and the Second Seminole War (1835–42). In his campaign against the Seminoles, Taylor requested permission to use bloodhounds to track the Indians through the swamps of Florida. Anti-Taylor forces made political capital of the episode in propaganda circulated during the presidential election of 1848. *Courtesy Library of Congress, LC-USZ62-89725.*

CALIFORNIA INDIANS AND THE GOLD RUSH

The bloodiest stage of westward expansion occurred during the settlement of California. On January 24, 1848, gold was discovered at the building site of Johann Sutter's mill, erected near Sacramento at the Maidu village of Kolo-ma. The discovery promoted a tidal wave of migration to the West. Some eighty thousand prospective miners, called "forty-niners," poured across the heartland, rushing to strike it rich. More fortune hunters followed. By 1850, California's population was larger than that of Florida or Delaware.[35]

The migrants encountered thousands of Native people, many of whom worked as laborers in the gold fields of northern California. The new prospectors ruthlessly exploited Indian labor, taking advantage of a state law that allowed whites to force intoxicated men and orphaned children into indentured servitude. As California's population grew, the state government subsidized vigilante groups of miners and ranchers, who raided and terrorized Indian villages. The militia units indiscriminately killed Indian men, women, and children, collecting bounties for harvesting scalps. Between 1845 and 1870, California's Indian population declined by 80 percent, from 150,000 to 30,000 people. Barred from testifying in courts against whites, California's Natives had no legal recourse when whites assaulted, raped, or murdered their people.[36]

California Indians often challenged the white invasion of their homelands. In 1850, in what is now known as the Yosemite Valley, conflict arose between white miners and traders and the Chauchila and Kau-í-a bands of Yokuts, Yosemite Paiutes, and members of three or four other small tribes. Two of the most outspoken local tribal leaders, José Rey and José Juarez, united Native peoples in the region and conducted numerous campaigns against miners. Juarez agreed that white settlement of his homelands was inevitable, but he continued to encourage the Chauchila band to resist the invaders. He was later killed in a battle with a two-hundred-man militia unit organized by James Savage, a white trader, near the Fresno River. Other Native leaders, including José Rey, were wounded in the engagement. In the Yosemite Valley, Chief Tenaya and his band resisted eviction until 1851, when they were discovered and sent to a reservation.[37]

The Gold Rush did not generate Anglo-Indian conflict in southern California to the same degree, but tensions flared between American settlers and *Californios*—the descendants of early Spanish settlers—with Native people caught in the fray. The Cupeño leader Antonio Garra attempted to form a pan-Indian alliance to repel invading Americans and to protest taxation, as Indians received neither representation nor citizenship. In an effort to unite bands of Cahuilla, Kumeyaay, Luiseño, and Quechan people, Garra traveled from the Pacific Coast to the Colorado River encouraging Indians to fight to preserve their lifeways. Garra even approached rival Cahuilla leader Juan Antonio, a longtime white ally, to join his resistance movement. Juan Antonio finally chose sides, capturing Garra and turning him in to local authorities. Garra was convicted of murder and theft and was executed the next day.[38]

American presidents and the federal government turned a blind eye to the violence committed against the indigenous peoples of California, allowing state and local governments to freely pursue a policy of genocide. Although federal commissioners negotiated treaties with eighteen California Indian groups, the U.S. Senate in 1852 declined to ratify them, bowing to pressure from white Californians opposed to giving land to Indians. A number of small reservations were later established, but the Indians held no title to the land and were constantly hectored by land-hungry whites. Ultimately, the federal government's hands-off policy placed the Indians' fate in the hands of men such as California governor Peter H. Burnett, who spoke for many when he said, "the war of extermination will continue to be waged until the Indian race becomes extinct."[39]

KANSAS: RAILROADS AND "INDIAN RINGS"

In the 1850s, Congress abrogated treaties with indigenous nations that had been forced out of their homelands and relocated west of the Mississippi River in Kansas and Oklahoma. Many of the displaced nations had prospered and enjoyed newfound security through treaties that pledged that they would never be expelled from their new homelands. Avarice and greed, however, knew no boundaries in mid-nineteenth-century America.

American presidents supported the westward movement of non-Indians to Indian lands and championed the development of transcontinental railroads to link eastern and western states. Congress, for its part, spent thousands of dollars on railroad surveys, and United States representatives created treaties to liquidate Indian land titles and foster development. Soon a triumvirate of land speculators, railroad companies, and politicians emerged to form the Indian Ring—a union of dishonor that bought off congressmen, bilked the public purse, and expropriated Indian homelands. Indian agents and railroad men engaged in blatantly corrupt insider deals. Using the form of a treaty, tribes would be induced to cede lands directly to railroads, which paid the Indians through future sales of the land. From these sales, thousands of acres went to corrupt politicians as payoffs.[40]

The Indian Ring was particularly effective in appropriating Indian lands in Kansas—a principal focus of railroad development during the 1850s, with east–west and north–south lines planned for the territory. The main obstacle to development: more than ten thousand Kickapoos, Delawares, Sacs, Foxes, Shawnees, Potawatomis, Kansas, Ottawas, Wyandots, Osages, and other Indians whose rights to Kansas Territory were guaranteed by treaties with the United States. Between 1854 and 1871, the Indian Ring used threats, bribes, and promises to force Native peoples to cede thousands of acres of land, ushering in a second era of Indian removal in which the federal government forcibly relocated all but a handful of Indian bands from eastern Kansas, opening the Territory for railroad development and white settlement.[41]

THE PACIFIC NORTHWEST

Lust for Native lands was not confined to Kansas. Between 1852 and 1856, under the administrations of Presidents Millard Fillmore and Franklin Pierce, government agents negotiated some fifty-two treaties with Native nations in the trans-Mississippi West, transferring to the United States more than 170 million acres of Indian homelands.[42] Much of the territory taken from the Native peoples of the Pacific Northwest was by the work of Isaac Ingalls Stevens, the thirty-seven-year-old governor of Washington Territory and the territorial Indian commissioner, and Oregon Superintendent of Indian Affairs Joel Palmer. Sent by Washington to secure lands for white settlement, Stevens held a series of rapid-fire treaty councils with Native leaders throughout the Northwest in 1855. In May and June, the pair met with the Cayuse, Umatilla, Yakama, Walla Walla, and Nez Perce Indians at Walla Walla, in present-day Washington State, to discuss land cessions.

A former surveyor for the transcontinental railroad, Stevens explained that the whites and their railroads were an unstoppable force of nature to which the Indians must yield. "Can you prevent the wind from blowing?" Palmer asked. "Can you prevent the rain

Treaty conferences were often marked by symbolic displays of Native power and pride. Arriving at a treaty council meeting in Washington Territory in 1855, the Nez Perce demonstrated a flair for horsemanship that white observers never forgot. First, tribal chiefs, including Utsinmalikin, Metat Waptass, Joseph, Lawyer, Old James, and Red Wolf rode in, dismounted, and were introduced in order of rank to the American representatives (shown at center, right). Then, mounted Nez Perce warriors hefting shields paraded past the dignitaries in single file. A breathtaking exhibition of equestrian skills followed the parade. The horsemen, one eyewitness recalled, "formed a circle and dashed around us. . . . They would gallop about us as if about to make a charge, then wheel round and round, sounding their loud whoops. Then some score or two dismounted, and forming a ring, danced for about twenty minutes, while those surrounding them beat time on their drums." The chiefs then retired to the tent of Isaac Stevens, governor and superintendent of Indian affairs for Washington Territory, who was charged with making treaties that freed Indian lands for railroads and white settlers throughout the region. The Nez Perce leaders smoked "a pipe of peace, in token of good fellowship" with Stevens and his associates, then returned to their camping ground to prepare for the further discussions.[43]

Nez Perce Indians parading before United States commissioners and tribal leaders prior to a treaty conference in the Walla Walla Valley, Washington Territory. By Gustavus Sohon (1825–1903). Pencil drawing and watercolor on paper, 1855. *Courtesy National Anthropological Archives, Smithsonian Institution.*

from falling? Can you prevent the whites from coming? You are answered No!"[44]

The American representatives strongly urged the Indians to surrender their lands and relocate to the Nez Perce, Umatilla, and Yakama reservations. Using a carrot as well as a stick, Stevens promised that the Indians would enjoy reservation life, where they could pasture their animals on land not claimed or occupied by settlers. He also promised that the United States would recognize the tribes' ancient right to their customary hunting, fishing, and gathering grounds, on and off the reservations.

Kamiakin, a Yakama/Palouse leader, did not want to surrender his people's land or freedom. Tall, handsome, and imposing, Kamiakin exuded an air of strength and determination, and many Native leaders looked to him for guidance. Stickus, a Cayuse chief, agreed with Kamiakin, remarking that he could not sell his people's land because "this is our mother." Owhi, a Yakama chief, asked, "Shall I give the lands that are part of my body and leave myself poor and destitute? Shall I say that I will give you my lands? I cannot . . . I am afraid of the Almighty." Unmoved, Stevens insulted, upbraided, and threatened. In the end, he and Palmer pressured the leaders into signing three treaties that turned over sixty thousand square miles to the United States for approximately three cents an acre. Kamiakin was so angry that he bit his lips until they bled, saying that he signed as an act of friendship but never agreed to cede tribal lands.[45]

When they realized they had been tricked into making enormous land concessions, Native groups around the Puget Sound, as well as Cayuse, Yakamas, and Walla Wallas farther inland, attacked white settlers and miners, triggering a bloody three-year war with the United States. The army, under Major Gabriel L. Rains, came ready for battle. A veteran of the war against the Seminoles, Rains promised that he would "war forever, until not a Yakama breathes in the land he calls his own."[46] American officers and volunteers massacred Cayuse, Nez Perce, Palouse, and Walla Walla villagers and murdered Chief Peo-Peo-Mox-Mox (Yellow Bird), who had attended and spoken at the Walla Walla treaty council in 1855. Soldiers dismembered his body, cutting off his ears, tearing out his eyes, and severing his hands. They flayed his skin and cut up pieces of his body as souvenirs to be displayed in Oregon towns.[47]

Later, Governor Stevens addressed several Native leaders who had fought against the United States. Claiming that he was interested only in their welfare, Stevens told them that the government would resettle them on reservations, where agents would civilize them. Tumneh Howlish, a Cayuse leader, declared, "Why are you talking to us? I have a head to think, a heart to feel, and breath in my body; I am equal to you. For that reason, as we are equal, I do not know why you are to tell me what to do."[48]

Native leaders repeatedly asserted their equality, humanity, and competency, but few whites listened. Americans clung tenaciously to the belief that Indians were "children" who needed their guidance and instruction. As their guardians, whites assumed control over Native people, lands, and resources, and instructed Native leaders to follow the wishes of the "Great White Father" in Washington, who always had their best interests at heart.[49]

PRESIDENT LINCOLN AND AMERICAN INDIANS

Abraham Lincoln is remembered as an enlightened, wise leader who removed the cancerous growth of slavery from the American Republic. Yet the Great Emancipator, as he is known, ignored America's other deformity—the dehumanization and decimation of American Indians. Preoccupied by the Civil War, the nation's sixteenth president had little time to address the ramifications of westward expansion, particularly the nation's dishonorable dealings with Native peoples. The challenges facing Indian nations when Lincoln took office in 1861 remained unresolved—and largely unexamined—when he was felled by an assassin's bullet at Ford's Theatre in 1865.

When the Civil War began, Lincoln withdrew federal troops from Indian Territory, betraying America's treaty obligation to protect Indian nations against intruders and leaving Indians loyal to the Union vulnerable to Confederate forces. Thousands of Delaware, Sac, Fox, Wyandot, Peoria, Osage, Seneca, Ottawa, Wea, Miami, Kickapoo, and other Native people fled to Kansas as they sought refuge from rebel troops, but Lincoln ignored their pleas for aid. Soon Indian Territory exploded in a horrendous civil war between

pro-Union and pro-Confederate factions of the Choctaw, Cherokee, Chickasaw, Muskogee, and Seminole nations. Lincoln belatedly realized his mistake in forsaking Indian Territory, but he still provided little aid, and during Reconstruction his Republican Party further punished the nations.[50]

Corruption ran rampant in the United States Indian Office during Lincoln's administration. Government officials, Indian agents, superintendents, traders, merchants, and politicians siphoned off treaty annuities and goods owed to Native nations as payment for land cessions. In Minnesota, public officials, private citizens, and others worked cooperatively to swindle Indians and enrich themselves. Consider the career of Henry Hastings Sibley, a manager for the American Fur Company in the Minnesota region. A man on the make, he entered politics and was elected territorial delegate to Congress in 1849. Retaining his financial interest in the fur trade, Sibley represented traders at the Minnesota Sioux treaty negotiations of 1851 and received $145,000 of the $475,000 the United States paid to the Sioux for ceding twenty-four million acres of land.

Sibley claimed the money was due him as the result of an overpayment for pelts purchased from the Sioux. The Indians objected, but Sibley's associate, Alexander Ramsey, United States Indian agent to the Sioux, approved the transaction. In 1858, Sibley became the first governor of Minnesota, narrowly defeating Ramsey, who became his successor in 1860.[51]

Ramsey's fortunes, too, were linked to the "Indian system." Appointed as a treaty negotiator with the Dakota Sioux, Ramsey engineered agreements in which the Dakotas ostensibly agreed to give up their lands for a pittance. He did this by encouraging illiterate chiefs to sign their x to a document that he claimed was a copy of the treaty. In fact, the chiefs had signed an agreement directing the United States to pay almost all of the tribe's money to Ramsey and his associates. When the chiefs discovered the swindle, they sent a message to President Lincoln and the Senate requesting that the agreement be set aside. The treaty remained in force, however, and Ramsey grew rich and powerful, serving in the Senate from 1863 to 1875 and as secretary of war under President Rutherford B. Hayes from 1879 to 1881. A shrewd businessman, he invested in real estate and built a fashionable home in the Irvine Park neighborhood of St. Paul, complete with hot and cold running water, gas lighting, radiators, and other Victorian-era conveniences. In 1872, his wife, Anna, went on a shopping spree in New York; her purchases filled two railroad boxcars.[52]

The Dakotas were less fortunate. Forced to cede millions of acres of their homelands in Minnesota and Iowa, they lost key hunting grounds and became increasingly dependent upon treaty annuities for procuring food. By 1862, the Dakotas were left with almost no land, no money, and no food, while all around them white settlers farmed and thrived on lands that were once theirs. Conditions grew more desperate when their crops failed during the summer and treaty annuities owed to them by the United States failed to materialize. In August, after a summer of desperation, the Dakotas demanded that the Indian agent distribute food stored in a government warehouse—it was theirs and they were starving—but a local trader, Andrew Myrick, said, "So far as I am concerned, if they are hungry, let them eat grass, or their own dung."[53] In desperation, four young

Dakotas attacked a white farm family who refused to give them food, killing all of them. Once lit, the flame of despair and resentment exploded into a wildfire. The four young men returned to their village and met with the head men and chiefs. The choices were grim: turn the four men in to the authorities, or go to war.

Ta-oya-te-duta (Little Crow, 1810–63), chief of the Mdewakanton (Santee) Sioux, had always counseled peace. He had signed treaties with the Americans, who poured by the thousands onto his people's homelands, with more coming every day. Members of his own family

Ta-oya-te-duta (Little Crow), leader of the Dakota conflict of 1862, Washington, D.C., 1858. *Courtesy National Anthropological Archives, Smithsonian Institution.*

had married whites; their children lived among his people. So, as before, Little Crow tried to convince his people that they could not prevail against the Americans; he tried to make them understand that if they took up arms, the United States would kill them all. But it was too late. Too many Dakotas were hungry and too many people were suffering. The Sioux believed that it was better to die as a warrior than to watch families slowly waste away from starvation. And so Little Crow told his people that since they were determined to fight, he would die with them.[54]

Many Dakota warriors followed Little Crow into battle. Before the fighting ended, more than five hundred Minnesota settlers would be killed. Many of them were squatters who had settled illegally on the Dakota reservation. President Lincoln sent soldiers to Minnesota to restore order, but the army was not interested in peace. "It is my purpose utterly to exterminate the Sioux," declared General John Pope. "They are to be treated as maniacs or wild beasts, and by no means as people with whom treaties or compromises can be made."[55]

Indian attacks became sporadic as thousands of troops and volunteers scoured the countryside for the Dakota warriors, killing them on sight. As the end drew near, Little Crow and some of his followers and family slipped off to Canada. A year later he and his youngest son returned to Minnesota, where he was shot down by a white settler eager for the bounty offered for Sioux scalps. The chief had been picking berries. His son escaped.[56]

Within a few weeks the fighting was over. Soldiers captured some fifteen hundred people, more than twelve hundred of whom were women and children. A military tribunal was set up to "try" the prisoners, who were charged with the civilian crimes of murder, rape, and robbery. The court heard evidence against 392 Dakotas. As many as 42 defendants were tried in a single day. Some cases were heard in five minutes. Ultimately, 323 Dakotas were convicted. Of these, 303 were sentenced to be hanged.[57]

Lincoln was appalled. The accused had no access to counsel, and each of the members of the military tribunal had fought the Dakotas during the uprising. Lincoln understood that the army and the settlers sought revenge, that the so-called trials had been conducted to provide the appearance of justice, and that bloodlust ruled the day in Minnesota. Accordingly, Lincoln directed his staff to review the trial transcripts. After careful reflection, he commuted the death sentences of all but 39 of the 303 condemned men, and ordered all others to be imprisoned. On the morning of December 26, 1862, the army hanged thirty-eight indigenous prisoners.[58]

The executions were the "first phase" in the forced removal of the Dakotas from their homelands, *Minisota Makoce* (Land Where the Waters Reflect the Skies).[59] After the executions, Dakotas judged guilty of crimes were sent to prison at Davenport, Iowa. Families were exiled to Dakota Territory. Those who had escaped capture

Wakanozanzan (Medicine Bottle), one of the men executed for participating in the Dakota conflict of 1862. Medicine Bottle retreated to Canada after the conflict, but was captured with the assistance of British authorities, imprisoned at Fort Snelling, Minnesota, and executed on November 11, 1865. A total of forty Dakotas were hanged in connection with the uprising, including thirty-eight who were brought to the gallows en masse, on December 26, 1862, the largest mass execution in American history. *Photo by Joel Emmons Whitney, St. Paul, Minnesota, 1864. Courtesy National Anthropological Archives, Smithsonian Institution.*

melded into western tribes or stayed in Canada, where they had found refuge from soldiers.[60] Even the neighboring Winnebago (Ho-Chunk) people, who lived in well-kept homes appointed with furniture, stoves, and other symbols of "civilized" life, were forced into permanent exile, despite the fact that they had not participated in the Dakota Sioux uprising.[61] Regardless, the Winnebagos were Indians, and Minnesotans seized the moment to remove them as well as the Sioux to Crow Creek, a barren wasteland in Dakota Territory.[62]

President Lincoln typically focused minimal attention on Indian affairs. Concerned with winning the war for the Union, he allowed army generals in the field to dictate Indian policy. In 1862, General James Carleton began a war against Apaches and Navajos in New Mexico, where gold had been discovered on Indian land. His instructions to Colonel Kit Carson were clear: "All Indian men . . . are to be killed whenever and wherever you can find them." Carson later led a scorched-earth policy that forced the Navajos from their traditional homelands to Bosque Redondo, a small reservation on the Pecos River in southeastern New Mexico. Ultimately, some eighty-five hundred Navajos would make the arduous three-hundred-mile trek, remembered as the Long Walk.[63] Later, Carleton sent gold

Navajo (Diné) captives under guard, Fort Sumner, New Mexico, ca. 1864–68. Some two thousand Navajos died of smallpox during their confinement at Bosque Redondo, which they called *Hweeldi*, the Place of Despair. In 1868, twenty-five Navajo headmen signed a treaty with the United States, which allowed the Navajo to return to their homelands. *Courtesy Palace of the Governors Photo Archives (NMHM/DCA), Neg. 028534.*

nuggets to members of Lincoln's cabinet, asking Treasury Secretary Salmon P. Chase to give the largest one to the president.[64]

Meanwhile, in Colorado, Lincoln's Indian agents exploited their positions for personal gain. Samuel Colley, the cousin of Lincoln's commissioner of Indian affairs, William P. Dole, had received a lucrative government position as an Indian agent, allowing him to both prospect for gold and line his pockets with cash siphoned from the Indian trade. Many alleged that Colley had diverted annuity goods to his son Dexter, a trader, who then sold the goods to Indians.[65]

When miners discovered gold on Pikes Peak, thousands of settlers infiltrated Cheyenne and Arapaho lands. Skirmishes led to intense fighting and resulted in the infamous Sand Creek Massacre in eastern Colorado. While American negotiators met with Cheyenne leaders, Colonel John M. Chivington led the Colorado militia against Chief Black Kettle (ca. 1812–68) and his band.[66] That morning, the great Cheyenne leader had emerged from his tipi holding an American flag; a white flag also fluttered on a pole over his home. At dawn on November 29, 1864, Chivington attacked Black Kettle's camp, killing and mutilating one hundred people, most of them women and children. Black Kettle managed to survive, but soldiers killed his wife, butchered children and pregnant women, and castrated and killed the men.[67]

As genocide continued in the West, Lincoln entertained delegations of Native leaders at the White House. In March 1863, he met a large group of Plains leaders in the East Room, where Natives spoke in amazement about the vast number of white people as well as the large and impressive buildings they had seen in Washington. "We pale-faced people think that this world is a great, round ball," Lincoln declared, as he brought out a globe to use in an impromptu lecture on geography and "civilization":

The pale-faced people are numerous and prosperous because they cultivate the earth, produce bread, and depend upon the products of the earth rather than wild game for subsistence. This is the chief reason of the difference; but there is another. Although we are now engaged in a great war between one another, we are not, as a race, so much disposed to fight and kill one another as our red brethren.[68]

Chief Black Kettle (Southern Cheyenne), seated second from left, with other Cheyenne and Arapaho chiefs at Camp Weld, Colorado, in 1864, eight weeks before the infamous Sand Creek Massacre. *Photo by Charles William Carter, Salt Lake City, Utah, 1864. Courtesy National Anthropological Archives, Smithsonian Institution.*

At that time, Civil War battle casualties amounted to more than one hundred thousand men—a figure that dwarfed casualties in wars between Indian nations or between American soldiers and Indian warriors. That Abraham Lincoln could make this assertion testifies to the pervasive blindness induced by nineteenth-century racial bigotry—a myopia that allowed whites to envision themselves as civilized people and Indians as savages.

In meetings with Indians, Lincoln demonstrated stereotypical attitudes toward indigenous peoples. During a meeting with Potawatomi leaders in 1861, Lincoln lapsed into a sort of pidgin English while replying to a head chief who had addressed the president in eloquent English: "Where live now?" He also asked the Potawatomi leader, "When go back Iowa?" Lincoln's private secretary, John Hay, found the exchange amusing.[69]

"THE ARTS OF CIVILIZATION":
PRESIDENT LINCOLN'S PRESCRIPTION FOR AMERICAN INDIANS

This Abraham Lincoln peace medal depicts a Native man scalping another, and compares it to a bucolic scene of an Indian farmer plowing his field. The imagery was intended to convince Indians to reject tribal culture and adopt the customs of "civilized" life, which for Lincoln included Christianity. In 1863, Lincoln told Congress that "sound policy and our imperative duty to these wards of the Government demand our anxious and constant attention to their material well-being, to their progress in the arts of civilization, and, above all, to that moral training which under the blessing of Divine Providence will confer upon them the elevated and sanctifying influence, the hopes and consolations, of the Christian faith."[70]

Abraham Lincoln peace medal (reverse side), ca. 1861.
National Museum of the American Indian, 24/1213.

Lincoln had long favored a homestead act, which Congress passed in 1862. In exchange for a small filing fee, a prospective homesteader could receive 160 acres of land that would become his after a five-year residency. Lincoln knew the act would promote westward expansion, and it did. The prospect of free land drew to the United States thousands of immigrants looking to build new lives as independent farmers in the Great Republic of the West—a life that was utterly unimaginable in Europe. But the culmination of their American dream had a dark side: the availability of free land depended on the continual dispossession of American Indians. As immigrants and settlers invaded Indian Country, Native people retaliated to defend their lands and their people. And when Native people took arms to protect their way of life, army troops and militia units attacked their villages, killing men, women, and children and exiling survivors to desolate locations spurned by whites.[71]

Starvation and suffering among Indians was also caused by rampant government corruption during the Civil War era. Lincoln knew that the Indian Service needed reform. Prominent activists such as Bishop Henry Benjamin Whipple, who championed the cause of Minnesota Indians in the 1860s, and John Beeson, the author of A *Plea for Indians* (1857), urged him to overhaul the system, but Lincoln replied, "If we get through this war and I live, this Indian system shall be reformed."[72]

As Lincoln's second term began in 1865, he accepted recommendations from congressmen for appointments to the Indian Service, continuing the political patronage that lay at the heart of government corruption. Perhaps Lincoln would have addressed the problem, had he lived. There is no way to know for certain. But we do know that Lincoln, like other Americans of his day, was steeped in a culture that celebrated white civilization and rejected Native American sovereignty and culture. As the historian David Nichols has observed, this culture shaped men like Lincoln, who "believed in a white, Christian, materialistic, and rapidly advancing civilization that was personified by homesteads, gold mines, and the transcontinental railroad." In this outlook, "the pursuit of political and financial gain at the expense of the Indian was both proper and inevitable." Indians—"savages"—were disappearing before the great juggernaut of white civilization. In a few years they would be extinct, and nefarious or shameful dealings with them would become a distant memory.[73]

PRESIDENT ULYSSES S. GRANT'S PEACE POLICY

President Ulysses S. Grant came to the presidency in 1869 as a great military hero and symbol of the Union's triumph over the Confederacy during the Civil War. President Grant brought part of his former military staff to Washington, including Ely S. Parker, a Seneca who had served as Grant's military secretary and who had produced the final copy of the surrender agreement that General Robert E. Lee signed at Appomattox, ending the Civil War. Grant appointed Parker commissioner of Indian Affairs, the first Native American to hold the post.[74] He also appointed fellow Civil War general William Tecumseh Sherman to head his U.S. Indian Peace Commission and General Phillip Sheridan to head the Department of the Missouri, a huge area that stretched from the Mississippi River to the Rocky Mountains.[75]

Grant's peace policy was intended, in part, to reform the Indian Bureau by replacing corrupt civilian agents with Christian missionaries who would now supervise the Indian reservations. In reality, the policy rested on the belief that Americans had the right to dispossess Native peoples of their lands, take away their freedoms, and send them to reservations, where missionaries would teach them how to

President Ulysses S. Grant, ca. 1869–77. President Grant's peace policy aimed to resolve "the Indian problem" by placing tribes on reservations, instructing Natives in farming and Christianity, and replacing government agents with religious missionaries dedicated to the "uplift of the Indians." *Photo by Matthew Brady. Courtesy Library of Congress, LC-USZ62-21986.*

farm, read and write, wear Euro-American clothing, and embrace Christianity. If the Indians refused to move to reservations, they would be forced off their homelands by soldiers.

Ironically, the peace policy produced some of the worst massacres and injustices against Native people, including actions against the Lakota and the Nez Perce. Indian leaders such as Sitting Bull, Gall, Chief Joseph, Geronimo, and Cochise all led their people in wars of independence against the United States, following a path they hoped would protect their lands and their way of life.

In 1870, President Grant entertained a delegation from the Sioux Nation that included the great Oglala war chief Red Cloud. A re-

Cheyenne and Arapaho leaders meeting with members of President Grant's Peace Commission at Fort Laramie, Wyoming Territory, 1868. Photo by Alexander Gardner. The commissioners (at center, from left) include Samuel F. Tappan, Major General William S. Harney, Lieutenant General William T. Sherman, General John B. Sanborn, Major General Christopher C. Augur, and Major General Alfred H. Terry. *Courtesy National Anthropological Archives, Smithsonian Institution.*

Chief Washakie (Flathead-Shoshone) standing at front, center, with his people, Wyoming, 1870. A loyal ally of the United States, Chief Washakie (1804–1900) lived in the Wind River Mountains of Wyoming, where he befriended the mountain man Jim Bridger as well as the trapper and scout Christopher "Kit" Carson. Under Washakie's leadership, the Shoshone guarded settlers moving west along the Oregon Trail and served as scouts for the U.S. Army. In 1878, President Ulysses S. Grant presented Washakie with a silver saddle and Camp Brown was renamed Fort Washakie, in recognition of the chief's loyalty. Washakie was buried with full military honors at the fort that bears his name. *Photo by William Henry Jackson. Courtesy National Anthropological Archives, Smithsonian Institution.*

porter from the *New York Herald* described the delegates, stating, "Physically, a finer set of men would be difficult to find. All were tall, full chested, and with features decidedly those of the American Indian." Indian Commissioner Ely Parker asked Chief Little Swan if he had become a great chief by killing people. "Yes," replied the chief, "the same as the Great White Father in the White House." Chief Spotted Tail told Grant that he tried to keep the peace but that white men continued to harass the Sioux. Grant responded by having an order sent out to all military commanders in the West that

"I WANT YOU TO TELL ALL THIS TO MY GREAT FATHER": MAKHPYIA-LUTA (RED CLOUD) SPEAKS, 1870

Red Cloud (ca. 1821–1909), one of the most prominent Oglala chiefs of the nineteenth century, was born near what is now North Platte, Nebraska. As a young man, he developed a reputation for bravery in wars against Pawnees and other tribes, and emerged as a leading warrior. His crowning military achievement occurred in the late 1860s, when his people forced the United States to abandon the Bozeman Trail, which snaked through Lakota territory to the gold mines of Montana. As wagon trains pushed into the Sioux homelands, Red Cloud launched assaults on the army forts, which had been established to protect the settlers. The attacks culminated in the 1866 massacre of eighty soldiers under the command of Lieutenant Colonel William Fetterman, an event that closed civilian traffic along the trail and forced the United States to negotiate with the Sioux. "I have more soldiers than the Great Father," Red Cloud asserted, "and he cannot take my lands against my will." Red Cloud, for his part, refused to bargain until the forts were closed. Finally, in a move that reflected Red Cloud's power, the United States abandoned the forts and negotiated the Fort Laramie Treaty of 1868, which recognized Lakota possession of what is now the western half of South Dakota, including the Black Hills, as well as lands in present-day Montana and Wyoming.

Red Cloud's war against the United States ended after the Fort Laramie Treaty, but the chief continued to champion his people's interests. In 1870, he and other Sioux chiefs traveled to Washington, where President and Mrs. Grant served them strawberries and cream at the White House. Though he said little during the reception, Red Cloud held forth the next day during a meeting with Secretary of the Interior Jacob Cox:

I came here to tell my Great Father what I do not like in my country. . . . The white children have surrounded me and have left me nothing but an island. When we first had this land we were strong, now we are melting like snow on the hillside, while you are grown like spring grass. . . . I was born at the forks of the Platte, and I was told that the land belonged to me from north, south, east, and west. . . . The railroad is passing through my country now; I have received no pay for the land—not even a brass ring. I want you to tell all this to my Great Father.

The men the Great Father sends to us have not sense—no heart. . . . They have promised me traders, but we have none. When you send goods to me, they are stolen all along the road, so when they reached me they were only a handful. They held a paper for me to sign, and that is all I got for my lands. I know the people you send out there are liars. Look at me. I am poor and naked. I do not want war with my Government.[76] ❧

they were to expel white intruders on Indian lands, by force if necessary. Red Cloud complained to Grant that his people were starving
and had no clothes because annuity goods promised the Sioux had
not been sent.

The Sioux delegation traveled from Washington to New York City,
where Red Cloud held an audience spellbound at Cooper Union.
He eloquently condemned American Indian policy, stating, "The
riches we have in this world . . . we cannot take with us to the next
world. Then I wish to know why agents are sent out to us who do
nothing but rob us and get the riches of this world away from us?"
Red Cloud's description of the suffering of indigenous peoples had

a strong emotional impact on his audience. One reporter noted it "was comparable to the public recital of a fugitive slave in former years."[77]

By 1880, most Native Americans resided on reservations, many of which were far from their homelands. The next twenty years were a period of enormous struggle, during which Native people worked against all odds to preserve their languages, customs, lifeways, and sovereignty. In many cases, Indians adopted certain American values and beliefs but changed them to meet the needs of their people. Rituals and ceremonies continued in private, in isolation, but people kept them alive. Languages suffered and in some nations few speakers survived when the long night ended. Others courageously retained their cultures and languages, passing them on to the next generation, who carried them into the twentieth century.

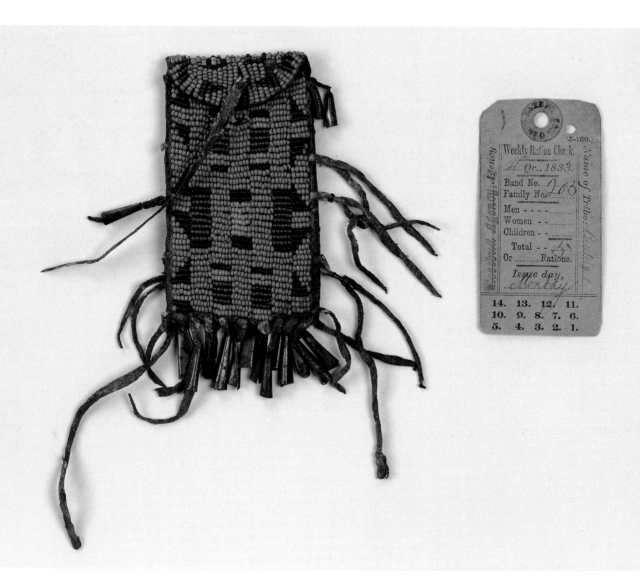

Brulé Sioux ration card and beaded case, Rosebud Agency, South Dakota, 1883. By the mid-1880s, some 243,000 Native people had been forced off their homelands onto 187 reservations embracing 181,000 square miles of land. Deprived of the ability to hunt, Indians became dependent on food and supplies distributed by government agents, who issued ration cards to each family. Some Native women made beaded cases for keeping the cards, transforming a badge of dependency into an article of pride. *Photo by Katherine Fogden. National Museum of the American Indian, 23/9391.*

CHAPTER III

DARK DAYS: AMERICAN PRESIDENTS AND NATIVE SOVEREIGNTY, 1880–1930

MATTHEW SAKIESTEWA GILBERT

In the late nineteenth and early twentieth centuries, American Indians regularly called on the president to uphold treaties and halt white settlement on Native lands. Since presidents seldom visited Native nations, Indian leaders often took the initiative to request—and at times demand—meetings in the nation's capital. Considering themselves equal to the presidents, Native leaders traveled great distances to speak with the president, congressmen, and other high-ranking government officials. The diplomatic missions rarely resulted in peace. Between 1880 and 1930, relations between Indians and the United States government were profoundly strained by policies that undermined Native self-determination and culture. Still, despite the forcible displacement of tribes, the creation of the reservation system, land loss, attacks on tribal culture and governance, and growing presidential disinterest in Indian diplomacy, Native Americans retained their identity as sovereign peoples through the Gilded Age and the onset of the Great Depression.

Indian leaders in these years viewed the protection of their territories as the most important issue they faced as representatives of sovereign nations. Through treaties and removal policies, the United States had acquired millions of acres of Native homelands, resulting in the relocation and death of thousands of Indian people. In the 1860s, government laws such as the Preemption and Homestead Acts provided "free" land—160 acres for minimal improvements—to white settlers in the West.[1] Although the government used acts of Congress to give land to white farmers and ranchers, American Indians did not consider their lands to be "free." To combat the government's land-acquisition campaign, Native people entrusted their leaders to negotiate and reason with the presidents of the United States and their representatives. When peaceful measures failed, Indians engaged in armed conflict with soldiers and state militia units to defend their lands and lives. And when the so-called "Indian Wars" ended in the late 1880s, Native leaders were forced to develop survival strategies that were consistent with the realities of life and power in an era of Indian reservations.

THE TRAVAIL OF THE PONCA NATION

By the 1870s, government efforts to remove Indian people from their ancestral lands had intensified. The battles of the Big Hole and Bear Paw, between the Nez Perce and the U.S. Army, served as a grim reminder to Indians everywhere that the government would not abandon its effort to destroy Native cultures and acquire Indian lands.

On the Great Plains, the Ponca Nation had made treaties with the government, desperately clinging to their lands in northeastern Nebraska, despite Sioux attacks to dislodge them.[2] In 1877, three commissioners arrived from Washington and informed Chief Standing Bear (1834–1908) and other Ponca leaders that President Rutherford B. Hayes had ordered the Ponca Nation to move south to

"I WANT TO SPEAK FOR MY PEOPLE": WOLF CHIEF, SCRIBE OF THE FORT BERTHOLD RESERVATION

In 1881, a Hidatsa man named Wolf Chief (ca. 1849–1934) wrote a letter to President James A. Garfield asking for a favor: Could the president secure for Wolf Chief's family a wagon from the Indian agent at the Fort Berthold Reservation in North Dakota? President Garfield was assassinated before Wolf Chief's letter reached the White House, but the Native American correspondent eventually received a reply from Washington. "The President did not see your letter, but . . . he would have been glad that an Indian boy has learned to write," the letter from the Office of Indian Affairs read. "We too are glad . . . and are writing [a] letter to your agent asking [that] he issue you a wagon."

Wolf Chief's missive was one of more than one hundred letters he sent to Washington during the course of his life. Wolf Chief apprised presidents, lawmakers, government bureaucrats, and newspaper editors of conditions on the Fort Berthold Reservation—home to Hidatsa, Mandan, and Arikara Indians—and gave voice to grievances shared by many Native Americans during the early reservation era. His letters tell of meager food rations, shady reservation traders, white ranchers trespassing on reservation lands, and the United States government's failure to live up to treaty agreements.

Wolf Chief showed deference when writing the White House, but always came to the point. An 1882 letter to President Chester A. Arthur began, "My name is Wolf Chief. I am poor. My agent is bad . . . he tells lies. . . . He says I am bad because I write." Six years later, he wrote President Grover Cleveland: "I want to speak for my people . . . the frost came and now we have no crop at all and we do not know what we will do this winter for food." In 1891, he told President Benjamin Harrison, "Our school houses are very old indeed. No good white man would keep children in such bad and dangerous buildings. Please, I wish to hear from you soon . . . I am your friend."

Wolf Chief's letter writing annoyed reservation officials. "There is no tribe or band of Indians on this reservation who have given me . . . as much trouble as Wolf Chief," one agent complained. The Hidatsa scribe, he said, was "a troublesome, meddlesome and dissatisfied Indian" who exercised an "evil influence" over "a certain class of our Indians viz. those who oppose everything." When the Office of Indian Affairs queried a Fort Berthold agent about a recent letter from Wolf Chief, the Indian agent explained that the "letter is simply Wolf Chief's annual eruption. He has contracted the letter writing habit and cannot be suppressed."

Wolf Chief continued to write to Washington, no matter what, and his letters got attention and results. His last letter, penned in 1934, was addressed to John Collier, commissioner of Indian affairs under President Franklin Roosevelt. In it, Wolf Chief described the terrible drought ravaging farms throughout the Midwestern and Southern Plains.[3]

Indian Territory. The Ponca chiefs insisted that they wanted to be left alone, and asked the commissioners to remind the president of the Ponca Treaty of 1865, in which the United States had promised their people that they would possess their lands "for as long as water should run or grass should grow." Rather than adhering to the treaty, President Hayes convinced the chiefs to visit the proposed reservation, assuring them that "if they were not satisfied with it, the tribe would not be disturbed."

In the winter of 1877, the Ponca delegation agreed to President Hayes's invitation and traveled to Oklahoma to look at the land set aside for their reservation. They didn't like what they saw. When the chiefs said so, government officials abandoned them, leaving them with no food, money, or transportation. Rather than remain in Indian Territory, the Ponca chiefs decided to walk home. While traveling on foot to northern Nebraska, the chiefs endured starvation and frostbite, but they finally arrived at their winter camps. Soon, soldiers

Chief Standing Bear, seated on floor, at right, with a Ponca delegation in Washington, ca. 1875. Also pictured, front row, from left: Big Elk (seated on floor), Standing Buffalo Bull, and White Eagle. Back row, standing, from left: Baptiste Barnaby and Charles Le Clair. *National Museum of the American Indian, P04485.*

Not all Indians were impressed by their encounters with the president. Sarah Winnemucca (ca. 1844–91), a Paiute activist who aroused humanitarian support for her people through lectures in Nevada, San Francisco, Boston, and Washington, D.C., from 1879 to 1886, was disappointed by an 1881 visit with President Rutherford B. Hayes. Serving as interpreter, Winnemucca and a Paiute delegation called on the president at the White House. When Hayes entered the room, he pontificated about Indian assimilation and left after five minutes. "That was all we saw of him," Winnemucca lamented. "That was President Hayes."[4]

Near right: **President Rutherford B. Hayes, ca. 1877–81.** *Courtesy Library of Congress, LC-USZ62-13019.*

Far right: **Sarah Winnemucca (Paiute), by Norval H. Busey.** Albumen silver print, 1883. *Courtesy National Portrait Gallery, NPG.82.137.*

came. They arrested the chiefs and confined them to prison and surrounded the Ponca camp, denying the Indians food and water until they agreed to move south. Seeing that men, women, and children were starving, the Ponca chiefs "consented" to leave their homes for the reservation President Hayes had designated for them in Indian Territory.[5]

But not every Ponca chief complied. Standing Bear and his followers refused to obey the president's order, for which Standing Bear was arrested and imprisoned. When he was finally released, government officials forced him and his Ponca supporters to walk five hundred miles to their reservation in Indian Territory. During the fifty-day journey and through the following year, more than one hundred Poncas died from exposure and disease, including Standing Bear's children.[6]

The Ponca situation outraged Indian leaders and white sympathizers, who called on the United States government to drastically reform Indian policy. In 1881, Helen Hunt Jackson wrote a scathing critique of the government's dealings with American Indian nations in *A Century of Dishonor*.[7] Jackson's book generated a groundswell of interest in and sympathy for American Indians, and came to be known as the "*Uncle Tom's Cabin* of Indian reform."[8]

DIMINISHING THE NATIVE ESTATE

In the 1880s, the federal government intensified efforts to acquire Native territories. Requiring tribes to abandon ancestral lands for Indian reservations did not satisfy demand. Congress also passed laws that reduced the size of Indian reservations, whose boundaries had been established in treaties with Native nations. The most significant of these laws was the General Allotment Act of 1887, also known as the Dawes Act, named for Senator Henry L. Dawes, chairman of the Committee on Indian Affairs from 1881 to 1893. The Dawes Act authorized the president of the United States to divide Indian reservations into single-family plots, or allotments, for distribution to tribal members. "Surplus" lands would be opened to white settlement.

Reformers hailed the measure as an engine of progress for Indian people. By breaking up communal ownership of land, each Indian family head would receive 160 acres, which he could farm just as did whites. Individuals over the age of eighteen were to receive eighty acres each. Native Americans would learn the values of individualism and private property and be freed of the tribal bonds that prevented their advancement toward "civilization."

Government officials worked quickly and aggressively. Surveying parties traveled to reservations to divide tribal lands into allotments while census takers collected the names of individual tribal members to determine who was entitled to a parcel. After the land was assigned

A NATIVE RECEPTION FOR PRESIDENT ARTHUR, 1883

Native American leaders typically traveled to Washington when they met with the president. In 1883, President Chester A. Arthur bucked the trend and stopped at the Wind River Indian Reservation, in Wyoming Territory, en route to Yellowstone National Park. The twenty-first president was welcomed by the Shoshones, many of whom carried umbrellas as shields against the summer sun. As president, Arthur championed the allotment of Indian reservations, a measure that, he believed, "would have a direct and powerful influence in dissolving the tribal bond, which is so prominent a feature of savage life, and which tends so strongly to perpetuate it."[9]

Mounted Shoshones greeting President Chester A. Arthur at Fort Washakie, Wyoming Territory, in 1883. *Photo by Frank Jay Haynes. Courtesy National Anthropological Archives, Smithsonian Institution.*

to the Indian allottees, the remaining territory was sold off to white settlers. In 1890, some thirteen million acres of Indian land were sold. In 1891, another twenty-three million acres fell under white control. A year later, some thirty million more acres changed hands.[10]

The Dawes Act provided American presidents with enormous arbitrary power over Native nations. As one contemporary critic observed, there "is not a word in the law requiring the consent of the Indian"—a fact that was not lost on Native leaders.[11] Although presidents argued that that they were working in the best interests of Native Americans, tribal leaders viewed the measure as the latest installment in America's ongoing effort to destroy tribal governments, undermine Native sovereignty, abrogate treaties, and take Native lands.[12]

Native opposition to allotment and other laws that diminished

President Grover Cleveland, 1888. The only president elected to two nonconsecutive terms (1885–89, 1893–97), Grover Cleveland was a strong advocate for the allotment of Indian lands. "Allotments in severalty," he declared in 1888, "proffers opportunity and inducement to that independence of spirit and life which the Indian peculiarly needs, while at the same time the inalienability of title affords security against the risks his inexperience of affairs or weakness of character may expose him to in dealing with others." *Courtesy Library of Congress, LC-USZ62-7618.*

tribal lands emerged quickly. In October 1888, sixty-one chiefs and subchiefs from the Lakota Sioux Nation in Dakota arrived in Washington to confer with President Grover Cleveland and Secretary of the Interior William Freeman Vilas. The chiefs—including Sitting Bull, Gall, Ma-tow-a-tak-pe, or John Grass, Wanigi-ska, or White Ghost, Swift Bird, and Swift Bear—hoped to present their objections to legislation which, if carried out, would result in the loss of eleven million acres of tribal land. At the White House, the delegation was welcomed by Secretary Vilas:

Tatanka Iyotanka, or Chief Sitting Bull (Hunkpapa Lakota). *Photo by William R. Cross, 1882. National Museum of the American Indian, PO6911.*

My friends, you have traveled a long way to visit Washington, and I am glad to see you. The Congress which makes the laws which govern this whole country has made this law [holding in his hand the act for the purchase of the reservation]. Congress saw that the time had come for the Sioux Indians to take sure steps toward civilization, and that the waste and unused lands of their reservation ought to be settled upon and made homes of.[13]

When Secretary Vilas finished speaking, Sitting Bull stood and shook hands with the secretary, the commissioners, and other government officials. Addressing the representatives of the United States government as his "friends," Sitting Bull stated, "I call you my friends because I am one of your people. I belong to the Government of the United States. As we have our own views of this new law we wish to speak to you as man to man. I hope everything will be done in a quiet manner. This is all I have to say."

Then it was John Grass's turn to speak. Saying that "he and his friends had been well taken care of since their arrival in Washington and [that] they all felt light-hearted," he turned to the matter at hand. "All of my friends know that I never intended to object to the new law as a whole," he said. However,

> Some of the clauses in it displeased me and I told my friends what they were. The first thing I want to mention is the treaty of 1868, and I ask you to promptly meet the obligation of that treaty. Pay us whatever rightfully belongs to us. And then [there was] the Black Hills treaty of 1876. Why is it that we are not paid what is due us under these treaties? What is lacking?[14]

Grass then took a map of the Dakota Territory and pointed to the Sioux reservation. He told the gathering that the reservation's "western boundary line" should be farther "west from its present location" and noted that "instead of there being only eleven million acres in the part which the Government proposed to buy, there should be much more." Declaring that government officials had "changed" the western boundary "without their knowledge or consent," Grass asserted that his people still owned the "lands far west of the present line."

Grass was not finished. He then reminded Secretary Vilas that the Sioux had previously requested $5.5 million "in one lump sum" for their lands, and that he and the other Sioux leaders had come to Washington to propose an even higher price. The United States government, at that time, was selling land for $1.25 per acre, and Grass demanded that the Sioux receive at least that amount. He also reminded officials that the government, in the Fort Laramie Treaty of 1868, had promised to establish schools on the Sioux Reservation and to provide teachers for twenty years, but the government had waited until 1878 to deliver on their promise. "Think of our fathers," he declared:

> They used to own all of these lands which the white man now lives upon. They were ours once, but we have been driven away from them. We are a poor and ignorant people, and you are the cause of our being poor. Looking back I say to you that whatever we ask should have due consideration. Put the key which opens our reservation in your pocket for a while. Do

not be in a hurry. Wait until these matters are well considered. Ascertain first whether after our lands are gone we will have enough left to do us.[15]

After Grass and the other chiefs had spoken, Secretary Vilas told the delegation that their words had been carefully recorded and that he would lay them before President Cleveland for his immediate "consideration." Two days later, on Wednesday, October 17, Secretary Vilas called the chiefs together to read and explain to them the president's amendment to the new law. Vilas told the chiefs that he had "consulted fully with the President" about their concerns, and that he had come to them with an answer. Vilas, according to a *New York Times* reporter, "read the proposed amendments one by one, explaining with great care and clearness wherein they differed from the law which the Indians had been asked to approve." Speaking for more than two hours, the interior secretary told the chiefs that President Cleveland had offered the Sioux Nation one dollar per acre for lands the government would purchase during the first three years, seventy cents per acre for lands purchased in the fourth and fifth years, and fifty cents per acre for lands purchased after the fifth year. When the council concluded, the chiefs took copies of the amendments and returned to their hotel to discuss the proposal in further detail.[16]

Three days later, on October 20, Secretary Vilas informed the public that Sitting Bull, John Grass, and others had "formally notified him that they had rejected by a large majority the proposition made by the President." Refusing to accept the government's original offer, the chiefs eventually agreed to accept the immediate payment of $1.25 per acre of their land. Vilas reported that the Sioux proposition "could not for a moment be entertained by the Government," and "expressed the opinion that one of the principal reasons for the rejection of the proposition was due to the fact that the execution of the law would break up tribal relations, thus depriving the chiefs of their present authority."[17]

THE WOUNDED KNEE MASSACRE, 1890

The campaign to take Indian lands led some Native people to seek answers and hope from spiritual sources. In the winter of 1889,

Benjamin Harrison, 1888.
Grandson of President William Henry Harrison, Benjamin Harrison declared that the United States should observe "with fidelity" its treaty obligations with American Indians, and should ensure that all legislation take into account the "best interests of an ignorant and helpless people." Assimilation, Harrison believed, was the only way to turn the Indian into "a self-supporting and responsible citizen. For the adult the first step is to locate him upon a farm, and for the child to place him in a school." *Photo by George Prince (1848–?). Courtesy Library of Congress, LC-USZ62-7611.*

shortly after President Benjamin Harrison took office, a Paiute man named Wovoka, from the Walker River Indian Reservation in Nevada, had a vision of being "taken up into the spirit world." Wovoka later told ethnographer James Mooney that while in the spirit world he saw "God and the dead of his nation, happily alive in a beautiful land abundant with game." When Wovoka returned from his experience, he told the Paiute people to "work hard, and to live in peace with the Whites and that eventually they would be reunited with the dead in a world without death or sickness or old age." In addition to his prophetic message, Wovoka returned with a ceremonial dance that he said would bring forth this transformation. News of the Ghost Dance spread quickly to other Indian nations throughout the Great Basin and beyond.

When Sioux and Pawnee people received the message and the dance, they adapted Wovoka's prophecy to reflect their own cultural and social situation. The Sioux and Pawnee people, according to historian Stephen Cornell, "gave to the prophecies a hostile content: In their version, the whites were to be annihilated by a massive whirlwind, and the Sioux in particular made much of the expected return of the buffalo—of little concern to the Paiutes—and great herds of horses."[18] Lakota anger stemmed, in part, from the United States' refusal to pay a just price for Sioux lands, as well as a legacy of broken promises to the Lakotas and other Native groups.

The expansion of the Ghost Dance movement, coupled with the Sioux and Pawnee interpretations of Wovoka's message, attracted the attention of officials in Washington, including President Harrison. Daniel Royer, an inexperienced Indian agent at Pine Ridge, South Dakota, feared that Wovoka's prophetic messages would ignite an "uprising" among Sioux warriors who had fought at the Battle of the Little Bighorn and asked the army to send troops to the reservation. The leaders of the Ghost Dance movement responded by retreating to the reservation's isolated northern boundary. Nearly three weeks passed without incident, but then James McLaughlin, an Indian agent at the Standing Rock Agency, in North and South Dakota, ordered agency police and troops to arrest Sitting Bull on the pretense that imprisonment would prevent him from joining the Ghost Dance movement. In the early morning of December 15, 1890, agency police "surprised" Sitting Bull at his house and proceeded to arrest him. In an act of resistance, Sitting Bull chastised the police, who then shot the chief at close range.

The murder of Sitting Bull angered Indian leaders and exacerbated tensions between the Sioux and United States soldiers. Some of the Ghost Dancers fled and joined Chief Big Foot's band on the Cheyenne River. As the soldiers approached, Chief Big Foot led his people on a 150-mile trek to the Pine Ridge Agency, where they hoped to join Chief Red Cloud of the Lakotas. On the morning of December 29, 1890, soldiers equipped with four Hotchkiss guns positioned themselves on top of a hill overlooking Big Foot's encampment. The soldiers ordered the Lakotas to put down their guns, but one warrior held his rifle over his head and defiantly fired a round into the air. Thomas H. Tibbles, a reporter for the *Omaha World-Herald*, observed that he "heard a single shot from the direction of the troops—then three or four—a few more—and immediately a volley. At once came a general rattle of rifle firing. Then the Hotchkiss guns." During the massacre that followed, soldiers shot unarmed elders, women, and children. Chief American Horse recalled that a "mother was shot down with her infant; the child not knowing that its mother was dead was still nursing. . . ."

> The women as they were fleeing with their babies were killed together, shot right through . . . and after most of them had been killed a cry was made that all those who were not killed or wounded should come forth and they would be safe. Little boys . . . came out of their places of refuge, and as soon as they came in sight a number of soldiers surrounded them and butchered them there.[19]

When the guns fell silent, 29 soldiers and approximately 146 Lakotas lay dead. Other Lakotas died later from their wounds.

President Harrison took no responsibility for the massacre at Wounded Knee, and Secretary of War Redfield Proctor exonerated the Seventh Cavalry for killing women and children. Proctor remarked that many of the Lakota men and women attempted to flee "on their ponies," which made it "impossible" for the soldiers to "distinguish buck from squaw." Officers had ordered their soldiers not to shoot women or children, Proctor explained, but some were "unavoidably killed and wounded." Ultimately, Proctor asserted, the "Indians themselves were entirely responsible" for the "unfortunate phase of the affair."[20]

Future president Theodore Roosevelt, who at the time was serving as United States Civil Service commissioner, remarked that he had been "inclined to think that the killing of Sitting Bull and of the Indians in the Forsyth fight [at Wounded Knee] was all right; but if all accounts are true there were peaceable men, or women and

We had some promises, but they are like all other promises of the Great Father. We are not fooled and we go home with heavy hearts. . . . We shall tell our people that we have got more promises. Then they will laugh at us and call us old men.[21]

—CHIEF YOUNG MAN AFRAID OF HIS HORSES (OGLALA SIOUX), COMMENTING ON HIS 1891 MEETING WITH PRESIDENT BENJAMIN HARRISON

Civilians loading victims of the Wounded Knee massacre into a wagon, Pine Ridge, South Dakota, 1891. The victims, including eighty-four men and boys, forty-four women, and eighteen children, were tossed into a mass grave and buried with no ceremony. *Photo by the Northwestern Photographic Company. National Museum of the American Indian, P12757.*

children killed under circumstances that ought to have called for the most rigid investigation." Roosevelt noted that, while he would "put down an Indian outbreak" as he would "put down a mob uprising with the strongest possible hand," he would also "strain every nerve and stretch the federal power to the utmost to protect and avenge the Indians when molested by lawless whites."[22]

President Benjamin Harrison, for his part, honored the Seventh Cavalry for their distinguished service in action at Wounded Knee Creek, and twenty soldiers later received the Medal of Honor for participating in what many contemporaries and some historians consider the last "battle" in the Indian wars of the nineteenth century.

The massacre at Wounded Knee was the last time United States soldiers systematically slaughtered Indian people, but it was hardly the last time American Indians and their leaders fought to save their ancestral lands and cultures.

ALLOTMENT IN INDIAN TERRITORY

In March 1893, President Grover Cleveland established the Dawes Commission to negotiate agreements for the allotment of land to members of the "Five Civilized Tribes." Half a century earlier, American presidents had promised the Chickasaw, Muskogee (Creek), Choctaw, Seminole, and Cherokee Nations that, if they moved to Indian Territory, they could live on their new lands "as long as grass grows or water runs."[23] But now the president was reneging.

The Five Civilized Tribes objected strenuously to the Dawes Act of 1887, so much so that they had been exempted from its provisions. But their reprieve lasted only six years. In May 1890, Indian Territory was divided into Oklahoma Territory and Indian Territory, ending the area's special status as a reserve for Native people. The availability of "new" land lured thousands of homesteaders. In 1890, some sixty thousand whites lived in Oklahoma Territory. Ten years later, the Territory was home to four hundred thousand white residents.[24]

Hunger for Indian land encouraged President Cleveland to extend allotment to the Five Civilized Tribes. Cleveland viewed allotment as a positive good for Indians. In his second inaugural address, in 1893, he declared that "humanity and consistency" required Americans, including government officials, to treat Indians with "forbearance," and "to honestly and considerately regard their rights and interests." Proclaiming that "every effort" ought to be made to lead Indian people "through the paths of civilization and education," Cleveland embraced programs that would make Indians self-supporting, independent citizens.[25] Allotment was such a program.

In May 1895, Senator Dawes, chairman of the Dawes Commission, wrote L. C. Perryman, chief of the Muskogee (Creek) Nation, noting that President Cleveland had expressed "great interest in the success" of the commission in "coming up" with an allotment agreement that would ensure the tribe's "just rights" and "highest welfare." When President Cleveland appointed the Dawes commissioners in 1893, he made it absolutely clear that they were to deal with the Indians in a fair manner, and avoid leading them into any action they did not "thoroughly understand" or "benefit" from. Although he realized that it would take valuable time to convince the Indians to accept allotment, Cleveland noted that a "slow movement of the kind fully understood and approved by the Indians is infinitely better than swifter results" that were "gained by broken pledges and false promises."[27]

It is to be regretted that the policy of breaking up the tribal relation and of dealing with the Indian as an individual did not appear earlier in our legislation. Large reservations held in common and the maintenance of the authority of the chiefs and headmen have deprived the individual of every incentive to the exercise of thrift, and the annuity has contributed an affirmative impulse toward a state of confirmed pauperism.

—PRESIDENT
BENJAMIN HARRISON,
1889[26]

The new agreement with the Creek Nation and the United States was signed and made public two years later. Under the terms of the agreement, government officials allotted "each citizen of the nation" 160 acres of land. The treaty stipulated that all "lands not taken in allotment" would be "sold to the highest bidder at no less than $1.25 per acre."

Allotment promoted profound social, economic, and cultural changes for the Creeks and other Native peoples. Land that the Creeks collectively possessed was divided into parcels and distributed to individual community members. As their tribal land base diminished, the Creeks saw their nation's sovereignty threatened, although it was not destroyed. While encouraging and forcing Native nations such as the Creeks to accept allotment, presidents and other officials urged Indian leaders to discard tribal management and adopt an American form of government. When they accepted allotment in 1897, the Creeks refused to discard tribal governance, and their nation continued to function as a sovereign entity. Many Americans were puzzled by the decision. "Whenever the Creeks abandon tribal government," a reporter for the *Chicago Daily Tribune* noted, "they will be allowed all the rights and privileges of citizens."[28]

Allotment challenged many Native nations in Oklahoma Territory, which, according to the *Chicago Daily Tribune,* held "eight or nine thousand square miles" of the "best land in the territory," perfectly suitable for growing "corn, wheat, sorghum, and grass." The Chickasaws and the Choctaws, the reporter predicted, "will undoubtedly soon follow the example of the Creeks and it is only a question of time how soon the whole Territory will be allotted and opened up to the white settlement with the Indians engaged in farming side by side with their white neighbors."[29]

"KILL THE INDIAN AND SAVE THE MAN": BOARDING SCHOOLS

The appropriation of Indian lands was paired with a vigorous campaign to extinguish tribal cultures. Government officials realized that the forced removal of Indians to reservations did not fully eradicate Native cultures or cause Indian people to embrace American values and customs. To rectify this, presidents such as Rutherford B. Hayes, along with the Office of Indian Affairs, established on- and off-reservation boarding schools for Native children.

The first non-reservation boarding school was established in 1879 in Carlisle, Pennsylvania, by Captain Richard Henry Pratt, an army officer who had run an Indian prisoner-of-war camp in St. Augustine, Florida. The Carlisle Indian Industrial School was founded to eliminate Indian cultures and assimilate Indian pupils into mainstream American society. Carlisle and other boarding schools were battlegrounds for the minds and affections of Indian pupils. White men who embraced Christian ideals drafted Indian education policies that determined what was beneficial for indigenous people. Government officials, including the presidents of the United States, did not consult Native leaders or parents when they developed the schools, nor did they seek the expertise of Indians in formulating curricula for Indian children. Instead, white educators and government bureaucrats unilaterally made decisions for a people they knew little about. Believing that Native cultures had little value in American society, Indian reformers and government officials viewed boarding schools as effective tools for wrenching Indians from their cultures and traditional practices. Carlisle's main objective, Pratt crowed, was to "kill the Indian and save the man."[30]

In the summer of 1879, Pratt arrived uninvited at the Rosebud and Pine Ridge agencies to secure Lakota children for his new boarding school.[31] Acting as the agent of the president, who approved of the "civilization" of Indian children, Pratt assured Lakota parents that their children would be well taken care of. Ultimately, Pratt secured "sixty boys and twenty-four girls from both agencies" to attend Carlisle. Many of the parents did not want their children to be taken, but they feared the consequences of resisting the demands of the federal government.

As a gesture of good will and out of a genuine desire for his children to learn English, the Lakota leader Spotted Tail (ca. 1823–81) permitted Pratt to take his four sons and one daughter to Pennsylvania. Shortly after his children arrived at the school, Spotted Tail became angry upon learning that "Episcopalians had baptized all the Sioux children at the school and had given them Christian names."[32] Spotted Tail considered this a cruel and disrespectful deed, for he "had sent his children to the school to be taught English and writ-

Sinte Gleska or Chief Spotted Tail (Brulé Sioux) with Richard Pratt, founder of the Carlisle Indian School, and the Longstrech sisters on the school's bandstand, ca. 1880. *Courtesy National Anthropological Archives, Smithsonian Institution.*

ing," and "not to be turned into imitation whites."[33] A delegation of the Pine Ridge and Rosebud agencies, including chiefs Red Cloud and Spotted Tail, quickly made plans to travel to Carlisle. When the delegation arrived in June 1880, the chiefs abhorred what they found. Amid the hundreds of Indian pupils, Spotted Tail "saw that his own children were dressed in military blue uniforms" and that their hair had been cropped. He abruptly removed his children from the school and vowed to "oppose any cooperation with Carlisle." Spotted Tail and the Lakota people associated the blue uniform of the United States military with years of suffering and bloodshed, and the Lakota chief made it clear that he did not approve of this or other aspects of Pratt's grand scheme.

Both Spotted Tail and Red Cloud, as leaders and representatives of a sovereign nation, took issue with Pratt's attempt to strip Lakota children of their indigenous culture and identity. Pratt, for his part, was infuriated by the chiefs' visit and complained that their remarks were "offensive and prejudicial to the discipline of the school."[34] Furthermore, the *New York Times* noted that Spotted Tail's removal of his children had resulted in "serious disapproval on the part" of some members of the tribe, who appealed to President Hayes to replace the Lakota chief with a "new one."[35]

Shortly after Spotted Tail, Red Cloud, and other Native leaders denounced Pratt and his school, President Hayes increased his involvement in the assimilation of Indian children. In October 1880, Hayes traveled by train to visit the Chemawa Indian School in Forest Grove, Oregon. After school officials introduced President Hayes to the crowd that had gathered to meet him, the president remarked that he had come to Chemawa to observe for himself how the government had been educating Indian children. Looking out toward the school buildings, Hayes told his audience that many Americans believed that it was "wise and just to make good citizens" of Indian boys and girls. Although some people in the United States had come to the conclusion that "God [had] decreed" that Indians "should die off like wild animals," Hayes reassured his audience that the government did not intend for that to happen. "If they are to become extinct," noted Hayes, "we ought to leave that to Providence, and we, as good patriotic, Christian people, should do our best to improve their physical, mental, and moral condition." Cries of "Amen!" filled the air. President Hayes further commented that white Americans should prepare Indian children "to become part of the great American family," and that if it turned out "that their destiny [was] to be different," the government will at least have done its "duty." The president reminded the crowd that America once belonged to Indian people, and that they owned the land as much as white men "owned their farms." Americans "have displaced them, and [we] are now completing that work," Hayes proclaimed. "I am glad that Oregon has taken a step in the right direction. I am glad that she is preparing Indian boys and girls to become good, law-abiding citizens."[36]

HOPIS: "HOSTILES" AND "FRIENDLIES"

The government's insistence that Indian children attend schools to become "good, law-abiding citizens" divided Native communities throughout North America. In 1890, eight years after President Chester A. Arthur established the official boundaries of the Hopi Reservation,[37] Kikmongwi (Village Chief) Loololma from the Hopi village of Oraibi, four chiefs from other Hopi villages, and a white tradesman named Charles Keams traveled to Washington. They made the trek to solicit Commissioner of Indian Affairs Thomas J. Morgan's help with Navajos who had raided their villages and destroyed their crops. After listening to the Hopi chiefs, Morgan recommended that the Hopis leave their homes on the mesas and disperse throughout the reservation to prevent additional Navajo encroachment.[38] Morgan also encouraged the chiefs to urge Hopi parents to send their children to government schools. Although Hopi leaders had come to Washington to seek redress from Navajo incur-

Hopi women at an outdoor market, Oraibi, Arizona, ca. 1890–1900. *Denver Public Library, Western History Collection, X-30791.*

sions, Morgan used the opportunity to lecture them that education and assimilation were in the best interests of the Hopi people.

Impressed with what he saw on his journey to Washington, Loololma returned home and called a meeting in one of the kivas at Oraibi with leaders from other Hopi villages. Loololma told of his recent trip, describing how the technology used by the white man allowed him to grow "acres and acres" of corn that was twice the height of two Hopi men standing on top of one another. After talking at length, Loololma asked those in the kiva how many white men existed. No one responded. Loololma then grabbed handfuls of sand from a pit at the center of the kiva, saying, "This is how many white men there are, and many more." He then asked the men to state the number of Hopis who lived on the reservation. Again, no one responded. Reaching down into the pit, Loololma took a pinch of sand: "That's how many Hopis there are."

Loololma had made his point. The "*pahaana* [white man's] way of life" was inevitable; the Hopi people "must accept that." Still, Loololma said, the Hopi should take heart—they could still "survive as a people" by learning the "white man's tongue" and the way in which he thinks. Hopis, Loololma said, must learn the white man's ways so that they could "also survive with it."[39]

United States officials believed that a compliant Indian chief, such as Loololma, had a greater ability to influence Indians than government agents. In the early 1890s, Commissioner Morgan invited chiefs from all of the Hopi villages to attend a meeting on the Hopi Reservation at the Keams Canyon Boarding School. Not every chief participated in the meeting, but those who attended had one primary issue on their minds: the mandatory schooling of Hopi children.[40] At the gathering, Hopi leaders were assured that the government had no intention of requiring their children to attend school.[41] Agents explained that education benefited Hopis by providing them with knowledge and skills to "meet the great, unavoidable problems of the future," most importantly the "preservation of the Indian race."[42] Although the leaders agreed that Hopi culture needed to be preserved, they suspected an ulterior motive was embedded in the government's plan for education: that the boarding schools were intended to eradicate Indian cultures. Soon they would also come to understand the

Girls praying at the Phoenix Indian School, 1900. When he visited the Phoenix Indian School in 1901, President William McKinley watched the seven hundred students perform military-style marching drills across the school's parade grounds. They also recited this pledge: "I give my head and my heart to my country; one country, one language, and one flag." *Courtesy National Archives, ARC ID #518925.*

great lengths to which the government would go to compel Hopi school attendance, such as withholding government food rations from those who refused to send their children to school.[43]

On September 8, 1906, shortly after the sun rose over the Hopi mesas in northeastern Arizona, two Hopi "factions" gathered outside the ancient village of Oraibi and engaged in a battle that forever changed the Hopi people. Considered by historians and anthropologists to be the oldest inhabited village in North America, Oraibi is located on the southern tip of Third Mesa, one of three mesas that comprise Hopi Reservation. For nearly thirty years prior to 1906, the two Oraibi factions fiercely disagreed over the growing influence of Christianity on the reservation and the mandatory enrollment of Hopi children at government schools. Government officials labeled the cooperative Indians "Friendlies" and those that opposed American rule "Hostiles." Although Hopis valued education, many people at Oraibi did not approve of the Americanized form of education offered at reservation day schools or off-reservation boarding schools. Concerned that the assimilation of Hopi children into mainstream white society would destroy Hopi culture, parents and village leaders not only opposed the government, but ran afoul of one another as they wrestled with the vexing issue of education and assimilation.

By the early twentieth century, internal divisions had intensified, and Hopi leaders concluded that the two factions could no longer live in the same village. Listening to the pleas of Christian missionaries and addressing the situation as Hopi people, leaders and elders agreed to settle the dispute in a uniquely Hopi way, which did not involve guns, knives, or other weapons. Instead, while more than five hundred men gathered outside the village, Hopi leaders poured a line of cornmeal on the ground, and the two groups positioned themselves on each side of the marker.[44]

Leigh Kuwanwisiwma, whose grandfathers participated in the dispute, recalled that Tawaquaptewa, *kikmongwi* of Oraibi and leader of the Friendly faction, and Youkeoma, leader of the Hostiles, stood chest to chest at the center of the line while their followers pushed them from behind.[45] Attempting to push their leader over the line, the Hopi factions understood that whichever side lost the confrontation would be forced to leave the village. Although some historians have suggested that the battle was "bloodless," many Hopis received injuries as others pulled, pushed, grabbed, and scratched them in the commotion. Furthermore, children who observed the battle from a distance saw their fathers, uncles, and grandfathers shoving each other from opposite sides. Kuwanwisiwma noted that the pushing battle went on for hours until the Friendlies pushed Youkeoma over the line and demanded that every Hostile family leave the village. Men, women, and children wept as their relatives quickly gathered their belongings and departed for a campsite two miles west of Oraibi. A few hours later, some of the Hostile families returned to the village for food and clothes, but the Friendlies told them to "get out," for they had "no business" at Oraibi anymore.

In Washington, Commissioner of Indian Affairs Francis E. Leupp carefully monitored the Hopi situation. For the commissioner, Tawaquaptewa had gone against the American legal system when he demanded that the Hostiles leave the village.[46] As a result, government officials turned against Tawaquaptewa, stripped him of his chieftainship, and banished the thirty-four-year-old Native leader to the Sherman Institute, an off-reservation Indian boarding school in Riverside, California.[47]

In November 1906, Tawaquaptewa and nearly seventy Hopi pupils left the reservation by wagon for Winslow, Arizona, where they boarded a Santa Fe train for California. Tawaquaptewa would spend nearly three years at Sherman, where he experienced firsthand the government's attempt to assimilate Indian people through the boarding school system. Although government officials had forced Tawaquaptewa to attend Sherman, they did not have the authority to strip him of his chieftainship. On the campus, Tawaquaptewa conducted himself as a chief and representative of a sovereign nation, and continued his leadership role with other Hopi children. In the *Sherman Bulletin*, the school's student-written newspaper, Indian pupils observed that Tawaquaptewa often called the Hopis together to give them instruction and sound advice. He told the Hopi children to do their very best at the school and to take advantage of their time at Sherman. With confidence and respect for their chief, the Hopi followers listened to Tawaquaptewa and made notable accomplishments at the school.

PRESIDENT THEODORE ROOSEVELT AND AMERICAN INDIANS

A year before the Oraibi split, President Theodore Roosevelt defeated Alton B. Parker for a second term as president of the United States. Roosevelt had an appreciation for American Indian cultures and had previously opposed the ruthless killings of women and children at Wounded Knee. To assure the American public that his administration supported the humane treatment of American Indians, Roosevelt invited several Native leaders to participate in his inauguration in Washington. A reporter for the *New York Times* observed that Roosevelt's inaugural committee had appropriated $2,000 for "six noted Indians" to ride horses in the president's inaugural parade.[48] Thousands of spectators viewed the procession, which, with the Indians' participation, looked more like Buffalo Bill's Wild West Show. But the Native leaders had come to represent sovereign Indian nations proudly, at a time when Americans believed that *real* Indians were vanishing.

Throughout his second term, President Roosevelt met with Indian leaders in Washington, although he seldom convened with Indian leaders who had accepted American citizenship. Once Indians received

American citizenship, President Roosevelt could no longer view them as representatives of sovereign Indian nations. In March 1905, a group of Sioux Indians from Yankton, South Dakota—including Eagle Track, Hollow Horn Bear, Yellow Thunder, Charging Bear, Shooting Hawk, Black Chicken, Big Tobacco, Iron Bear, White Swan, Red Owl, and five others—traveled to Washington to speak with President Roosevelt.[49] The Sioux leaders noted that the "principal object" of their journey was to obtain redress from "white men and half-breeds" who had "contested the rights" to their land and had taken away their homes. Prior to their visit, the group had written government officials in Washington to state their case, but Commissioner Leupp telegraphed the Indian agent on the reservation and told him not to let the delegation come to Washington. The Sioux came anyway and demanded a hearing. Neither President Roosevelt nor Leupp would see them. A reporter for the

"I WANTED TO GIVE THE PEOPLE A GOOD SHOW":
PRESIDENT THEODORE ROOSEVELT'S INAUGURAL PARADE, 1905

Some thirty-five thousand people participated in President Theodore Roosevelt's inaugural parade in 1905, including cowboys, miners, members of Roosevelt's legendary Rough Riders, politicians, and six Indian chiefs. The chiefs astride horses were Geronimo, the great Apache medicine man and fighter, who at that time was a prisoner of war at Fort Sill, Oklahoma; Quanah Parker, a Comanche from Anadarko, Oklahoma, who was the last to surrender during the Red River Indian War; Buckskin Charlie, a Ute from Durango, Colorado; Little Plume, a Blackfoot from Browning, Montana; American Horse, an Oglala from Pine Ridge, South Dakota; and Hollow Horn Bear, a Brulé Sioux from Rosebud Agency, South Dakota. Wearing full regalia, the six Native leaders turned in their saddles and waved as they passed Roosevelt, "uttering whoops as they did so," according to the *New York Times*. "They were like Remington's pictures, only endowed with life and motion," noted a reporter for the *Washington Post*. The parade, which lasted for more than three hours, included students from the Carlisle Indian School as well as members of the Seventh Cavalry, Lieutenant Colonel George A. Custer's old unit, which had participated in the massacre at Wounded Knee, South Dakota, fifteen years

Native American leaders riding horses in President Theodore Roosevelt's inaugural parade, Washington, D.C., 1905. From left: Buckskin Charlie, American Horse, Quanah Parker, Geronimo, and Hollow Horn Bear. Little Plume is not shown. *Courtesy Library of Congress, LC-USZ62-56009.*

before. When asked why he had invited the Indians to participate, Roosevelt replied: "I wanted to give the people a good show."[50]

Washington Post noted that the Indians were the "first delegation to have come to Washington as private citizens and not as representatives of any tribe"; to this fact they attributed their failure to meet with the president, "with whom they desired to talk business."

Angered by the way they had been treated, the Sioux delegation reminded government officials that since they had accepted allotment, they possessed American citizenship and the right to vote. They noted that many Indians in South Dakota belonged to the Democratic Party, but that they were "strong Republicans" who looked favorably on Roosevelt.[51] The delegates believed that if they "were good enough to vote," then they "were good enough to come to Washington" to discuss their "troubles." A reporter for the *Washington Post* recalled that when the "Indians stalked into the President's office building, they formed the most picturesque sight seen in Washington for many days." The Indian leaders "were in the full dress of the Sioux" and "every man wore a bonnet of dyed feathers, [varied]-colored blankets, gaudy moccasins, and lurid-looking beads and fur pieces" that hung "attached to their raiment." They had also brought a peace pipe and a large bag of tobacco to share with the president. But Roosevelt would not meet them.

Goyathlay, or Geronimo (Chiricahua Apache), and his family standing in a melon patch at Fort Sill, Oklahoma Territory, ca. 1895. *National Museum of the American Indian, P13115.*

"IF I MUST DIE IN BONDAGE":
GERONIMO'S PLEA TO PRESIDENT THEODORE ROOSEVELT, 1907

In 1907, the great Chiricahua Apache warrior Goyathlay (also known as Geronimo, ca. 1829–1909) dictated his memoir. A prisoner of war since 1886, Geronimo and 469 other Chiricahua Apaches had been exiled from their homelands in Arizona and held captive in military internment camps in Florida, Alabama, and, finally, at Fort Sill in Oklahoma. At Fort Sill, Geronimo supported his family by raising garden crops and selling autographed photos to tourists. He also appeared at the St. Louis World's Fair and participated in President Theodore Roosevelt's inaugural parade in 1905. Despite his celebrity, Geronimo longed for home. Hoping to call attention to his and his people's plight, the now aging warrior arranged to tell his story to Stephen Melvil Barrett, the superintendent of schools at Lawton, Oklahoma. When army officers at Fort Sill objected, Barrett sought and received permission from President Theodore Roosevelt, to whom *Geronimo's Story of His Life* was dedicated. In the book, Geronimo pleaded with the president to free and return the Chiricahua Apaches to Arizona, but it was not to be. Geronimo died a prisoner of war at Fort Sill on February 17, 1909. Four years later, Congress released the remaining Apaches, twenty-seven years after they had been taken into custody. It was the longest captivity of any Indian group in American history.

I am thankful that the President of the United States has given me permission to tell my story. I hope that he and those in authority under him will read my story and judge whether my people have been rightly treated. . . . I think that my people are now capable of living in accordance with the laws of the United States, and we would, of course, like to have the liberty to return to that land which is ours by divine right. We are reduced in numbers, and having learned how to cultivate the soil would not require so much ground as was formerly necessary. We do not ask all of the land which the Almighty gave us in the beginning, but that we may have sufficient lands there to cultivate. What we do not need we are glad for the white men to cultivate. . . .

It is my land, my home, my fathers' land, to which I now ask to be allowed to return. I want to spend my last days there, and be buried among those mountains. If this could be I might die in peace, feeling that my people, placed in their native homes, would increase in numbers, rather than diminish as at present, and that our name would not become extinct.

I know that if my people were placed in that mountainous region lying around the headwaters of the Gila River they would live in peace and act according to the will of the President. They would be prosperous and happy in tilling the soil and learning the civilization of the white men, whom they now respect. Could I but see this accomplished, I think I could forget all the wrongs that I have ever received, and die a contented and happy old man. . . . If this cannot be done during my lifetime—if I must die in bondage—I hope that the remnant of the Apache tribe may, when I am gone, be granted the one privilege which they request—to return to Arizona.[52]

—Geronimo, 1907

CITIZENSHIP

In 1924, Congress passed the Indian Citizenship Act, which extended American citizenship to all Native people. Prior to 1924, approximately two-thirds of the Native population held American citizenship through treaty stipulations or individual acts of Congress.[53] Some Native people felt empowered when the United States government extended the franchise to them, and were encouraged to approach presidents with concerns that went beyond the issues of land and assimilation. Two years after William H. Taft became president in 1909, a delegation of Cheyenne and Arapaho Indians came to Washington to meet with Commissioner of Indian Affairs Robert G. Valentine and President Taft about a "small land issue" in Oklahoma.[54] Unbeknownst to government officials, the delegation had a second issue to address: movies. American movie producers were making films that often portrayed American Indians as uncivilized savages, and this group of Cheyenne and Arapaho leaders was concerned that Indians were "discreditably depicted in moving pictures." The group met with Indian Commissioner Valentine, who sympathized with their concern, recalling that he had "seen productions wherein the Indian was pictured as a cannibal, thief, and almost every evil thing one can imagine," but had "seen only a few wherein he [had] been favorably represented."[55]

To further demonstrate their point, chiefs Big Buck and Big Bear accompanied a *Washington Post* reporter to a "moving picture" on life in the American West. The movie featured a young Indian woman who had fallen in love with a white man taken prisoner by her tribe. After she discovered that the man was married, she "stabbed his wife with a poisoned arrow" so that he would be free to marry her.

The chiefs watched the film with disdain. Big Buck noted that, "If the white people would only take the pains to study Indian characteristics . . . he could possibly produce something worthy of presentation to the public." Big Bear told the reporter that they might "go to President Taft in the morning and ask him to close up" the movie house. "It is bad to be lied about to so many people," said Big Bear, and be "helpless to defend yourself."

Movie producer F. Thomas Moore disagreed with both men. "All the shows in which Indians are portrayed are good clean productions

President Woodrow Wilson, ca. 1913. *Courtesy Library of Congress, LC-USZ62-20570.*

passed on by the National Board of Censorship."[56] President Taft's own response to the protest is unclear, but censoring depictions of Indians in movies was clearly not one of his administration's top priorities.[57]

The extension of citizenship to Indians encouraged some American presidents to view Native people as "Americans" rather than "wards of the government" or members of tribal nations. Shortly after his inauguration, President Wilson recorded a "welcome message" on a phonograph record that was played on each of the 189 Indian reservations registered by the Indian Bureau. Wilson's message—part of an "expedition of patriotism" to Indian communities organized by Rodman Wanamaker, heir to the Philadelphia department store dynasty—was played on a state-of-the art phonograph, donated by Thomas Edison, during a ceremony held beneath an American flag. As they gathered around the wooden console, Indians listened to Wilson's recorded voice, hailing them for their "remarkable progress" in "education, agriculture, and the trades" and for taking "their places in civilization alongside their white neighbors." To signal this achievement, Wilson emphasized that he would now call Indians his "brothers," not his "children," because "you have shown in your education and in your settled ways of life, staunch, manly, worthy qualities of sound character. . . ." Although Wilson admitted that there were "some dark pages in the history of the white man's dealings with the Indian," he was certain that the nation's Indian policies had been "wise, just, and beneficent," and that white men and Indians now shared the same rights, privileges, and "devotion to our common country."[58]

After World War I, an increasing number of Indians who visited the White House had been educated at white-run schools. In 1921, Zitkala-Ša (Gertrude Simmons Bonnin), a Yankton-Nakota woman who had attended the Quaker-sponsored White's Indiana Manual Labor Institute in Wabash, Indiana, came to Washington to beseech President Warren G. Harding and Congress to forbid the use of peyote, a cactus used by some Natives for religious purposes.[59] A year later, Jim Thorpe, the great all-American Sac and Fox athlete who earned fame at the Carlisle Indian School and at the 1912 Olympics, met with President Harding, following in the footsteps of other Indian leaders and representatives who had made the journey to Washington before him.

Although American citizenship was extended to Native people in 1924, the road to Indian self-determination remained littered with obstacles. The early twentieth century saw the continued depletion of tribal lands through allotment as well as increased government efforts

Robert Yellowtail (Crow).
Photo courtesy Hardin
Photo Service.

"OUR LAST STAND AGAINST THE EVER-ENCROACHING HAND": ROBERT YELLOWTAIL AND INDIAN SELF-DETERMINATION, 1919

During World War I, more than ten thousand Native American men—almost twenty-five percent of the eligible Indian population— answered the nation's call to serve in the armed forces. The irony of fighting to defend democracy abroad was clear to many Native Americans, whose lives were circumscribed by the iron hand of government Indian agents. After the war, a new generation of young, educated Indian leaders, influenced by the democratic wartime rhetoric of President Woodrow Wilson, emerged to demand positive change in Indian Country. One of them was Robert Yellowtail (1889–1988).

A member of the Crow Tribe of Montana, Yellowtail was educated at a reservation school and then attended the Sherman Institute, the government boarding school in Riverside, California. Yellowtail later spent three years studying law in Southern California, then returned to Montana in 1910 to raise cattle. More interested in politics than ranching, Yellowtail became involved in tribal affairs and soon emerged as a leading opponent of efforts to open Crow lands to white settlement. When local politicians pushed for federal legislation to diminish Crow Reservation lands, Yellowtail led a delegation to Washington, D.C., where he spoke out in opposition to the measure before the Senate Committee on Indian Affairs.

Yellowtail's speech, excerpted below, drew upon President Woodrow Wilson's postwar vision of a new democratic world order in which all subjected peoples would enjoy the right to national self-determination. Using Wilsonian rhetoric to demand Indian rights, Yellowtail, as the historian Frederick E. Hoxie has observed, "translated the Crows' political ideals into terms other American politicians could not ignore."

In his speech to lawmakers, Yellowtail noted that President Wilson had "assured the people of this great country, and also the people of the whole world, that the right of self-determination shall not be denied to any people, no matter where they live, nor how small or weak they may be, nor what their previous conditions of servitude may have been." Then, the young tribal leader asked whether Wilson's commitment to self-determination extended to American Indians:

I and the rest of my people sincerely hope and pray that the President, in his great scheme of enforcing upon all nations of the earth the adoption of this great principle of the brotherhood of man and nations, . . . will not forget that within the boundaries of his own nation are the American Indians who have no rights whatsoever. . . . I hold that the Crow Indian Reservation is a separate semi-sovereign nation in itself, not belonging to any State, and that no Senator, or anybody else . . . has any right to . . . tear us asunder by the continued introduction of bills . . . without our consent . . . neither has he the right to dictate to us what we shall hold as our final homesteads in this our last stand against the ever-encroaching hand, nor continue to disturb our peace of mind by a constant agitation to deprive us of our lands, that were, to begin with, ours, not his, and not given to us by anybody. This nation should be only too ready, as an atonement for our treatment in the past, to willingly grant to the Indian people of this country their unquestionable and undeniable right to determine how much of their own lands they shall retain as their homes and how much they shall dispose of to outsiders. . . .[60] ❧

to assimilate Indians into mainstream American society. By the 1920s, the outlook for Native people was grim. Indians had long blamed federal Indian policies for the loss of their lands and for undermining their tribal cultures. But now a new generation of white reformers, socialized during the Progressive Era of the 1890s through the 1920s, emerged to support Indian demands for change.[61] Those demands found expression in a pivotal report on Indian affairs commissioned in 1926 by Hubert Work, secretary of the interior under President Calvin Coolidge. The study, conducted by the Institute of Government Research, was led by the anthropologist Lewis Meriam and a team of researchers, including Henry Roe Cloud, a Winnebago who cofounded the Society of American Indians. Their report, published in 1928, pilloried United States Indian policy and set in motion a wave of reforms that would affect American Indian nations in the 1930s and beyond.

Crow and Sioux chiefs presenting a tobacco pouch to President Harding as Indian Commissioner Charles Burke looks on. The delegates were in the nation's capital to attend the burial of the Unknown Soldier at Arlington National Cemetery, 1921. *Courtesy Library of Congress, LC-USZ62-83673.*

WARRIOR TO WARRIOR:
CHIEF PLENTY COUPS PAYS HOMAGE TO THE UNKNOWN SOLDIER

In 1921, the last hereditary chief of the Crow Nation traveled east to participate in a ceremony to honor the Unknown Soldier at Arlington National Cemetery, west of Washington, D.C. An old warrior of great distinction, Plenty Coups (1848–1932) had been invited to participate in the event, but organizers insisted that the chief remain silent throughout the ceremony. The day began with a solemn parade for the unidentified soldier, who had been killed in France during the final days of World War I. Leading the way was a horse-drawn caisson carrying the soldier's remains. Behind walked President and Mrs. Warren G. Harding, Vice President and Mrs. Calvin Coolidge, and Chief Justice (and former President) William H. Taft. Former President Woodrow Wilson, crippled by a devastating stroke, trailed behind, seated in a car. War veterans, politicians, military bands, mothers, members of social and professional organizations, and other parade participants filed past throngs of onlookers, as the caisson pushed west toward Virginia.

Some one hundred thousand spectators gathered at the cemetery to watch the proceedings, which began at noon. After observing two minutes of silence, the crowd sang "America," and President Harding and other dignitaries delivered speeches. Representatives of foreign governments honored the deceased soldier's memory by presenting their nations' military medals. Finally, the coffin was placed in a marble sarcophagus, and a military chaplain recited prayers.

Dressed in beaded buckskin, Chief Plenty Coups rose, placed his eagle-feather headdress and warrior coup stick on the sarcophagus, and began speaking to the crowd in his Native language. A translation reads, "I am glad to represent all the Indians of the United States in placing on the grave of this noble warrior this coup stick and war bonnet, every eagle feather

Chief Plenty Coups (Crow) greeting Marshal Ferdinand Foch, Crow Agency, Montana, 1921. Foch, the French hero of World War I, came to visit the Indian warrior in Crow Country shortly after the two met at the burial of the Unknown Soldier at Arlington National Cemetery, 1921. *Courtesy National Anthropological Archives, Smithsonian Institution.*

of which represents a deed of valor by my race." The chief added this prayer: "I hope that the Great Spirit will grant that these noble warriors have not given up their lives in vain and that there will be peace to all men hereafter."

By participating in the commemoration, Plenty Coups appeared as an ally of the United States. But, as the historian Frederick E. Hoxie has noted, his bold decision to speak was an act of opposition that turned the occasion "to his own and to his community's advantage." The chief not only celebrated time-honored Native American warrior traditions, but established himself as the representative of sovereign Indian nations—the equal of the presidents, politicians, military officers, and foreign dignitaries who attended the ceremony. Through his act of independence, Plenty Coups cast a spotlight on Native Americans at a time when Indians had been largely consigned to the margins of American society.[62] ➤

President Franklin D. Roosevelt shaking hands with Chief Noah Bad Wound (Oglala Sioux, 1867–?) in Bismarck, North Dakota, during a tour of drought-stricken areas of the United States, 1936. During the New Deal, the United States repudiated earlier Indian policies that broke up tribal lands and undermined Native culture and sovereignty. Under Roosevelt's administration, American Indian cultures were to be respected, and tribal economic and political power enhanced. After World War II, the pendulum swung back as Congress and the presidents attempted to terminate federal services and protections for tribes, and encouraged Indians to assimilate into mainstream American life. *©Bettmann/CORBIS.*

CHAPTER IV

FROM FULL CITIZENSHIP TO SELF-DETERMINATION, 1930–75

DUANE CHAMPAGNE

American presidents in the twentieth century rarely met with Indian leaders to discuss tribal issues. As the leaders of a dynamic industrialized nation with burgeoning worldwide influence, the presidents increasingly relied on government officials and White House advisors to formulate and execute policy. Though their involvement in Indian affairs diminished, presidents continued to focus attention on Indian Country and adopted various strategies to address relations between Native nations and the United States government. All of the presidents between 1930 and 1970 expressed concern over the Office of Indian Affairs' heavy-handed control of tribal communities, and all articulated a range of goals and strategies for promoting the well-being of Indian people. The key point of divergence among presidents focused on whether Native nations should retain their own governments and cultures, or whether Indians should participate as full citizens in American society.

For most presidents, these choices were clear and mutually exclusive; one policy would be chosen over another. By the late 1960s, however, Presidents Johnson and Nixon outlined a strikingly new approach that invited Indians to participate as American citizens and, at the same time, retain their rights to tribal self-government and traditional culture. The new commitment to self-determination—the result of growing political assertiveness among tribal leaders, Native communities, and Indian organizations—laid the foundation for Indian policy for the remainder of the twentieth century and continues to shape the relationship between Indian nations and the presidents in our time.

THE MERIAM REPORT AND PRESIDENT HERBERT HOOVER

Between 1880 and 1920, United States Indian policy encouraged Native people to reject traditional culture and tribal governance in order to assimilate into mainstream American society. The federal government, with the encouragement of presidents, forced thousands of Indian children to attend boarding schools where teachers required students to speak English and develop skills appropriate for life and work in white America. At the same time, government divided tribal lands into parcels, or allotments, which were distributed to individual tribal members. The allotment policy encouraged tribal members to take up farming, dissolved the tribe's collective control of land, promoted individualism, and distanced many Indians from traditional community and kinship relationships.

These policies came under increasing scrutiny during the 1920s, as Native American organizations and non-Indian reformers called for an overhaul of Indian affairs. The rising reform chorus generated an investigation of conditions on Indian reservations, which resulted in the publication in 1928 of *The Problem of Indian Administration*.[1] Prepared by Lewis Meriam and nine other scholars, the Meriam Report documented a litany of "deplorable" conditions on Indian reservations and recommended that Congress allocate additional funding for Native communities, reform Indian policy, and reorganize the Office of Indian Affairs.

Chief American Horse (Oglala Sioux) giving information to allotment officer Charles Bates (center), with Billy Garnett, an interpreter (left), at Pine Ridge, South Dakota, in 1907. Established in 1868, the 2.7-million-acre Pine Ridge Reservation was divided into 8,275 individual parcels, amounting to 2.3 million acres, during allotment, which lasted from 1904 to 1916. Approximately 182,653 acres of land were sold to the government, and another 146,633 acres remained in tribal hands. Allotment eroded the Native estate throughout Indian Country. Between 1887, when the General Allotment Act was passed, and 1934, when allotment was repealed under President Franklin Roosevelt, the Native land base shrank from approximately 138 million acres to 52 million acres. *Photo by Edward Truman. Courtesy Denver Public Library, Western History Collection, X-31717.*

All presidents in the post–Meriam Report era sought solutions
to the difficult conditions of life on Indian reservations. The first
was Herbert Hoover, the only president who lived for a time on an
Indian reservation. Hoover was born in Iowa in 1874, and brought
rock-ribbed Republican values to the White House in 1929. His
mother, Hulda Hoover, was a Quaker minister who instilled in her
son the Quaker values of honesty, simplicity, diligence, and generosity. When Hoover's father died in 1880, his uncle, Laban Miles,
took him to live on the Osage Reservation, in Indian Territory, where
Miles served as Indian agent to the Osage Nation. The young Hoover
spent eight months on the reservation, playing and making friends
with the Indian boys who attended the agency's school. The Osage
boys taught Hoover how to fish, a pastime the future president
would pursue throughout his life. As a Quaker pacifist, Hoover was
not allowed to carry a gun, but the Osages taught him how to make
bows and arrows, which he used for hunting rabbits, pigeons, and

Herbert Hoover listening to a radio, ca. 1925. "A certain amount of time of every President every week, from George Washington down, has had to be devoted to 'Indian Affairs,'" Hoover lamented in his memoirs. "Certainly our 400,000 Indians consume more official attention than any twenty cities of 400,000 white people." *Courtesy Library of Congress, LC-USZ62-111716.*

prairie chickens. In his memoirs, Hoover recalled that his interest in Indians dated to the time he lived with the Osages. During Hoover's presidency, Osages visited him at the White House, posing for photographs in full Indian regalia—a symbol of honor and respect.[2]

As president, Hoover initiated a discussion that defined the terms of United States Indian policy for the next forty years. Federal Indian policy, Hoover observed, "vibrated from a yearning . . . to perpetuate . . . tribal organization and customs, to a desire, at the other pole, to make industrious citizens of them and thus fuse them with the general population." Hoover sided with those who believed American Indians should be invited to join American society as full and productive citizens. "The objective of the administration must be to make the Indians self-supporting and self-respecting," he said. "They were to be viewed no longer as wards of the nation, but as potential citizens."[3]

Hoover appointed Charles J. Rhoads, a Quaker, philanthropist, and president of the Indian Rights Association, to serve as commissioner of Indian affairs. Like Hoover, Rhoads was heir to a centuries-old Quaker tradition of respecting Native land and treaty rights. "Quakers," Hoover noted, "had always been the defenders of the Indians since the beginning of American history."[4] After examining issues in Indian Country, Rhoads concluded that the Hoover administration should concentrate on making Indians self-supporting and removing them from the authority of the Office of Indian Affairs. To that end, Hoover increased funding for health care and education, the latter to provide training to Indian youth, who would be better prepared to work and function in mainstream society. Indians would now be encouraged to abandon tribal communities—as well as the paternalism of the federal agency that administered them—and to embrace independence, self-sufficiency, and citizenship rights in the wider society.[5]

In addition to supporting full citizenship for Indians, the Hoover administration moved to protect Indian property rights from further exploitation, and to reaffirm Indian treaty rights.[6] Hoover decried the fact that Native peoples had lost more than ninety million acres of land through the government's allotment policy between 1887 and 1928 and railed at the often fraudulent means by which Indian lands had been acquired. Indian communities, he observed, "were infested with human lice" who illegally sold alcohol or married Indian women to gain control of their land and mineral rights.[7] He blasted profit-sharing lawyers who helped push Indian land claims through Congress, and, as president, supported legislation that provided Indians with enhanced protection from exploitation.[8] Ultimately, Hoover viewed Indians as potential citizens who deserved equal treatment under the law rather than members of Native nations who wanted to retain their culture, government, land, and resources. "It is the purpose of the United States Government to do justice by the Indians," Hoover insisted, and to "assist them to citizenship and participation in the benefits of our civilization."[9]

These views were shared by Hoover's vice president, Charles Curtis. A descendant of Kaw and Osage Indians, Curtis was a long-time Republican who had served as a congressional representative and senator from Kansas and as a member of the Kaw tribal community, located near Topeka, Kansas. Although the vice president's

The United States Indian Band with Vice President Charles Curtis, Washington, D.C., 1929. The band, representing thirteen Native tribes, called at the U.S. Capitol to serenade Curtis, part Kaw and Osage Indian, during a tour of the United States. *Courtesy Library of Congress, LC-DIG-ppmsca-05083.*

Indian policies were compatible with Hoover's, Curtis played a minor role in Indian affairs and wielded little influence within the Hoover administration.[10] An Indian who had more influence with the Hoover administration was Will Rogers (Cherokee), the enormously popular humorist and newspaper columnist as well as a stage, radio, and motion picture star.

In the early years of the Great Depression, Rogers supported President Hoover's philosophy of denying direct government aid to the unemployed, appearing with Hoover on a national radio program in which the president trumpeted his alternative to government-

"MY CHEROKEE BLOOD": WILL ROGERS AND THE PRESIDENTS

Born near Oolagah, Cherokee Nation, Will Rogers (Cherokee, 1879–1935) was the son of a prosperous rancher, banker, and activist in tribal affairs. Clement V. Rogers entered tribal politics in 1877, when he became a judge for the Cooweescoowe District, and later served five terms in the Cherokee senate. He was an influential public official who frequently associated with the principal chiefs of the Cherokee Nation and other tribal leaders. Living on the family's ranch on the Verdigris River exposed the young Will Rogers to cattle, horses, and cowboys, and he soon developed a knack for roping—a skill that served him well as a trick roper in circuses and Wild West shows in the early 1900s. Rogers's lasso work, however, gradually took a backseat to his satirical commentaries about life, people, and politics. Delivered in a down-home, folksy style, Rogers's humor appealed to audiences throughout the United States, and by 1914 he had become one of the most popular entertainers in vaudeville.

Rogers began acting in silent films in 1918 and transitioned successfully to the "talkies." By 1934, he had appeared in some seventy-one films and was voted the most popular actor in Hollywood. He also launched a successful career as a writer. In 1919, he published two books, *The Cowboy Philosopher on the Peace Conference* and *The Cowboy Philosopher on Prohibition,* and later began writing a weekly newspaper column, which became nationally syndicated. In 1926, the *Saturday Evening Post* sent him to Europe as an unofficial ambassador for President Calvin Coolidge; his dispatches for the magazine were later published in *Letters of a Self-Made Diplomat to His President.* An international celebrity and renowned political pundit, Rogers was frequently a guest at the White House and counted Presidents Calvin Coolidge and Franklin D. Roosevelt as

Best known for his folksy humor, Will Rogers (Cherokee) was an acquaintance of and advisor to three presidents. *Courtesy Library of Congress, LC-USZ62-20553.*

friends. When Roosevelt was elected president, Rogers emerged as a champion of poor farmers, unemployed workers, and others dislocated by the Great Depression.

Rogers publicly identified himself as a Native American but rarely spoke out about Indian issues. Once, while discussing the site of the Pilgrims' landing, Rogers quipped: "Now I hope my Cherokee blood is not making me prejudiced. I want to be broad-minded, but I am sure that it was only the extreme generosity of the Indians that allowed the Pilgrims to land. Suppose we reversed the case. Do you reckon the Pilgrims would have ever let the Indians land? Yeah, what a chance! What a chance! The Pilgrims wouldn't even allow the Indians to live after the Indians went to the trouble of letting 'em land."[11]

supported unemployment relief: private charity.[12] During the program, Rogers delivered what became known as the "Bacon, Beans, and Limousines" speech, which referenced the nation's seven million unemployed and decried the growing rift between rich and poor.[13] The speech struck a chord with listeners and became one of Rogers's best-known political addresses. When Hoover lost the presidential election of 1932 to Franklin D. Roosevelt, Rogers told critics that he admired Hoover and believed that his administration had been hampered by a series of bad breaks. "We have been a fortunate nation," Rogers observed. "We have always had good presidents."[14]

PRESIDENT FRANKLIN D. ROOSEVELT AND THE INDIAN NEW DEAL

Franklin D. Roosevelt had developed a friendship with Rogers before he was elected president in 1932. As governor of New York, Roosevelt invited Rogers to visit him in Albany, where the two discussed a range of issues, including treatment for one of Rogers's relatives who had been stricken with infantile paralysis.[15] Roosevelt suggested treatment at Warm Springs, Georgia, where he often went to receive treatments for polio. In the spring of 1931, Roosevelt in vited Rogers, saying, "Come and talk to me of cabbages and kings! I want to see you, Oh, most excellent of philosophers!"[16]

As the Depression worsened, Rogers had begun to favor public works projects as well as direct and immediate government relief for unemployed workers, all financed by an income tax on the rich. Believing that the Hoover administration was giving insufficient aid to meet the challenges confronting the nation, Rogers looked increasingly for pragmatic solutions to immediate social needs caused by the Depression. Soon after the presidential election of 1932, Rogers sent a telegram to the victorious Roosevelt containing a spate of humorous advice and suggestions for the new president and the nation.[17] For Rogers, Roosevelt was a local humanitarian, a man who would fix attention on America's internal woes. Hoover's problem, Rogers opined, was that he was a world humanitarian who was overly concerned with international affairs.[18]

Rogers's daily and weekly newspaper commentaries were required reading for the new administration.[19] Although the White House did not always agree with him, the humorist's commentary was always good for a chuckle. In addition to his wry wisdom, Rogers's knowledge of Indian Country most likely came up in conversation with Roosevelt and may have influenced the president's thinking. But whatever influence Rogers may have had was short-lived. On August 15, 1935, he died in a plane crash while flying to Barrow, Alaska. Rogers was an American Indian who had the ear of several presidents. There would be no comparable Indian voice in national affairs for many years to come.

President Franklin Roosevelt moved quickly to change the nation's Indian policy. Shortly after taking office, the president transferred the powers of the Board of Indian Commissioners—which had been established by Congress in 1869 to provide humanitarian and Christian oversight to Indian affairs—to the secretary of the interior. The move centralized authority over Indian policy in the offices of

Commissioner of Indian Affairs John Collier with, from left, Hopi Chiefs Lemahaftewa and Kol Chaf Towa, at the cornerstone-laying ceremony for the new Interior Department Building in Washington, D.C., 1936. *©Bettmann/CORBIS.*

the secretary of the interior and the commissioner of Indian affairs, and provided greater scope for change.[20] Roosevelt also appointed John Collier, an Indian rights activist, as commissioner of Indian affairs. Collier had led the Indian Defense Association, which helped defend Pueblo lands, and from 1926 to 1933 edited *American Indian Life*, a magazine that advocated for Indian rights. As commissioner of Indian affairs from 1933 to 1945, Collier implemented the Indian New Deal—an initiative that moved Indian policy toward preserving Indian culture and self-government, respecting Indian land and treaty rights, and ending the policy of mandatory assimilation imposed on Indian communities since the nineteenth century.[21]

The keystone of the Indian New Deal was the Wheeler-Howard Act, commonly called the Indian Reorganization Act of 1934, or IRA. Collier succeeded in maneuvering the heavily marked-up and compromised bill through a rather unwilling Congress, which passed what became the most significant policy statement on Indian affairs during the Roosevelt administration. President Roosevelt had encouraged lawmakers to pass the bill, which, he believed, embodied new standards for relations between Indians and the United States government and provided a measure of long overdue justice to American Indians. "We can and should, without delay, extend to the Indian the fundamental rights of political liberty and local self-government and the opportunities of education and economic assistance that they require in order to attain a wholesome American life," the president declared.

> That is but the obligation of honor of a powerful nation toward a people living amongst us and dependent on our protection. . . . Certainly the continuance of autocratic rule, by a Federal Department, over the lives of more than two hundred thousand citizens is incompatible with American ideals of liberty. It is also destructive of the character and self-respect of a great race.[22]

Roosevelt singled out the allotment of reservation lands as particularly detrimental to Indians and called for its abolition, as provided in the Wheeler-Howard Act. Excessive poverty and poor health on

Representatives from the Flathead Reservation in Montana, including Chief Bear Track and Chief Three Eagles, at left, an unidentified man, and Chief Kustada, at far right, receiving a tribal constitution and by-laws, made under the Indian Reorganization Act, from Secretary of the Interior Harold Ickes in 1935. The Kutenai and Salish Tribes of the Flathead Reservation had the first tribal government established under the Indian Reorganization Act, passed in 1934 as part of President Franklin D. Roosevelt's New Deal. *Courtesy Library of Congress, LC-USZ62-11598.*

Indian reservations, the president noted, also called for new measures and new policies which, to be successful, required the active consent and cooperation of Indian people. Under the Wheeler-Howard Act, Roosevelt explained, tribal communities could adopt new constitutional governments, create economic corporations, enjoy opportunities to manage their own political and economic affairs, and affirm their rights to local self-government. "I do not think such changes can be devised and carried out without the active cooperation of the Indians themselves," Roosevelt asserted. "It allows the Indian people to take a responsible part in the solution of their problems."[23]

FDR, SEMINOLES, AND CATTLE TICKS

President Franklin D. Roosevelt typically left Native American policy to his commissioner of Indian affairs, John Collier, but on at least one occasion, the president intervened directly to press for positive change in Indian Country. It happened in 1942, when the state of Florida and the United States Bureau of Animal Husbandry announced plans to kill deer suspected of carrying cattle ticks on Florida's Seminole Reservation. Displaying a flair for executive leadership, Roosevelt dashed off the following letter to Secretary of Agriculture Claude Wickard, ordering him to halt the deer kill:

Dear Claude:

Tell your Bureau of Animal Husbandry that I do not want any deer killed on the Seminole Reservation in Florida until this war is over. Tell them to have the proposed amendment put on by the House eliminated in the Senate—$5,000. Tell them that if the thing stays in the bill I will impound the money. The point is that no one knows whether these unfortunate animals are hosts to cattle ticks or not. The investigation ought to teach us more about it. You might also tell the Bureau of Animal Husbandry that they have never proved that human beings are not hosts to cattle ticks. I think some human beings I know are. But I do not shoot them on suspicion—though I would sorely like to do so!

Always sincerely,

Franklin D. Roosevelt[24]

The Indian New Deal received mixed reviews from tribal communities. Some Native people were stunned by the prospect of the United States government fostering tribal cultures and governments it had tried for decades to eradicate. When an elderly resident of the Pine Ridge Reservation was told of Collier's Indian New Deal, he sat for a moment, collected his thoughts, and responded with the Lakota equivalent of, "Well, I'll be damned."[25] Ultimately, some 164 Native communities decided to organize under the IRA. At the same time, 94 Native tribes rejected reorganization, a decision that staggered Collier, who assumed he knew what was best for Native people. Although many tribal communities welcomed New Deal jobs programs, they were suspicious of new American-style constitutional forms and policies that were not grounded in treaty rights, and preferred to work within time-honored forms of governance that were more congruent with tribal traditions and cultures.[26]

By the late 1930s, support for the Indian New Deal was waning.

Tlingit carvers standing with an Abraham Lincoln totem pole, 1939. The carvers, Charles Brown (right) and James Starrish, were employed by the Civilian Conservation Corps (CCC), a New Deal program that provided jobs for the unemployed. Between 1933 and 1942, some eighty-five thousand Indians participated in similar jobs programs. In southeastern Alaska, CCC workers restored plank houses and totem poles, including this Abraham Lincoln pole, which was raised over Tongass Village in the nineteenth century. *©Bettmann/CORBIS.*

A less-supportive Congress allocated fewer dollars for Indian affairs, particularly after the onset of World War II. When the war ended in 1945, Congress increasingly rejected New Deal Indian policy in favor of moving Indians toward full citizenship and full participation in American life. That perspective, strongly supported by former President Herbert Hoover, soon gained sway with the new president, Harry S. Truman.[27]

PRESIDENT HARRY S. TRUMAN AND
FULL CITIZENSHIP DURING THE COLD WAR

President Harry S. Truman had no formative experiences or strong personal contacts with American Indians. Members of his family had pioneered the state of Missouri, and Truman sometimes told stories of relatives who hunted, traded, and occasionally encountered hostile Indians. Yet Truman believed that Native Americans had been treated disgracefully. Far from being an inferior race, Indians, for Truman, were people of wisdom who produced great leaders and lived under almost ideal forms of government. They were intelligent and brave people, who, he believed, should have been allowed to maintain themselves on their lands.[28]

Truman liked to tell a story about campaigning on an Indian reservation. After each promise of what he'd do for Indians if elected, the crowd shouted, "Oompah! Oompah!" The louder the chorus grew, the more inspired Truman's speech became. As he left, the candidate had to cross a corral filled with horses. "Careful," his Indian escort told him. "Don't step in the oompah."[29]

Although Truman supported the right of Indians to hold their lands, he believed that the future of Native people lay in entering and participating as equals in America's burgeoning economy. For Truman, American Indians were a racial minority whose lives could be improved through federal policies that guaranteed equal civil rights and full participation in American life. Truman's commitment to equal rights for Native Americans was shown in 1951, when the president intervened on behalf of the family of Sergeant John Raymond Rice, a Winnebago (Ho-Chunk) Indian from Thurston, Nebraska, who was killed in action during the Korean War. When Rice's body was returned home, the managers of a Sioux City, Iowa, cemetery refused to bury him, claiming that their policy restricted burials to whites. Word of the incident sparked outrage near and far. When President Truman heard about it, he arranged to have the eleven-year Army veteran buried at Arlington National Cemetery.[30]

Truman's action reflected growing pressure for equal treatment of racial minorities in post–World War II America. Revelations of Nazi atrocities during World War II had prompted Americans to re-examine anti-Semitism in the United States, and African American

From left: Ish-Ti-Opi (Choctaw), Reginald Curpy (Ute), and Julius Murray (Ute) presenting a pipe to President Harry S. Truman, 1946. The pipe, said to have been smoked by Chief Sitting Bull, was presented shortly after Truman signed legislation authorizing the Indian Claims Commission. *Courtesy Library of Congress, LC-USZ62-105437.*

participation in the war effort sparked efforts to abolish discriminatory racial practices. During the Cold War, Soviet propaganda underscored racial inequities in American society and highlighted the economic plight of minorities, including American Indians. Principles of racial equality were also written into the charter of the new United Nations, which set standards for treatment of racial and cultural minorities.[31]

Many American Indians were ambivalent about Truman's civil rights approach to Indian affairs because it failed to recognize long-standing Native desires for retaining tribal lands, self-government, and traditional culture. Far from supporting Indian self-government and community programs or consolidating Indian lands and tribal sovereignty, Truman dismantled Roosevelt's Indian New Deal and returned to policies established by President Hoover. Under Truman, American Indian policy would once again focus on providing full civil rights to Native people, dismantling reservations, and encouraging

Indians to embrace American life. For Truman, as for Hoover, Native American wardship status had subjected Indians to overbearing administrative constraints and created an economic burden on the federal government. Moving American Indians into full citizenship was more consistent with the equalitarian spirit of the age.[32]

Truman's commitment to full citizenship was also reflected in his support of the Indian Claims Commission Act of 1946. Passage of the act addressed a long-standing Indian grievance. For many years, American Indian tribes could not collect compensation for unpaid treaty agreements or lands lost through congressional legislation or through cases brought before the United States Court of Claims. By an act of 1863, Indian tribes could not bring suit against the government through the Court of Claims over issues stemming from treaties. The only way tribes could bring a cause of action against the United States was through congressional acts.

By creating a special Indian Claims Court empowered to hear and adjudicate Indian land cases, the Indian Claims Commission Act provided Native people with a mechanism through which to bring land-related grievances before the United States and secure compensation. Truman and congressional policy makers favored a final settlement of Indian land claims as a step toward assimilating American Indians and dismantling the Office of Indian Affairs. Once Indian land claims were settled, Truman believed, Indians would assume full citizenship, and would no longer require Indian status.

Many Indian leaders supported the Indian Claims Commission Act as a means of redressing long-standing land grievances. The president of the National Congress of American Indians (NCAI), a multitribal lobbying organization incorporated in 1944, was present when Truman signed the act into law. At the signing ceremony, Truman explained that the measure would affirm Indian property rights in the same manner that the federal government protected the property of all American citizens, and he invited Indians to submit any overlooked or outstanding land claims to the impartial court that the act created. "I hope that this bill will mark the beginning of a new era for our Indian citizens," Truman declared.

They have voluntarily served on every battlefront. They have proved by their loyalty the wisdom of a national policy built upon fair dealings. With the final settlement of all outstanding claims which this measure ensures, Indians can take their place without special handicap or special advantage in the economic life of our nation and share in its progress. [33]

In 1949, the federal government changed the name of the Office of Indian Affairs to the Bureau of Indian Affairs (BIA), and the following year President Truman appointed Dillon Myer as commissioner of Indian affairs. Myer implemented the reorganization of the BIA, promoted employment training, and introduced a relocation program that encouraged Indians to leave reservations and seek work in cities. Myer also worked to implement President Truman's policy of promoting full citizenship by removing American Indians

"INDIAN CULTURE HAS BEEN SWEPT AWAY": THE HOOVER COMMISSION REPORT, 1949

When President Harry Truman took office in 1945, Congress, as well as many Americans, felt that the federal government had grown too large, too bureaucratic, and too expensive. It was time to streamline government and eliminate what conservatives viewed as the excesses of the New Deal. Concerns about big government and presidential power encouraged Congress to create the Commission on the Organization of the Executive Branch of the Government, also known as the Hoover Commission, after its chairman, former President Herbert Hoover. The Hoover Commission's report, issued in 1949, included recommendations for sweeping changes in federal Indian policy. The commissioners blasted the New Deal's celebration of tribal cultures and asserted that assimilation of Indians into American society must once again become the cornerstone of federal policy. "The basis for historic Indian culture has been swept away," the Commission declared. "Traditional tribal organization was smashed a generation ago." In an effort to cut government spending for Native American programs, the commission recommended that the United States remove itself from the regulation of Indian affairs. These recommendations found support in the Republican-dominated Congress, and helped usher in a new era in American Indian policy, in which lawmakers sought to terminate federal involvement in Indian affairs.[34]

from federal supervision and ending Indian wardship status. Commissioner Myer called the program "termination."

Termination found support among many members of Congress who viewed it as an effective way to reduce government costs while conforming to domestic and international pressures for greater equality for racial minorities.[35] For Truman, termination removed the federal government from the administration of Indian affairs, advanced the civil rights of a racial minority, and affirmed full citizenship and economic opportunity for American Indians.[36]

The Truman administration developed long-term plans for the termination of Indian tribes but made no immediate changes in the status of Indian reservations. Those changes—and Native efforts to prevent them—took place under the administration of President Truman's successor, Dwight D. Eisenhower.

PRESIDENT DWIGHT D. EISENHOWER AND TERMINATION

The victorious commander of Allied forces in Europe during World War II, Dwight D. Eisenhower came to the White House in 1953 as a war hero who proclaimed America's commitment to world peace. Born in Texas in 1890, Eisenhower grew up in Abilene, Kansas.

Dwight D. Eisenhower kicking a football as a cadet at West Point, ca. 1911–15. *Courtesy Eisenhower Library, Abilene, Kansas.*

Jim Thorpe (Sac and Fox), top right, and members of the Carlisle Indian Industrial School football team in formation, 1912. *Cumberland County Historical Society, Carlisle, Pennsylvania.*

He excelled in high-school sports and upon graduation attended West Point. His most celebrated encounter with Indians occurred on the gridiron in 1912, when the future president and five-star general was a cadet and football player at the military school.[37] On November 19, the cadets were playing against the Carlisle Indian School, whose star player was the already famous Olympic champion Jim Thorpe. A member of the Sac and Fox Nation, Thorpe had won several gold medals that summer in the 1912 Stockholm Olympics and was pronounced the greatest athlete in the world by the king of Sweden. For some, the West Point–Carlisle game symbolized the historic rivalry between American Indians and the United States Army, and the outcome was invested with no little importance.

The game was competitive and hard-fought. Eisenhower played linebacker and, together with other defensive players, planned to team-tackle Thorpe, hitting the Carlisle star hard enough to neutralize him, if not take him out of the game. Thorpe was big and strong, and it often took two well-placed tacklers to bring him down. Eisenhower and another linebacker got a good hit on Thorpe, who took an injury time-out. Leveling Thorpe was Ike's greatest football memory.

In a subsequent play, Eisenhower and a fellow West Point linebacker positioned themselves to hit Thorpe again, but the Indian deftly moved to the side; both linebackers collided violently and had to be removed from the game. With the two best West Point linebackers sidelined, the Indian team took control and the contest turned into a rout. Carlisle won 27 to 6.

As president, Eisenhower demonstrated a commitment to consult with tribal leaders and communities in 1953, when he objected to sections of Public Law 83-280, which gave criminal and civil jurisdiction involving Indians over to certain states, without Indian consent.[38] The prospect of states unilaterally imposing their powers over tribal communities unsettled Native leaders, who viewed local government authorities as traditional opponents of tribal sovereignty.[39] Tribal leaders also viewed the new law as the first step toward complete termination, in which the federal government would sever ties to Indian communities and withdraw federal support for tribal governments.

President Eisenhower supported the law, which he viewed as a step toward "complete political equality" for Indians, but asked Congress to amend the measure to require states to consult with tribal communities and gain federal approval before conferring jurisdiction over Indian reservations.[40] Congress did not respond to the president's request to modify the law until 1968, when under the administration of Lyndon B. Johnson a clause requiring consent from tribal governments was passed into law as part of the American Indian Civil Rights Act. Meanwhile, some tribes, including the Confederated Tribes of Warm Springs Reservation and the Red Lake Chippewa, acted quickly to remove themselves from the bill. The South Dakota Sioux fought for nearly a decade to avoid state extension of criminal law over their reservations, and in 1958 the Quinault Indian Reservation's general council voted against the law, arguing that it infringed on the inherent powers of tribal government.[41]

Congressional efforts to implement termination through legislation continued in 1953, when the House of Representatives enacted House Resolution 108, which outlined a far-reaching plan to remove

Indian reservations from federal supervision, abolish the wardship status of American Indians, dismantle Indian reservations, and turn tribal property into private holdings by tribal members. Lawmakers followed with acts to terminate individual tribal communities that were considered ready to manage their own affairs. President Eisenhower did not play a direct role in conceptualizing or implementing these measures, but he agreed in principle with the goals of termination policy: moving Indians out of wardship status, distributing tribal assets to tribal members, and removing Indian lands from federally protected trust status. When Eisenhower signed a bill that terminated federal supervision over the Menominee Tribe of Wisconsin on June 17, 1954, he acknowledged that the tribe had demonstrated an ability to manage its assets without federal supervision. The Menominees, Eisenhower remarked, had "opened up a new era in Indian Affairs—an era of growing self-reliance." The termination bill would not solve all the problems of Indian administration, Eisenhower conceded, but the act would provide a model for other tribes who wanted to assume management of their own assets and affairs like other Americans.[42]

Over the next twenty years the federal government terminated about 110 Indian reservations. In 1957, the Southern Paiutes became the first tribe to be formally terminated. Formal termination for the last group, the Menominees, went into effect in 1961.[43]

Most Indian communities were unwilling and unprepared for termination, and many organized to oppose it. The NCAI organized national opposition to termination throughout Indian Country, insisting that the federal government honor treaties with Indian nations, consult with tribal leaders, and dismantle no Indian reservation without consent from the tribal community.[44] Early in 1953, the NCAI convened a meeting in which Indian delegates representing 183,000 tribal members gathered to oppose termination. The gathering adopted a Declaration of Indian Rights, which NCAI President Joseph Garry (Coeur D'Alene) later sent to President Eisenhower. The Declaration blasted termination as a basic violation of Indian treaty agreements and offered the president a refresher course in American Indian history. "The Government of the United States first dealt with our tribal governments as sovereign equals," the Declaration declared:

In exchange for federal protection and certain benefits our ancestors gave forever to the people of the United States title to our beloved country. . . . Today the federal government is threatening to withdraw this protection and these benefits. . . . These proposals do not have Indian consent . . . [and] if adopted, will tend to destroy our tribal governments [and] leave our older people destitute . . . [and] force our people into a way of life that some of them are not willing or not ready to adopt."[45]

The NCAI's struggle against termination was led by Garry, who served six consecutive terms as president of the NCAI—from 1953 to 1959—and who denounced termination in speeches and meetings throughout the country. He was assisted by Helen Peterson

The leaders of the National Congress of American Indians (NCAI) defended Native American sovereignty during the termination crisis of the 1950s. From left: Helen Peterson, D'Arcy McNickle, Joseph Garry, Louis Bruce, and Ruth Muskrat Bronson, ca. 1954. *Courtesy Smithsonian Photo Services.*

(Oglala Sioux), who, as executive director of the NCAI from 1953 to 1961, managed a small staff that analyzed congressional bills, advised tribal delegations on lobbying strategies, and distributed information through mass mailings.[46]

The NCAI gathered considerable support from Indian Country and enlisted many state governments that opposed termination because it shifted the cost of supporting often-impoverished Indian people from the federal government to the states. By 1958, American Indians and state alliances coalesced to curtail additional congressional efforts to terminate Indian reservations.

Many tribal communities continued to fight termination while others, such as the Colville Reservation, Washington State's largest Indian reservation, struggled internally to define an appropriate response. Washington senator Henry Scoop Jackson had supported termination of the Colville Reservation since the early 1950s and by the mid-1960s had garnered congressional and Colville tribal support. Jackson, however, had not reckoned on Lucy Covington, a Colville tribal member who launched a political campaign to inform tribal members about the negative effects of termination. By inviting leaders and witnesses from terminated tribes to visit the Colville Reservation, Covington was able to gain enough political support to elect an anti-termination tribal government, and to reject the termination bill in the Colville Reservation's tribal elections of 1968.[47]

The movement to reject termination promoted widespread discussion among Indian leaders, organizations, and youth groups. Regional meetings were organized, and a pivotal national meeting was held at the University of Chicago in June 1961. Sol Tax, a University of Chicago anthropologist who supported contemporary Indian reform efforts, helped organize a steering committee to determine the content of the upcoming national meeting, in addition to scheduling preliminary regional meetings, enlisting support from scholarly organizations, and securing funding from foundations. He and other conference organizers stressed that they were assisting in organizing the event, but that the voice of the gathering would be left to the Indians themselves.[48]

Tribal people from all walks of life attended the Chicago conference, which began on June 13, 1961. Seventy-nine tribes were represented and 439 Indians were registered, although perhaps as many as 700 attended the seven-day meeting. The participants included Vine Deloria, Jr. (Standing Rock Sioux), a writer, lawyer, and, later, executive director of the NCAI from 1964 to 1967; Ada Deer (Menominee), an activist and later the U.S. assistant secretary for Indian affairs; Jack D. Forbes (Powhatan-Delaware), a historian and activist; William L. Paul (Tlingit), a lawyer; Helen Peterson, executive director of the NCAI; and the anthropologist D'Arcy McNickle (Flathead).[49]

The conference participants considered current policies and issues in Indian Country and drafted a policy statement entitled the "Declaration of Indian Purpose," which rejected termination and requested government recognition of Indian cultures as well as greater Native participation in Indian policy making.[50] McNickle had worked for John Collier, the commissioner of Indian affairs under President Franklin Roosevelt, and brought many perspectives of the New Deal to the conference. A strong advocate for local self-government and cultural autonomy, McNickle opposed both termination and the full citizenship policies of the Truman and Eisenhower administrations. As chair of the American Indian Chicago Conference's steering committee, he played a pivotal role in developing and refining the Declaration of Indian Purpose. "McNickle never received the acknowledgment he deserved for putting the hours of discussion into the clear and eloquent prose of the final document," one conference organizer recalled. "Although the conference would not have been possible without Tax's initial vision and skill as strategist and fundraiser, it was McNickle's unobtrusive guidance that kept the conference on course as a truly Indian endeavor."[51]

In language redolent of the U.S. Constitution, the Declaration stated:

> We, the Indian People, must be governed by principles in a democratic manner with a right to choose our way of life. Since our Indian culture is threatened by presumption of being absorbed by the American society, we believe we have the responsibility of preserving our precious heritage. . . . We believe in the inherent right of all people to retain spiritual and cultural values, and that the free exercise of these values

is necessary to the normal development of any people. . . . We believe that the history and development of America shows that the Indian has been subjected to duress, undue influence, unwarranted pressures, and policies which have produced uncertainty, frustration, and despair. . . . What we ask of America is not charity, not paternalism, even when benevolent. We ask only that the nature of our situation be recognized and made the basis of policy and action.[52]

The Declaration demanded that Congress revoke the legislation that authorized termination and recommended new Indian policies to promote education, economic development, tribal law, and stronger support for tribal self-government. Although Indians wanted to participate as citizens of the United States, the Declaration asserted, American's Native people did not want to give up their culture, community, lands, or tribal governments.

PRESIDENT JOHN F. KENNEDY

The Declaration of Indian Purpose was finalized during the early days of President John F. Kennedy's administration, which began in 1961 and ended after little more than one thousand days.[53] Like Truman and Eisenhower, Kennedy approached Indian policy much as he did policies for social minorities: by advocating solutions that promoted civil rights and citizenship, and increased federal aid. His emphasis on equal rights responded, in part, to Cold War pressures for the United States to live up to its democratic ideals.

Soon after taking office, Kennedy appointed a task force to study and make recommendations on the status of Indian America. He also appointed Phileo Nash—an anthropologist, task-force member, friend of Sol Tax, and organizer of the American Indian Chicago Conference—as commissioner of Indian affairs.[54] A strong opponent of termination, Nash would assist the Menominees in their struggle against termination in the mid-1960s.

The Kennedy administration observed the American Indian Chicago Conference but made no immediate policy changes. Likewise, the President's Task Force on Indian Affairs recommended ending termination policy and emphasized greater government support for and attention to economic development for reservation communities, but in the short run, the President's Task Force made no substantive policy changes, although Kennedy did meet with Indian leaders.[55] On August 15, 1962, on the south lawn of the White House, he greeted an NCAI delegation who wished to discuss the Declaration of Indian Purpose, which had been drafted at the Chicago conference the year before.[56] Delegates representing some ninety Indian tribes were led by Robert Burnette, executive director of the NCAI (1961–64) and past president of the Rosebud Sioux tribe. Burnette introduced Denny Bushyhead (Cherokee), who read the Declaration aloud to make sure the president had received the Indians' message.

The president congratulated the delegation and the conference participants for affirming their strong love for the United States and acknowledged Indian Country's need for improved housing, education, health, security, old age support, and other services that would help Native people to live full and productive lives as American citizens. In a phrase that caught on with writers, the president suggested there was much "unfinished business" in Indian affairs and recommended

President John F. Kennedy greeting American Indian representatives at the White House in 1962. Representatives of ninety tribes visited the president to deliver a copy of the Declaration of Indian Purpose. The representatives pictured here are, from left, Eleanor Red Fawn Smooth (Mohawk/ Cherokee), Calvin McGhee (Creek), and an unidentified Native woman. *©Bettmann/ CORBIS.*

increased federal aid to Native people to alleviate economic and social disadvantages, improve civil rights, and provide opportunities for Indians to benefit from American citizenship.[57]

President Kennedy would not have the opportunity to complete the "unfinished business." On November 22, 1963, he was assassinated as his motorcade passed through Dealey Plaza in Dallas, Texas. His successor, Lyndon B. Johnson, would fulfill many of Kennedy's policy goals and would articulate a new and definitively modern policy that governed relations between Native nations and the U.S. government.

INDIANS AND PRESIDENT JOHNSON'S "GREAT SOCIETY"

Lyndon B. Johnson became president in 1963 and worked tirelessly during the next five years to transform the United States into a "Great Society," in which "the meaning of man's life matches the marvels of man's labor."[58] Johnson pushed for an ambitious legislative agenda that included a new civil rights bill, antipoverty and urban renewal programs, and a range of other federal initiatives aimed at improving education, health care, conservation, and other concerns. Early in his administration, President Johnson adopted the perspectives of his immediate predecessors, who considered Indians disadvantaged citizens. At a meeting at the White House with two hundred delegates from the NCAI, Johnson declared that it was "a fact that America's first citizens, our Indian people, suffer more from poverty than any other group in America."[59] Pledging to provide greater opportunity for Indian Country, Johnson declared that he would put Native Americans at the forefront of his administration's war on poverty.

Leaders of the National Congress of American Indians were active in reforming Indian affairs during the Johnson administration. Robert Burnette worked well with Congress and with Secretary of the Interior Stewart Udall, and gained support for improvements in Indian education.[60] A strong voice against corruption and abuse of power among tribal leaders and governments, Burnette worked to strengthen the movement for tribal self-determination and lobbied for an American Indian Civil Rights Act, which passed in 1968.

In the 1960s, a younger generation of NCAI activists emerged, hoping to provide more forceful leadership to American Indian politics. Vine Deloria, Jr., was elected executive director of the NCAI on a reformist ticket in 1964, defeating Joseph Garry and Helen Peterson, both of whom had been active in NCAI leadership since the early 1950s. For Deloria, Indian policy was controlled largely by churches, the Indian Rights Association, and the Association on American Indian Affairs (AAIA), which did little to significantly change Indian policy. To break from the past, Deloria received advice from Robert K. Thomas and Clyde Warrior (Ponca), a political activist, as well as support from the National Indian Youth Council (NIYC), represented by Mel Thom (Paiute) and Wendell Chino, chair of the Mescalero Apache tribe. "My objective was to expand the horizons of the NCAI membership so that tribes would think of other things than the constant fight against the Bureau of Indian Affairs," Deloria declared. "The poverty programs were in full swing, and the message I wanted people to hear was that the BIA could be played off against other agencies."[61]

In 1966, President Johnson appointed Robert Bennett (Oneida), a longtime officer of the Indian service, as commissioner of Indian affairs. The only Native American to be appointed commissioner of Indian affairs since Ely Parker served under President Grant, Bennett was given the green light to reorganize the BIA. "Do anything you have to," Johnson told Bennett. "If there are cobwebs in the Bureau, then clean them out."[62] After Bennett's appointment, few non-Indians would be appointed to administer the BIA.[63]

During the mid-1960s, tribal communities pushed for and took advantage of many antipoverty programs created under the Johnson administration. During the summer of 1964, some eight hundred Indian activists and non-Native supporters attended the Indian Capitol Conference on Poverty to lobby Congress to add Indians to the Economic Opportunity Act. Tribal leaders sought inclusion in order to gain access to antipoverty funds as well as greater tribal government autonomy and recognition from federal agencies. The conference "really started the modern movement that stressed sovereignty and self-determination with many tribes in this country," recalled Helen Scheirbeck (Lumbee), an Indian activist and educator. As a result of the meeting, Scheirbeck recalled, "an Indian desk was created in the Office of Economic Opportunity (OEO) and, for the first time, moneys were earmarked for . . . federally recognized Indians."[64]

The BIA had long managed funding for tribes, but this began to change during the Johnson years, when tribal governments became eligible for programs administered by a host of other government agencies. The change enabled tribal governments to assert more control and administrative oversight and to hire tribal members to deliver services to the reservation community in more culturally appropriate ways. The BIA also began to accommodate tribal governments that wanted greater scope to make decisions about local programming as well as the allocation of funds. Some tribes, like the Zuni Pueblos, began to contract for services with the federal government, enabling them—rather than the BIA—to assert control over social programs. In short, President Johnson's Great Society program turned tribal governments into social-service providers and helped establish the modern tribal governments we know today.[65]

On March 6, 1968, President Johnson delivered a pivotal address that would lay the groundwork for change in American Indian

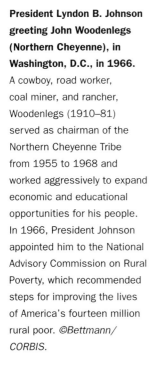

President Lyndon B. Johnson greeting John Woodenlegs (Northern Cheyenne), in Washington, D.C., in 1966. A cowboy, road worker, coal miner, and rancher, Woodenlegs (1910–81) served as chairman of the Northern Cheyenne Tribe from 1955 to 1968 and worked aggressively to expand economic and educational opportunities for his people. In 1966, President Johnson appointed him to the National Advisory Commission on Rural Poverty, which recommended steps for improving the lives of America's fourteen million rural poor. *©Bettmann/ CORBIS.*

policy. In his "Special Message to the Congress on the Problems of the American Indian: 'The Forgotten American,'" Johnson proposed "a new goal" for United States government Indian programs—one that "ends the old debate about 'termination' of Indian programs and stresses self-determination; a goal that erases old attitudes of paternalism and promotes partnership and self-help."

The goals of Johnson's new Indian policy were, first, for Indians to enjoy living standards equal to those of other Americans. The president also declared that he wanted Indians to have the choice of whether to live in their reservation homelands or to migrate to towns and cities where they could live in dignity and equality. Declaring that Indians should be offered full participation in American economic and social life, Johnson advocated "programs of self-help, self-development, [and] self-determination."[66]

Johnson outlined his plans to coordinate federal programs and services to better serve Indian communities, promote greater participation of Indian leaders in community development, and solicit greater involvement of tribal governments and organizations in the administration of federal programs. "Indians must have a voice in the making of the plans and decisions in programs that are important to their daily life," the president declared. Emphasizing the concept of self-help in community development, Johnson lauded tribes that had "begun to administer activities which Federal agencies had long performed in their behalf." He singled out the Crow Creek, Lower Brulé, and Fort Berthold reservations in the Dakotas for "imaginative new work-experience programs, operated by Indians themselves," which provided jobs "for Indians once totally dependent on welfare." He also recognized the Warm Springs Tribes of Oregon for a program that repaired flood damage to their reservation, the Oglala Sioux and the Zunis for contracting to provide law enforcement for their communities, and the Navajos for furnishing community services that had once been provided by the federal government. "Passive acceptance of federal service is giving way to Indian involvement," Johnson observed. "More than ever before, Indian needs are being identified from the Indian point of view—as they should be."[67]

Making the federal government a responsible partner with Indian communities was the essence of President Johnson's Indian policy.

In this relationship, Indians would be treated as full citizens who were completely capable of setting the pace and direction of change and development within their communities. They would be allowed to assert their rights as American Indians while enjoying the benefits of United States citizenship. The federal government, for its part, would respect the uniqueness of Indian citizens and preserve the special relationship between Native nations and the United States. "We must affirm the right of the first Americans to remain Indians while exercising their rights as Americans," Johnson said. "We must affirm their right to freedom of choice and self-determination."[68]

President Johnson laid out a thoughtful and informed Indian policy that showed that he had listened to Native voices during his administration. He charted a new course toward greater choice for Native individuals and communities, and toward greater respect for Native culture and tribal government. In so doing, Johnson went a long way toward settling the policy debate that advocated assimilation and citizenship for Indians on the one hand, and local self-government for Indians on the other.

PRESIDENT RICHARD M. NIXON AND TRIBAL SELF-DETERMINATION

Like Presidents Truman, Eisenhower, Kennedy, and Johnson, Richard M. Nixon confronted international and Cold War pressures to provide opportunities to American minority groups. Nixon's Indian policies, however, went far beyond previous programs of citizenship, civil rights, and economic opportunity to embrace self-determination for American Indian nations. His Indian policy, unveiled in 1970, transformed the federal government's relationship with tribal governments and continues to have considerable influence in Indian Country today.

Best known for his role in the Watergate scandal that ended his presidency, Richard M. Nixon is also remembered as a sympathetic president who took an active role in the administration of Indian affairs. His interest in Indians is a subject of considerable speculation. One view suggests that he wanted to demonstrate his administration's concern for minority groups, and that Indians, as one of the most vulnerable groups, were a good target for policy change.[69] Others suggest that Nixon's motivation flowed from personal associations with Indians and his religious faith. As a student and football player at Whittier College, Nixon developed a strong relationship with his football coach, Wallace "Chief" Newman, a member of the La Jolla Band of Mission Indians.[70] "I think I admired him more and learned more from him than from any man I have ever known aside from my father," Nixon recalled in his memoirs.

Newman was an American Indian, and tremendously proud of his heritage. . . . He inspired in us the idea that if we worked hard enough and played hard enough, we could beat anybody. . . . There is no way I can adequately describe Chief Newman's influence on me. He drilled into me a competitive spirit and the determination to come back after you have been knocked down or after you lose. He also gave me an acute understanding that what really matters is not a man's background, his color, his race, or his religion, but only his character."[71]

President-elect Richard M. Nixon with his Whittier College football coach Wallace "Chief" Newman, 1969. *Courtesy Whittier College.*

Wallace Newman was born on the La Jolla Reservation to a mother who was of Basque and Luiseño Indian heritage. At age eleven, he attended the Sherman Indian School near Riverside, California, and finished at Riverside Polytechnic, where he excelled in sports, including football. Newman's athletic ability won him a scholarship to the University of Southern California (USC), where he became captain of the football team. One day USC's football coach, Elmer Henderson, introduced the Native player to a teammate as "chief," and the nickname stuck. In 1929, Newman was hired as an athletic coach at Whittier College, a position he held until his retirement in 1951.[72]

Newman was well versed in Luiseño and other Native tribal history and traditions. His great aunt "Yela" Maria Antonio Nelson taught him the Luiseño language and family and tribal customs and traditions. Known for his temper, Newman often became upset when critics made disparaging remarks about Indians. "Foreigners said and wrote that Indians were lazy," Newman said, "but it was the Indians who did all the hard work building Father Serra's missions."[73]

Nixon played on the Whittier football team in 1932, 1933, and 1934. He seldom played in games, but always participated in team scrimmages and practices. "He took real beatings when we scrimmaged and always came back for more," Newman recalled. "He was smart enough, but he didn't have the size, the skills, or the speed. He did have the integrity."[74]

Newman later worked in all of Nixon's political campaigns, from 1946—when Nixon was a candidate for the United States House of Representatives—to Nixon's 1968 election to the presidency. For Nixon, Newman was "a close friend and an inspirational leader of men who [had] given him strength at times when needed."[75]

President Nixon's personal attention to and concern for Indians may also have derived from his religious faith. Reared in a small Quaker community in Yorba Linda, California, Nixon received the faith from his mother, a devout Quaker, and his father, who had converted to Quakerism. At Whittier College, Nixon attended Quaker religious meetings at which he may have learned about William Penn's efforts to uphold treaties and maintain honorable relations with American Indians in Pennsylvania during the colonial era. Later, as a congressman, Nixon would have known that Quaker organizations, including the

American Friends Service Committee, the Friends Committee on National Legislation, and the Associated Executive of Friends Committee on Indian Affairs, opposed Indian termination legislation in 1953 and organized events in Native communities to discuss the policy's negative effects. Ultimately, Nixon asked for and supported legislation that officially ended termination policy in the 1970s.[76]

Nixon's favorable perspective on American Indians was tested soon after his election to the presidency. In 1969, a group of Native American students occupied Alcatraz Island, reclaiming it as Indian land. According to author Jerry Reynolds, the eighteen-month-long occupation gained international attention and "put Indian claims to cultural identity and land rights before the Nixon administration in a way that would not be ignored."[77] The event set the stage for Nixon's successful proposal to repeal termination and acted as a catalyst for congressional action on Nixon's Indian reform proposals.[78]

On July 8, 1970, President Nixon presented his landmark Indian policy statement in a special message to Congress. Nixon characterized first Americans as the most marginalized and deprived minority in the nation, peoples who had suffered centuries of injustice through loss of lands and control over their communities and lives. While American history was littered with acts and policies of aggression toward Native communities and interests, American Indians had endured and survived. "Both as a matter of justice and as a matter of enlightened social policy," Nixon intoned, "we must . . . break decisively with the past . . . and create conditions for a new era in which the Indian future is determined by Indian acts and Indian decisions."[79]

Nixon said he rejected the policy of termination because it was based on a false premise, that the federal trustee relationship with American Indians was an act of generosity by the federal government toward a disadvantaged minority and could be withdrawn at any time. Instead, Nixon argued, the special relationship between Indians and the federal government was the result of written treaties and agreements—"solemn obligations" which the United States was committed to uphold. "To terminate this relationship would be no more appropriate than to terminate the citizenship rights of any other American," Nixon declared.

Native American protestors in a multilevel cellblock on Alcatraz Island, 1969.
In 1969, Native American activists took over Alcatraz, an island in San Francisco Bay that had been the site of a federal prison from 1934 to 1963. The activists held "the Rock" for eighteen months, reclaiming the land for all American Indians and inspiring Native protest throughout the United States. *Photo by Art Kane. National Museum of the American Indian, P28162.*

Nixon also castigated termination because Indian tribes and tribal members typically became more impoverished after termination, often because the policy inhibited institution building and economic investment on Indian reservations. "The threat of termination stifled long term progress and planning on Indian reservations," Nixon proclaimed. "In the end, termination tended to foster continuing dependency on Federal programs."[80] Rejecting termination on one side and federal paternalism on the other, Nixon hoped to establish a middle ground in which tribal communities could "become more self-reliant and self-sufficient, without the threat of [losing] community, identity, tribal land, and self-government." The United States "must make it clear that Indians can become independent of Federal control without being cut off from Federal concern and Federal support."[81]

NIXON AND "RED POWER," 1969–75

Richard M. Nixon's years in the White House were marked by a dramatic increase in Native American militancy. In 1969, "red power" activists took over Alcatraz Island, reclaiming the land for its original inhabitants. Following the Alcatraz occupation, the American Indian Movement (AIM) became the center of American Indian activism. In November 1972, this group, led by Russell Means (Lakota), Hank Adams (Oneida), and Sid Mills (Yakima), organized the Trail of Broken Treaties, a car caravan that traveled from San Francisco, California, to Washington, D.C. The caravan leaders intended to meet with President Nixon and present him with a list of Indian grievances, but they soon learned that President Nixon was out of the country, and that arrangements for food and sleeping accommodations had not been procured. Frustrated, they sought a visible target to highlight their dissatisfaction, and on November 2, 1972, they occupied the Bureau of Indian Affairs headquarters building in Washington, D.C. During the seventy-two-hour-long occupation, they sought evidence of broken treaties and misuse of Indian trust money, removed vast numbers of records concerning the BIA and Indian Health Service, and caused extensive damage to the building.

Also in 1972, the BIA backed the questionable election of Richard Wilson as tribal chairman of the Oglala Sioux Nation. Wilson saw his election as a validation of his pro-reform Indian government, and the Oglala Nation split along the lines of progressives and traditionalists who preferred the old form of Indian tribal leadership. The situation was further exacerbated by the killings of two Lakota men, Wesley Bad Heart Bull and Raymond Yellow Thunder. Tribal members felt that the sentences meted out to the killers were inappropriately light, and they turned to AIM for justice. On February 27, 1973, AIM leaders and about two hundred activists from the Sioux Nation declared themselves independent from the United States and occupied the village of Wounded Knee, South Dakota.

The Nixon White House, the Department of Defense, and the Department of Justice coordinated efforts throughout the Wounded Knee occupation. Whereas the occupation of Alcatraz Island had been nonviolent, the Wounded Knee occupants were armed and considered dangerous. The government responded in kind: weapons, personnel, and equipment—including armored personnel carriers, helicopters, and grenade launchers—were supplied by the Department of Defense. During the seventy-day occupation, U.S. Marshal Lloyd Grimm sustained a wound that paralyzed him from the waist down, and two Indian men, Frank Clearwater (Cherokee) and Lawrence Lamont (Lakota), were killed. Following the two deaths, both sides agreed to a tenuous cease-fire. Between April 28 and May 5, negotiations took place between members of the Nixon administration, Oglala elders, and members of AIM. On May 5, Leonard Garment, senior White House consultant to President Nixon, sent a letter stating that White House representatives would meet with the Lakota leadership to discuss past treaty violations. In response, the Wounded Knee occupiers would be required to surrender their weapons and leave Wounded Knee. By May 8, 1973, the occupation had ended, doomed by hunger, low morale, and the inability to bring Indian reinforcements onto the compound.

Following the Wounded Knee occupation, Congress passed the Indian Self-Determination and Education Assistance Act, which expanded tribal control over tribal governments and education. The act encouraged the development of human resources and reservation programs and was hailed by many as the most important piece of Indian legislation passed in the twentieth century.[82] ⫘

Russell Means (Lakota), holding poster of President Richard Nixon during the occupation of the Bureau of Indian Affairs headquarters, in Washington, D.C., 1972. ©*Bettmann/CORBIS.*

To implement his policy, Nixon asked Congress to pass a resolution that rejected termination and affirmed that the United States government would not abridge any historic treaty or other agreement with Indian nations without the consent of Native people. Nixon suggested that Indians had the right to manage federal programs that served their communities and that many federal programs should be turned over to tribal administration. He also proposed settling a long-standing issue by returning sacred land around Blue Lake to Taos Pueblo and providing additional funding for Indian education, economic development, health programs, and aid to urban Indians. Finally, the president suggested the establishment of an Indian trust counsel authority to resolve issues between federal and tribal interests, and favored elevating the commissioner of Indian affairs to the

"THE HEART OF OUR RELIGION":
PRESIDENT RICHARD NIXON RETURNS TAOS BLUE LAKE, 1970

For centuries, Taos Indians conducted an annual pilgrimage to Blue Lake, a sacred site in northern New Mexico where the Creator made their people. There, in late summer, the pilgrims prayed, made offerings, sang, danced, and renewed their ties to a sacred Native landscape, performing an annual ritual which, they believed, would ensure the well-being of their people.

In 1906, President Theodore Roosevelt transferred ownership of the sacred lake, as well as forty-eight thousand acres in New Mexico, to the newly created Carson National Forest. Soon sports fishermen, lumberjacks, and miners entered the Taos Reserve, hiking and logging trails were carved into the land, and the lake's turquoise waters were sullied by trash and bottles. The leaders of Taos Pueblo as well as sympathetic non-Indians launched a battle to regain the sacred lake and the land that surrounded it. "The lake is our church," one tribal elder declared. "The evergreen trees are our living saints. We pray to the water, the sun, the clouds, the sky, the deer. Without them we cannot exist. Blue Lake is the heart of our religion."

The Pueblos repeated their demand for the return of Blue Lake at meetings, congressional hearings, and in court documents—all to no avail until 1970, when President Richard Nixon seized upon the issue as a symbol of his administration's policy of supporting Indian rights. In a meeting with Leonard Garment, his Indian affairs advisor, the president had expressed interest in returning the lake. "A new Indian policy needs a starting point," Nixon told Garment. "Blue Lake is just that—strong on merits, and powerfully symbolic." Finally, on December 15, 1970, President Nixon signed an order that returned Blue Lake, as well as forty-eight thousand acres that surrounded it, to the Taos Pueblo.[83] ≈

Fed by the sacred Blue Lake, the Rio Pueblo flows past Taos Pueblo, New Mexico, which has been continuously inhabited for more than one thousand years. On December 15, 1970, President Richard M. Nixon signed an order that returned Blue Lake to the Taos Pueblo. *Photo by Bobak Ha'Eri, 2005.*

rank of assistant secretary of the interior to signify the increased importance of Indian affairs in American government.[84]

Above all, Nixon emphasized the importance of involving Native people in the decisions that affected their communities. "It is essential that the Indian people continue to lead the way by participating in policy development to the greatest degree possible," Nixon said. "In place of policies which oscillate between the deadly extremes of forced termination and constant paternalism, we suggest a policy in which the Federal government and the Indian community play complementary roles."[85]

Presidents Johnson and Nixon developed some of the most comprehensive and innovative Indian policy statements in the history of the United States. By rejecting termination and federal paternalism in favor of greater decision making and local control by tribal governments, they transformed the ways presidents had thought about Indian policy: as a choice between full citizenship and tribal governance. From Richard Nixon's administration through today, American presidents have tended to view full citizenship and tribal self-determination as the foundation of U.S. Indian policy. Richard Nixon's role in this transformation was pivotal.

The move toward self-determination did not spring full-blown from the Oval Office or even from President Nixon's special assistants. It resulted, instead, from consultation with Indian leaders whose perspectives helped to shape the administration's vision of Indian affairs. The national mobilization and participation of Indian leaders and community members during the 1950s and 1960s generated intense policy discussions in Indian Country, producing a vision of a future with greater possibilities for upholding tribal culture and community and for building stronger tribal governments. By 1970, President Nixon's Indian policy proposals incorporated many Indian views about self-government, treaty obligations, and greater local control and management of programs—ideas that would more fully mature in the White House under the administration of President Nixon's successor, Gerald R. Ford.

Bobby Onco (Kiowa), a member of the American Indian Movement (AIM), hefting an AK-47 during a cease-fire between Indian militants and federal marshals at Wounded Knee, South Dakota, in 1973. ©Bettmann/CORBIS.

CHAPTER V

THE ERA OF SELF-DETERMINATION: 1975–TODAY

TROY JOHNSON

American presidents in the post-Nixon era came into office during a period of hope and restrained excitement for Indians. The Indian activism of the 1960s had promoted greater self-awareness among Native people and attracted support from many non-Natives, including students influenced by the black power, LaRaza, and nascent feminist movements that held sway on college campuses across the United States. Phrases such as self-determination and tribal sovereignty had become part of the conversation at Native community gatherings, tribal council meetings, and meetings between Indian leaders and state and federal officials. At the White House, Presidents Gerald Ford, Ronald Reagan, George H. W. Bush, Bill Clinton, and George W. Bush officially recognized Native nations as sovereign entities, resuscitating a once-vibrant presidential perspective that had eroded during the nineteenth and early twentieth centuries. The road to recognition as self-governing nations was not smooth, and not supported by all. But the modern-day presidents' acknowledgment of tribal self-determination has resulted in positive gains for Native nations and Native people throughout the United States.

PRESIDENT GERALD R. FORD AND AMERICAN INDIAN ACTIVISM

The first of these modern-day presidents came to the White House in an unusual manner. At 8 P.M. on August 15, 1974, Richard M. Nixon sat down to dinner in his home in San Clemente, California. Among those in attendance were his wife, Patricia; his daughters, Tricia and Julie; close friend Charles "Bebe" Rebozo; and his life-long friend and mentor, Wallace Newman, former chairman of the La Jolla Band of Mission Indians. Wallace had been Nixon's college football coach and instilled in Nixon the tenacity that had driven him throughout his life, especially the belief that preparation and hard work led to great personal victories. These principles had served Nixon well.

The occasion of this dinner, however, was not one of celebration. Thirteen hours earlier, Nixon had resigned as president of the United States. The mantle of authority and the weight of the leadership of the western world had passed to Gerald R. Ford.

Ford had never aspired to become president. Born on July 14, 1913, in Omaha, Nebraska, and raised during the Depression era, his highest aspiration was to serve in the United States Senate. Although he never accomplished that goal, Ford spent twenty-five years in the U.S. House of Representatives, beginning in 1948, when he was elected for the first of thirteen terms. In 1974, his stated goal was to be elected for a fourteenth term and then retire with his wife Betty to western Michigan.[1]

Ford's future was changed forever on October 11, 1973, when Vice President Spiro T. Agnew resigned amid rumors that he had accepted bribes and falsified federal tax returns. On October 12,

President Gerald R. Ford conferring with White House chief of staff Donald Rumsfeld (at left) and deputy chief of staff Dick Cheney in the Oval Office, in 1975. When it came to Indian policy, President Ford relied on White House counsel Leonard Garment and Bradley H. Patterson, Jr., special assistant for Native American programs. *Courtesy Gerald R. Ford Library.*

1973, President Nixon nominated Ford to fill the vacancy. Congress approved the nominee on November 17, 1973, and one hour later Gerald Ford took the oath of office as vice president of the United States. Less than one year later, he took the oath of office as the thirty-eighth president of the United States.

Gerald Ford inherited administration officials chosen by his predecessor. Familiar with many of President Nixon's cabinet, advisors, and aides, Ford did not ask any of the Nixon appointees to resign. Nor did he reassign anyone. Instead, he emphasized his reliance on existing cabinet officers and presidential advisors. This was especially true for members of the White House staff for Native American affairs.[2]

In the Ford administration, as in the Nixon administration, Indian affairs were handled by a small cadre of individuals, including Leonard Garment, White House counsel, and Bradley H. Patterson, Jr., special assistant for Native American programs.[3] During interviews conducted in 1993, Garment and Patterson recalled that neither President Nixon nor President Ford issued specific instructions, directions, or decisions when it came to Indian affairs, and that they were both so "in tune" with the presidents' feelings that they needed little or no direct guidance. When issues arose, Patterson made the decisions, clearing them with Garment.

"THIS WAS SUPPOSED TO BE A DESK JOB?"
AN INSIDER'S VIEW OF INDIAN AFFAIRS AT THE WHITE HOUSE

During the twentieth century, American presidents increasingly relied on White House staff to formulate Indian policy. As executive assistant to White House Counsel Leonard Garment from 1969 to 1974, Bradley H. Patterson, Jr., was intimately involved in the development of President Nixon's policy of Indian self-determination, and also served as White House coordinator for Native American policy and programs under President Ford. In these positions, Patterson opened the doors of the White House "to people from outside the government," including historian Alvin Josephy, Jr.; the writer and scholar Vine Deloria, Jr., (Standing Rock Sioux); Ada Deer (Menominee); Charles Lohah (Osage); LaDonna Harris (Comanche); Ernest Stevens, Sr. (Oneida of Wisconsin); Sandy McNabb (Micmac); Rose Crow-Flies-High, chairperson of the tribal business council of the Three Affiliated Tribes of the Fort Berthold Reser-vation; Laura Bergt and Don Wright of the Alaska Federation of Natives; Bob Jim, tribal chairman of the Yakima Nation; and Wendell Chino, tribal chairman of the Mescalero Apache. Patterson also met and listened to people he described as "dissidents—the angry and the discontented," Native people who "were not the regular government or Indian bureaucrats one might expect to be coming in and out of our precincts." Some of these leaders, Patterson recalled, "were raucous and rough, often discourteous, even pugnacious. . . ." As coordinator of a White House staff team that was sent to negotiate an end to the occupation of Wounded Knee, in 1973, Patterson recalled that a group of Lakotas "separated me from my colleagues, surrounded me, brusquely pressed against me, [and] demanded that I give them back the Black Hills NOW—on the spot. I thought to myself: 'This was supposed to be a desk job?'"[4]

Written responses or plans of action were formulated and presented to both presidents for signature, announcement, or promulgation. Additional input from other White House staff was rarely required.[5] Such was the case on October 29, 1974, when the first issue concerning Native Americans came before President Ford: appropriations legislation for the Indian Claims Commission.[6]

Created in 1946, the Indian Claims Commission provided the United States with an opportunity to redress an old wrong committed against Native Americans: the loss of tribal homelands. The problem was rooted deeply in American history and involved many Native nations, including the Lakota (Sioux) Indians. Under the Fort Laramie Treaty of 1868, the United States had pledged that the Great Sioux Reservation, including the Black Hills of South Dakota, would be

Harney Peak Lookout, Black Hills National Forest, South Dakota, 2003. The highest point in South Dakota, the 7,242-foot Harney Peak towers over the Black Hills. Whites named the peak for Major General William S. Harney (1800–89), who served as a United States peace commissioner during discussions that led to the Fort Laramie Treaty of 1868. Red Cloud and other Sioux leaders left the treaty conference assured that their people had secured the Black Hills for all time, but the United States soon negotiated a new agreement with a small group of Sioux chiefs, and claimed possession of the Black Hills. Since 1874, Lakota people have consistently maintained the United States stole the Back Hills, and continue to assert their rights to the land. *Photo © Karen Wattenmaker.*

set apart for the absolute and undisturbed use and occupation of the Sioux Nation. Under the agreement, no treaty for the cession of any part of the reservation would be valid unless executed and signed by at least three-fourths of the adult male Sioux population. The treaty also reserved the Sioux's right to hunt in certain unceded territories. Subsequently, the United States developed a new agreement, signed by only ten percent of the adult male population, which provided that the Sioux relinquish their land rights to the Black Hills and their hunting rights in the unceded territories. In exchange, the Indians would receive subsistence rations for as long as they would be needed.[7] Congress passed a law implementing the new agreement in 1877—an act which, in effect, abrogated the Fort Laramie Treaty.

Although the Sioux long regarded the 1877 act as a breach of the Fort Laramie Treaty, they and other American Indians had no legal mechanism through which to litigate claims against the United States until 1920, when Congress passed the Sioux Jurisdictional Act. That year, the Sioux brought suit in the United States Court of Claims, alleging that the government had taken the Black Hills without just compensation—a violation of the Fifth Amendment, which protects property against illegal government seizure. In 1942, the Court of Claims dismissed the claim, stating that the court was not authorized to hear the question of compensation. Finally, in 1946, Congress created the Indian Claims Commission to hear Native American grievances, including claims involving Indian-owned or occupied lands taken by the United States. The Sioux Nation immediately filed a claim before the commission.[8]

In 1974, the Indian Claims Commission ruled that the United States took the Black Hills illegally. The 1877 value of the land—and the gold found on it—was established at $17.5 million, which, with accumulated interest, boosted the value to approximately $103 million. But there was a hitch. Included in the Claims Commission Act was a provision requiring the government to supply food and other provisions to offset the Indians' claims. The provisions supplied were estimated at $54 million, which appeared to wipe out the original $17.5 million claim.[9]

When he signed the Indian Claims Commission appropriations legislation on October 29, 1974, President Ford placed into record a statement, prepared by White House Counsel Leonard Garment, that said it would be unfair and unjust to avoid paying the original value of the Lakota land by deducting the cost of previously supplied provisions. President Ford stated that he was pleased to take advantage of the opportunity to right a past wrong, and asserted that "while this nation cannot undo the injustices of American history, we can insure that the actions taken today are just and fair."[10]

Coming to the Oval Office in the middle of a presidential term, President Ford quickly received an education in American Indian activism, which shaped his philosophy on handling American Indian issues. Both Leonard Garment and Bradley Patterson schooled Ford in the forces that had given birth to the red power movement, as well as the activist philosophies and tactics that fueled the occupation of Alcatraz Island, the takeover of the BIA building in Washington, D.C., and the violent confrontation at Wounded Knee Village in South Dakota. Patterson convinced the president that restraint rather than force, coupled with negotiation without specific promises and deadlines, would lead to peaceful settlement of most if not all of the Indian complaints or demands.[11]

This policy of restraint would be tested in a confrontation at Bonner's Ferry, Idaho, where the Kootenai were challenging an 1885 action that resulted in the loss of 1.6 million acres of northern Idaho tribal lands. At the time, the Canadian Pacific Railway ran through Indian land in various places. One of those was Kootenai homeland. The Canadian government paid compensation to white property owners whose land had been taken but refused to acknowledge ownership by the Kootenai, who ardently continued to claim the territory.[12] In 1974, Congress considered giving the tribe a parcel of land for a reservation. Insulted, the Kootenai responded on September 20, 1974, by declaring war on the United States. Assisted by activists such as Leonard Peltier, the Indians placed roadblocks around Bonner's Ferry. The governor of Idaho quickly deployed seventy state troopers armed with mace and shotguns. The Kootenai called for outside Indian activists to come to their aid. Fearing an outbreak of violence, Patterson advised President Ford to exercise patience, coupled with legislation, to defuse the situation, and urged him to respond positively to the Indians' demands. Ultimately, President

Ford signed a bill that transferred twelve and a half acres of federal land into trust status for the Kootenai, built a road to the new reservation, funded a $100,000 community center, and authorized spending of $7,000 per tribal member over a twelve-month period. With this strategy, President Ford, assisted by Bradley Patterson, ensured that Bonner's Ferry did not escalate into violence.[13]

The Ford-Patterson model would be tested again in May 1974, when Mohawk activists occupied an abandoned camp near Eagle Bay in Adirondack State Park, New York, demanding the return of land that they claimed had been illegally taken by New York State. The seventy-five Mohawk occupiers demanded the return of the land, on which they planned to rebuild a traditional community. President Ford, on Patterson's advice, decided not to enter into the discussions and turned the task of settling the dispute over to New York secretary of state Mario Cuomo. Through patience and negotiation, Cuomo and the Mohawk chiefs arrived at an agreement that led to the establishment of a second permanent community for the Mohawk Nation.[14]

The incidents at Bonner's Ferry and Eagle Bay reminded President Ford and Bradley Patterson that they needed to remain sensitive to Native American issues. In 1975, the Ford-Patterson team once again exhibited professional sincerity in their dealings with Native peoples, this time with the Havasupai Indians of Northern Arizona.

Prior to leaving office, President Nixon had indicated that he was interested in expanding the land holdings of the Havasupai Indian Reservation. President Ford took up the cause, and in 1975 signed a bill that enlarged Grand Canyon National Park and added 185,000 acres to the Havasupai Indian Reservation. Both the Department of Agriculture and the Office of Management and Budget had opposed the bill as setting an undesirable precedent of giving public lands to specific groups for their exclusive use. William Byler, executive director of the Association of American Indian Affairs, regarded the bill as a stunning victory achieved against all odds.

President Ford's crowning achievement in Native American affairs was the signing of the Indian Self-Determination Act of 1975. By signing the act, the president aligned his administration with the policy of President Nixon and moved the United States forward

Beaver Falls, near the Havasupai Indian Reservation, Grand Canyon, Arizona. In 1975, Congress returned 185,000 acres of land taken in 1882, when the government relocated the Havasupais to a 518-acre reservation at the bottom of the canyon. Today, 450 of the Havasupais' 650 enrolled members live on the reservation, the only community in the United States that has mule-train postal delivery service. *Courtesy Havasupai Tribe.*

toward a progressive approach to Indian self-determination and government-to-government relations with Native nations. "The enactment of this legislation marks a milestone for Indian people," Ford declared. "It will enable this Administration to work more closely and effectively with the tribes for the betterment of all the Indian people by assisting them in meeting goals they themselves have set."[15]

PRESIDENT JIMMY CARTER AND AMERICAN INDIANS, 1976–80

President Ford failed in his bid for election to the presidency in 1976, and the direction of America's Indian policy moved to a new administration. President James Earl "Jimmy" Carter, Jr., took the oath of office as America's thirty-ninth president on January 20,

1977. Leonard Garment, Bradley Patterson, and other key advisors who had served President Ford had left the White House, taking with them years of experience and insight in American Indian policy. Prior to leaving his post, however, Bradley Patterson met with David Berg, a member of President Carter's staff, to discuss American Indian issues. Based on this discussion, the staff drew up a position paper that endorsed the Indian self-determination policy initiated by President Nixon and signed into law by President Ford.[16]

Unlike Nixon and Ford, Carter chose to leave unfilled the position of special assistant on Indian Affairs, previously held by Bradley Patterson. Carter explained that the appointment of special counsels and commissions in Indian affairs would lead to pressure to create similar positions for other special-interest groups. For Carter, primary responsibility for Indian affairs would reside with Secretary of the Interior Cecil Andrus and his appointees. To convey policies, Andrus relied on Stuart E. Eizenstat, the assistant to the president for domestic affairs.[17] Within Eizenstat's offices, questions arising at the White House concerning Indian affairs were fielded by Kathy Fletcher and Marilyn Haft.[18] This decentralization of power reflected President Carter's belief that responsibility for Indian affairs rested outside of the Oval Office.[19]

South Dakota senator James Abourezk became an important voice in Indian affairs during the Carter administration. Of all of the president's Indian affairs advisors, Senator Abourezk was the only one with experience in Native American affairs.[20] Abourezk had been an advisor to President Richard Nixon during the tumultuous years of the red power era and had served as the chair of the Indian Affairs Subcommittee that investigated the Wounded Knee occupation and the resulting trials. During Carter's administration, Senator Abourezk capitalized on the public awareness generated by Wounded Knee and used it as a catalyst to move Indian legislation through Congress.[21]

Senator Abourezk also recommended that Carter appoint an Indian to be assistant secretary of Indian affairs. Carter nominated Forest Gerard, a member of the Blackfeet Tribe of Montana. Gerard's appointment was in keeping with Carter's campaign commitment to place responsibility for Indian affairs in the hands of American Indians or those who were thoroughly conversant with Native American problems and committed to their solution.

During his first year in office, President Carter made no mention of American Indians in public or private addresses, causing concern among Indian leaders. In his State of the Union message on January 19, 1978, Carter noted briefly that "the Administration has acted consistently to uphold its trusteeship responsibility to Native Americans."[22] The inclusion of the brief reference to Native Americans in the State of the Union address was the work of Chris Matthews, President Carter's speechwriter.[23] More importantly, Carter elevated the commissioner of Indian affairs to the level of assistant secretary of the interior.[24] Nevertheless, many Native Americans viewed President Carter's first year in office as a disappointment. That assessment was summed up by Ernest L. Stevens, director of the American Policy Review Commission, who concluded that the Carter administration's watchwords were "Indians, No Participation."[25]

Indian criticism of Federal government inaction, particularly in the wake of the turbulent red power movement, targeted Carter for his early inattention to Native issues. Vine Deloria, Jr. (Standing Rock Sioux), a noted American Indian scholar at the University of Colorado, Boulder, chided the Carter administration for failing to announce an Indian policy.[26] LaDonna Harris (Comanche), an outspoken advocate on Native American issues, also wrote President Carter, advising him of the unhappiness in Indian Country and encouraging him to issue a major policy statement as past presidents had done. Such concerns went unheeded.[27]

President Carter's State of the Union address in 1979 became more proactive and set the tone for later legislative action. Carter acknowledged that the federal government had a special responsibility to Native Americans and pledged to seek negotiated settlements with tribal leaders in conflicts over land, water, and other resources. He also acknowledged the trust relationship that exists between the federal government and Indian nations and stated that the United States government had a commitment to promoting Indian self-determination.[28]

Native American tribal leaders and activists worked to influence the Carter administration, as many believed that President Carter did not have a fully coherent Native American policy. LaDonna Harris, Floyd

PASSAMAQUODDY AND PENOBSCOT INDIANS
DEMAND TWO-THIRDS OF MAINE, 1980

Using a feather pen, President Jimmy Carter signed legislation in 1980 that resolved long-standing tribal claims to two-thirds of the land in the state of Maine. The origins of the land claim dated to 1791, when the Passamaquoddy Nation ceded all but twenty-three thousand acres to Massachusetts, which had jurisdiction over Maine. Similarly, the Penobscot Nation ceded all but five thousand acres of land to Maine in treaties and land sales in 1796, 1818, and 1833. The agreements went unchallenged until 1972, when tribal attorneys asked the United States to file suit against Maine for violating the Indian Trade and Intercourse Act of 1790, a law that required congressional approval for all Indian land transfers. Since Congress had not approved the old agreements, tribal lawyers argued that Maine had illegally appropriated the land. In 1975, both a federal district court and a federal appeals court held in favor of the tribes. For the next four years, tribal leaders, lawyers, congressmen, state officials, and the president engaged in discussions. Carter worked hard to broker an agreement—so hard that, in the words of Charles Wilkinson, he "probably spent more time on an Indian issue than any president in the twentieth century." In the end, Carter signed the Maine Indian Claims Settlement Act in October 1980. Under the law, the Passamaquoddy Tribe and Penobscot Nation agreed to give up their claims to land in exchange for $81.5 million, which could be used to purchase three hundred thousand acres from current landowners. The tribes also received federal recognition, entitling them to participate in government programs. However, provisions in the agreement that limited tribal sovereignty in Maine have been controversial. Since 1980, approximately twenty-four Native American tribes have filed claims to recover lands taken by states through treaties that violated the Non-Intercourse Acts. All but one tribe, the Mashpee of Massachusetts, won settlements.[29]

President Jimmy Carter signing the Maine Indian Claims Settlement Act, 1980. *©Bettmann/CORBIS.*

Correa (Laguna Pueblo), and Peter MacDonald (Navajo), among others, developed the idea of forming the Council for Energy Resources Tribes (CERT) to assist tribes in acquiring the most favorable financial returns for the extraction of natural resources located on tribal lands. CERT became a reality during the Carter administration, not as an action by the president, but as an initiative of American Indian leaders who were impatient with the president's pace on Indian affairs.

Another American Indian activist, Suzan Shown Harjo (Cheyenne and Hodulgee Muscogee), worked more directly with the White House. In 1976, just weeks before the presidential election, Harjo organized a meeting of Indian leaders with then Democratic candidate Jimmy Carter in Albuquerque, New Mexico. At the meeting, Harjo asked Carter if he would sign an American Indian Religious Freedom Act as president. Carter said he would.[30] Between 1976 and 1978, Harjo worked with the legislative leaders who would introduce the bill to Congress in August 1978. Before the measure reached the Senate floor, Washington representative Thomas Foley lobbied Representative Morris Udall to kill the bill. Foley promoted the United States Forest Service, which opposed legislation to protect Indian sacred sites on National Forest land in California. Ultimately, Udall convinced Harjo that a modified bill was better than no bill at all, so, as written, the American Indian Religious Freedom Act failed to protect sacred sites.[31] Nevertheless, it was a landmark to practitioners of Indian spiritual ceremonies across the country.

While a victory was achieved, the new American Indian Religious Freedom Act (AIRFA) had no teeth. After passage of the act, the United States Supreme Court held in favor of the United States Forest Service in a lower court case involving the sacred sites.[32] In *Lyng v. Northwest Indian Cemetery Protection Association* (1988), tribal religious practitioners asserted that the AIRFA protected sacred sites, including the Chimney Rock area of the Six Rivers National Forest in northwest California—land that had historically been used by the Karok, Tolowa, and Yurok tribes for religious rituals. However, the Supreme Court gave government agencies the green light to build a road through the heart of a sacred site, notwithstanding that tribal religious practices required privacy, silence, and an undisturbed natural setting.

President Carter supported American Indian aspirations on other issues. Under his administration, the federal government was tasked to ensure that Native Americans were treated fairly and that treaty promises were fulfilled.[33] A key issue among these promises was water rights.

Rights to water running through or adjacent to Indian reservations were guaranteed by treaty, and in *Winters v. United States* the United States Supreme Court held that the government had created an "implied reservation" of water rights when it created Indian reservations.[34] In a 1978 message to Congress, President Carter declared that his general water policy would include "an instruction to Federal Agencies to work promptly and expeditiously to inventory and quantify Federal reserved and Indian water rights." Unfortunately, as with many of his initiatives, Carter did not get to deliver on that promise. With only two exceptions, Carter proved unable to overcome strong opposition from western congressional delegations in water-rights controversies. Carter's one-term presidency and the demanding foreign policy issues of the late 1970s limited the promise of his fundamental sympathy for American Indian aspirations.[35]

"MAYBE WE SHOULD NOT HAVE HUMORED THEM": PRESIDENT RONALD REAGAN AND AMERICAN INDIANS

President Ronald Reagan took the oath of office on Tuesday, January 20, 1981, and once again, for his second term, on January 20, 1985. Although his Indian policies and initiatives were numerous and significant, Reagan's actions were overshadowed by a speech he delivered in the Soviet Union, at Moscow State University, in May 1988. During the address, Reagan stated,

> We have provided millions of acres of land for what are called Reservations . . . and they're [the Indians] free also to leave the reservations and be American citizens among the rest of us, and many do . . . maybe we made a mistake. Maybe we should not have humored them in wanting to stay in that kind of primitive lifestyle. Maybe we should have said, no, come join us, be citizens along with the rest of us.[36]

Native American leaders were unsettled by the president's remarks. For one thing, his assertions flew in the face of the fact that the United States did not "give" Indians land; rather, Native Americans had given the United States more than one billion acres of land through treaties and agreements. The president's speech also ignored the fact that many American Indians had become citizens during the allotment period beginning in 1887, that more became citizens during World War I, and that the United States extended citizenship to all American Indians in 1924. "I was appalled by the president's performance but not surprised," declared Suzan Shown Harjo, then executive director of the National Congress of American Indians. "He has headed the worst administration for Indians since the days of outright warfare and extermination."[37]

Tribal leaders reacted to President Reagan's uninformed depiction of Indian people as non-American citizens living in a primitive lifestyle by requesting a face-to-face meeting at the White House. After a preliminary discussion with Indian leaders at the president's California ranch, White House spokesman Marlin Fitzwater and M. B. Oglesby, the deputy chief of staff, agreed to arrange a meeting with tribal leaders and President Reagan at the White House.[38] The meeting—held in December 1988, just days before the president moved out of the White House—lasted all of twenty minutes, and included Ivan Sydney, chairman of the Hopi Tribe; Phillip Martin, tribal chief of the Mississippi Choctaw; Wilma Mankiller, principal chief of the Cherokee Nation; Edward Thomas, president of the Tlingit/Haida Central Council; and Assistant Secretary of the Interior for Indian Affairs Ross Swimmer (Cherokee).

During the meeting, President Reagan apologized for his earlier inaccurate statements, praised the achievements and contributions of Indian people, and explained that his remarks did not reflect the thrust of his administration's Indian policy. Reading from a prepared statement, the president reiterated his 1983 Indian policy statement, that Indians should have the right to choose their own life and the right to have a say in what happens in Indian Country. Native tribes, the statement declared, needed the freedom to spend the monies available to them. To create a better quality of life, Reagan said, Native American tribes—not the federal govern-

"YOUNG CHEROKEE GIRLS WOULD NEVER HAVE THOUGHT . . .": WILMA MANKILLER, PRINCIPAL CHIEF OF THE CHEROKEE NATION, 1987–95

In the final weeks of his second term, President Ronald Reagan met to discuss Indian grievances with sixteen tribal chiefs, including Cherokee principal chief Wilma Mankiller, who had been selected as one of the group's three spokespersons. The meeting, held at the White House, was little more than a "photo opportunity," said Mankiller, who expressed dismay at the president's apparent disinterest in Indians. Yet when photos showing Mankiller seated next to the president appeared in the morning papers, her image as an inspired and tenacious Indian leader was hardwired into public consciousness.

The first female principal chief of the Cherokee Nation of Oklahoma, Wilma Mankiller has made a career of making history. Born in 1945 in Tahlequah, Oklahoma, Mankiller came to adulthood in San Francisco, a center of social activism during the 1960s. Inspired by the Indian occupation of Alcatraz Island in 1969, Mankiller said that she was "totally engulfed by the Native American movement" and was propelled along a path that would lead her back to Oklahoma and, in 1987, into the principal leadership position of the second-largest Indian tribe in the United States.

During her tenure as principal chief, from 1987 to 1995, Mankiller opened health clinics, improved schools, supported economic self-sufficiency, and expanded the Cherokee Nation Community Development Department, of which she was founding director. Her emphasis upon the balance of male and female roles working together for the community good—the Cherokee concept of *gadugi*—strengthened her tribal government and brought attention to "women's issues" such as health care and education.

Chief Mankiller also met with President George H. W. Bush and was active in Arkansas governor Bill Clinton's presidential campaign in 1992. Under the Clinton administration, Mankiller communicated directly with the president and cabinet officials—connections that made her, according to one writer, "the most influential Indian leader in the country." In 1998, President Clinton awarded her with the Presidential Medal of Freedom, America's highest civilian award.

A popular author, activist, and lecturer, Mankiller now lives with her husband, Charlie Soap, on family land in the Cherokee Nation. Reflecting upon her own legacy, Mankiller observed, "Prior to my election, young Cherokee girls would never have thought that they might grow up and become chief."[39]

President Ronald Reagan meeting at the White House with Wilma Mankiller, principal chief of the Cherokee Nation; Leonard C. Burch, chairman of the Southern Ute Tribe (far right); and Interior Secretary Donald P. Hodel (far left), on December 12, 1988. *Photo by Cliff Owen. ©Bettmann/CORBIS.*

ment—should make the key social and economic decisions that affect their people.[40]

President Reagan's American Indian policy statement of 1983 was the handiwork of Morton Blackwell (Cherokee), who served as special assistant to the president. Blackwell held more than one hundred meetings with tribal leaders—including Peter MacDonald, chairman, Navajo Nation; Ned Anderson, chairman, Arizona Inter-Tribal Council; John Sloat, vice president, United Tribes of Western Oklahoma and Kansas; Russell Jim, chairman, Northwest Affiliated Tribes; Nelson Angapak, chairman, Alaska Federation of Natives; and Delfino Lovato, president, All Indian Pueblo Council—to ensure that the administration addressed the concerns of the American Indians.

The tribal leaders raised a host of issues, from reaffirming the government-to-government relationship of Indian tribes with the United States to the repudiation of the government's policy of tribal termination; from the fulfillment of the federal trust responsibility to Indian nations to the strengthening of tribal governments; from direct funding rights for block grants for Indian tribes to the development of Indian-owned energy resources; and from the preservation of Indian water rights to the coordination of federal Indian programs through the Cabinet Council on Human Resources. President Reagan included all of these issues in his Indian policy statement of 1983.[41]

During the Reagan presidency, budget cuts severely handicapped the progress of tribal programs on Indian reservations, generating far-reaching consequences. Reagan believed that tribes should fully enter the world of private enterprise, reduce their dependence on federal funding, and attract more private business to Indian reservations. He characterized the nation's Indian policy as paternalism and branded the United States' policy of treating Indians as wards of the government a colossal failure.[42] Yet while he spoke of government-to-government relations between the federal government and Native nations, Reagan supported states' rights over the rights of Indian reservations.[43]

Reagan's philosophy was reflected in the appointment of James G. Watt as secretary of the interior. Watt, like Reagan, favored cutting government assistance to American Indians as well as promoting

"WE MUST DO IT OUR OWN WAY": PETER MACDONALD, SR., AND INDIAN SELF-DETERMINATION

One of the most prominent and controversial Native leaders of the twentieth century, Peter MacDonald, Sr. (Navajo, b. 1928), served as Navajo tribal chairman from 1970 to 1991 and played an important role in asserting and establishing self-determination for his people. Born in the small Arizona community of Teec Nos Pos, MacDonald was reared on the seventeen-million-acre Navajo Reservation, which sprawls across northern Arizona as well as parts of Utah and New Mexico. His people, traditional sheepherders, sent him to a boarding school in Shiprock, New Mexico, but MacDonald ran away and later enlisted to fight in World War II, serving as a Navajo code talker. After the war, MacDonald attended college, earned a degree in engineering, and moved to Southern California, where he worked as an electrical engineer on the Polaris nuclear missile project for Hughes Aircraft. Longing for home, he returned to Navajo Country in 1963.

MacDonald was drawn permanently into tribal affairs during a contentious Navajo council meeting, when a frustrated BIA official lost his temper and declared, "If you guys continue to act like children, I'm going to throw every one of you out of this council chamber and I'm going to put a padlock on it." In 1965, MacDonald took the helm of the Office of Navajo Economic Opportunity, a federally funded economic development program managed by Navajos which improved the lives of thousands of reservation residents and put MacDonald at the epicenter of tribal politics. In 1970 he won the race for tribal chairman, demanded that the BIA turn over the council chamber to the tribe, and then changed the locks.

As tribal chairman, MacDonald moved the Navajo Nation toward greater self-determination. Navajos must no longer "depend on others to run our schools, build our roads, administer our health programs, construct our houses, manage our industries, sell us cars, cash our checks, and operate our trading posts. We must do it our own way," he insisted. "And we must do it now."

Prominent in national Republican Party circles, MacDonald served on the committee to re-elect the president and lauded President Nixon as "the Abraham Lincoln of the Indian people" for his support of Indian self-determination. With the backing of powerful friends in Washington, MacDonald persuaded lawmakers to double federal spending on the Navajo Nation, America's biggest Indian tribe. The influx of federal dollars enabled the tribal government to initiate programs that emphasized Navajo control of education and resources. Dozens of new schools were opened, including Navajo Community College, the first tribally controlled institution of higher education. MacDonald also fought to assert Navajo control of reservation resources, and, through his chairmanship of the Council of Energy Resources Tribes (CERT)—a consortium of Native nations dedicated to maximizing revenue generated from the extraction of resources on tribal lands—helped Native nations receive a fair share of what was rightfully theirs.

By the early 1980s, Peter MacDonald had become one of the most powerful Indian leaders in the United States. With his penchant for pin-striped suits, MacDonald—whom political enemies dubbed "McDollar"—traveled in a private jet and dealt as an equal with corporate leaders, politicians, and presidents. His power, authority, and effectiveness as a leader helped him win an unprecedented four terms as Navajo tribal chairman. Despite his achievements, MacDonald was constantly challenged by political rivals and dogged by allegations of corruption. In 1989, the Navajo Nation Council suspended him from office, pending resolution of corruption charges. The following year, a tribal court found him guilty of accepting bribes, violating ethics laws, and conspiracy. In 1993, he was convicted of separate charges in federal court and was sentenced to fourteen years in federal prison. After serving eight years, MacDonald's sentence was commuted by President William J. Clinton.[44]

economic development on Indian reservations. And like the president, Watt also made inflammatory statements that raised Native ire. In a January 19, 1983, radio interview with host Richard Viguerie, Watt described Indians as "incompetent wards of the government" and cited Indian reservations as examples of "the failures of socialism." Despite federal subsidies, Watt said, reservations were hotbeds of unemployment, alcoholism, adultery, divorce, drug abuse, and venereal disease.[45] American Indian leader LaDonna Harris called the statements "unacceptable," "inexcusable," "a slap in the face," and a "genocidal racist slur."[46]

Assistant Interior Secretary Kenneth L. Smith (Warm Springs Wascoe) carried the president's message to the National Congress of American Indians in 1983, stating that while the administration intended to support Indian self-determination, the priority would be to reduce Indian dependency on federal staff and funds. As president, Reagan oversaw a severe downsizing of the federal budget for social service programs aimed at assisting Indian tribes; his Indian policy was devoted to reducing tribal reliance on federal support.

An unforeseen consequence of Reagan's Indian policy was the tremendous growth of gaming on Indian reservations. Reagan's administration encouraged tribes to consider establishing gaming operations patterned after the high-stakes bingo parlor operated by the Seminole Tribe of Florida.[47] Although this did not come to full fruition during Reagan's administration, Indian gaming would grow to have a profound economic and political impact on Indian nations across the United States in the decades that followed. By 2008, some 250 tribes owned casinos, many of them comparable to the glittering establishments of Las Vegas and Atlantic City, which earned revenues in excess of $25 billion. Once the stepchildren of individual states, Indian tribes would now support numerous tribal political, economic, and cultural initiatives. They could even assist in balancing state budgets, contributing from fifteen to thirty-three percent of gaming profits to state coffers.

President Reagan cut funds for Indian programs, but he stood firmly opposed to past termination policies. In January 1983 he spoke of encouraging tribal self-reliance and urged Congress to replace legislation that "established the now discredited policy of ter-

Lucky Blanket, **1998, by Marcus Amerman (Choctaw, b. 1959).** Beadwork on roulette table cover. *National Museum of the American Indian, 25/7257.*

minating the federal-tribal relationship."[48] Indian people had good reason to fear the return or continuation of termination. While self-determination was now official government policy, an anti-Indian backlash in Congress seemed to foretell support for "termination through legislation." Washington representative John E. Cunningham proposed legislation to "abrogate all treaties with Indians" living in Washington State as a way to end federal paternalism.[49] He ironically called the act the Native American Equal Opportunity Act. Lawmakers introduced eleven other bills that sought to abrogate Indian treaties or deny federal support to Indians. One of these bills, introduced by Washington representative Lloyd Meeds, was intended to deny southwestern Indian tribes' water rights secured by treaty.[50] President Reagan, following the precedent set by former President Nixon, called for Indian self-determination without termination and stated that a lingering threat of termination has no place in the administration's policy of self-government for Indian tribes.[51] This was Reagan's shining moment in Indian affairs, one for which he will be remembered.

Reagan also made positive attempts to improve his image with American Indian people. For the years 1986 through 1988, he proclaimed a National American Indian Heritage week, each time calling upon the country to honor the achievements of American Indians and to acknowledge their contributions to American life. Reagan noted that Indians had served with valor in the armed forces and that their diverse heritages had made lasting contributions to the nation. In a 1988 proclamation, he acknowledged that the government-to-government relationship between the United States and Indian tribes had endured, despite periods of conflict and changes in Indian affairs, and that the United States Constitution, treaties, and laws, as well as Supreme Court decisions, consistently recognized a unique political relationship between tribal governments and the United States.[52]

Citing this unique relationship, Reagan encouraged the use of direct tribal contracts for administering domestic programs on Indian reservations. In 1980, tribes were contracting $203 million in federal programs. In 1984, this amount grew to $315 million, and in 1985 five Oklahoma tribes negotiated a contract to assume full responsibility for all direct services provided by the local Shawnee Agency. This represented a major milestone in the Reagan presidency, and placed the federal government's policy of Indian self-governance on the road to becoming a reality.[53]

Despite these developments, President Reagan was unable to erase the stain of his 1988 Moscow speech, which remains embedded in the collective memory of Native America.

"YOU GET BLAMED IF THINGS GO WRONG . . . ": PRESIDENT GEORGE H. W. BUSH

Born in Milton, Massachusetts, on June 12, 1924, George Herbert Walker Bush was sworn in as the forty-first president of the United States on January 21, 1989. Prior to becoming president, Bush served two terms as vice president under President Ronald Reagan, during which he took no active role in Indian affairs. His stated position was, "Don't take on fixed responsibilities as vice president. You get blamed if things go wrong, and you don't get credit if things go right."[54] Biographers make little mention of President Bush's Indian policies, and his autobiography is silent about American Indians.[55] To find evidence of his contributions, one must turn to the rather cold and stilted *Public Papers of the Presidents of the United States.*

President Bush's approach to Indian affairs closely mirrored that of the Carter administration. He delegated responsibility for Indian affairs to Secretary of the Interior Manuel Lujan, continuing President Reagan's policy of governing by committee. Lujan appointed Eddie F. Brown (Pascua Yaqui) as assistant secretary for Indian affairs. The appointment of Cliff Alderman and Mary McClure to the Office of Intergovernmental Affairs to handle Indian affairs rounded out the presidential steering group.

American Indian leaders, including LaDonna Harris, became concerned that the move toward tribal self-determination might become stalled under a president whose main concern was foreign policy. Harris called upon President Bush to issue a policy statement delineating his stand on Indian affairs. Rather than issuing such a statement, however, President Bush referred Harris to President Reagan's Indian policy statement, saying that he had supported Reagan's position and still did.

Mary McClure, speaking on behalf of President Bush, harkened even farther back in time, emphasizing the administration's strong commitment to the principle of Indian self-determination set forth by President Nixon in 1970. This statement raised more concern among American Indians, who continued to fear the legislative termination of Indian tribes. In 1991, Oren Lyons, faith keeper of the Turtle Clan and member of the Onondaga Council of Chiefs, led a delegation of Native leaders to meet with President Bush in Washington, D.C., where they called, once again, for a formal presidential policy statement on Indian affairs.

Lost among the calls for a presidential policy statement was George H. W. Bush's crowning achievement in Indian affairs. On November 28, 1989, the president signed an act of Congress that established the Smithsonian Institution National Museum of the

"WE COMANCHES BELIEVE EVERYONE HAS MEDICINE": LADONNA HARRIS, ACTIVIST

Cutting her political teeth in the 1960s as aide and advisor to her husband, former Oklahoma senator Fred Harris, LaDonna Harris (Comanche) carved out a career as an advocate for Native Americans as well as the poor, underprivileged, and disadvantaged everywhere. Inspired by the optimism of President Kennedy's New Frontier as well as the reform energy of President Johnson's War on Poverty, Harris worked tirelessly to develop community action programs and organizations such as Oklahomans for Indian Opportunity (OIO) to address the health, economic, and educational needs of Oklahoma Indians.

As a senator's wife in Washington, D.C., Harris rubbed shoulders with the leading lights of social reform during the 1960s, enjoying close relations with the families of New York senator Robert Kennedy; Sargent Shriver, then head of the Office of Economic Opportunity; and Secretary of the Interior Stuart Udall, whose agency oversaw the BIA. Her experience developing grassroots organizations soon caught the eye of President Johnson, who appointed her chair of the National Women's Advisory Council of the War on Poverty and named her to the newly created National Council on Indian Opportunity. When the latter fell stagnant during President Nixon's administration, Harris created Americans for Indian Opportunity (AIO), based on OIO's model but with a national focus. President Gerald Ford also recognized Harris's leadership skills, appointing her to the U.S. Commission on the Observance of International Women's Year. In 1980, Harris was nominated as the vice presidential candidate of the Citizens Party for her leadership on social issues and environmental advocacy, two leading concerns in her work with Native people.

Harris continued to work with AIO during the 1980s and 1990s, assisting tribes in establishing government-to-government relationships with federal agencies, educating government

LaDonna Harris, president of Americans for Indian Opportunity (at right), with Chilean Indigenous Leader Clara Bulnes at a ceremony celebrating the approval of the United Nations Declaration of Indigenous Peoples' Rights, Tiwanaku, Bolivia, 2007. *(AP Photo/Dado Galdieri).*

officials about the benefits of providing funding directly to tribes—rather than through the BIA—and launching a program that uses traditional tribal values to develop the leadership abilities of Native youth. In recent years, Harris has become a recognized advocate for the indigenous peoples of the Americas, applying lessons learned in Oklahoma and Washington to Native people throughout the Western Hemisphere. "We Comanches believe everyone has medicine," she declared, "and it is everyone's responsibility to help everyone else cultivate their strengths and their medicine."[56]

American Indian, to be built on the National Mall in Washington, D.C. Hawaii senator Daniel Inouye, Colorado representative Ben Nighthorse Campbell (Northern Cheyenne), and Congressional Delegate Eni Faleomavaega (American Samoan) coauthored the bill that led to the act establishing the Museum. When he signed the act, President Bush stated, "From this point, our Nation will go forward with a new and richer understanding of the heritage, culture, and values of the peoples of the Americas of Indian ancestry."[57]

Also obscured by the clamor for an official American Indian policy was the passage of an act designating the month of November as National American Indian Heritage Month. The act, which President Bush signed in 1990, was later expanded to include the heritage, history, art, and traditions of American Indians and Alaska Natives. That year, President Bush also signed into law the Native American Language Act, which formally recognized the language rights of American Indians, Alaska Natives, Native Hawaiians, and Pacific Islanders and encouraged the use of Native languages in schools with large enrollments of Native children.[58]

Two years later, President Bush took a bolder step and issued a proclamation designating 1992 as the Year of the American Indian. At the signing ceremony, he stated:

The National Museum of the American Indian, Washington, D.C. In 1989, President George H. W. Bush signed legislation that established the Smithsonian's National Museum of the American Indian (NMAI)—the first national museum dedicated to advancing knowledge and understanding of the Native cultures of the Western Hemisphere, past and present. Opened on the National Mall in 2004, the NMAI maintains a collection of more than 800,000 objects representing Native cultures throughout the Americas. The Museum's founding legislation and a 1996 amendment mandated that the NMAI return objects of special cultural significance to Native communities. The policy has resulted in the repatriation of approximately 2,700 items, including human remains, sacred and funerary pieces, and other singular objects, to more than 120 tribes and communities. *Photo by Maxwell MacKenzie © Maxwell MacKenzie.*

The contributions that Native Americans have made to our Nation's history and culture are as numerous and varied as the tribes themselves. . . . They have added to their ancient wealth of art and folklore a rich legacy of service and achievement. Today . . . we salute the Navajo Code Talkers of World War II and all those Native Americans who have distinguished themselves in service to our country . . . such as the great athlete Jim Thorpe and our thirty-first vice president, Charles Curtis—who have instilled pride in others by reaching the heights of their respective fields.[59]

Another noteworthy event went largely unheralded: the commemoration of Native warriors who died at the Battle of the Little Bighorn in 1876. Efforts to honor the Indian warriors date back at least to 1925, when Mrs. Thomas Beaverheart (Northern Cheyenne) requested that a marker be erected on the battlefield to indicate the spot where her father, Lame White Man, had fallen during the battle against troops under the command of Lieutenant Colonel George A. Custer.[60] At the time, the Custer National Cemetery was under the auspices of the secretary of war, who protected the graves of the Seventh Cavalry troops at the battle site. When Mrs. Beaverheart received no response from the superintendent of the cemetery, she pursued her request through the army, this time asking for grave markers showing where other American Indian warriors had fallen. Her request was met with silence. Although army officials met with members of the Northern Cheyenne at the battlefield in 1926, no markers for Indians were authorized. Markers began to appear at the battlefield in 1945, most likely placed there by descendants of the fallen warriors.

The National Park Service took over management of the Custer Battlefield National Monument in the 1940s, and for the next four decades, various groups lobbied to have the American Indian participants in the battle officially recognized. In 1988, members of AIM cemented a metal plaque onto the base of the memorial that marks the mass grave of the Seventh Cavalry soldiers. Finally, on December 10, 1991, President Bush authorized legislation that changed the name from the Custer Battlefield

National Monument to the Little Bighorn National Monument, and called for a new monument to honor the Indian participants in the battle.[61]

Not every piece of legislation proposed by a president becomes law. In 1992, President Bush proposed legislation to set aside 8.6 million acres of public lands in Oregon, Utah, Wyoming, and Nevada, to be designated as wilderness areas. The measure, supported by Secretary of the Interior Lujan, would have provided Indian people with access to wilderness areas for traditional cultural and religious purposes. Three successive congresses received the American Wilderness Protection Act, but each time the measure died on the floor.[62]

President George Herbert Walker Bush's name is largely absent from the drafting of legislation proposed on behalf of American Indians. During his term in office, his administrative staff and steer-

Seventh Cavalry Monument at the Little Bighorn Battlefield, Montana, 2005. The monument was erected in 1881 to honor the memories of the 263 U.S. soldiers who lost their lives during the Battle of the Little Bighorn in 1876. *Photo by Sharon A. Small.*

The *Spirit Warriors* sculpture, part of the Indian Memorial at the Little Bighorn Battlefield National Monument, Montana, 2005. Perched on a ridge overlooking the Little Bighorn River, and silhouetted against the ever-changing Great Plains sky, the *Spirit Warriors* sculpture honors the Lakota, Cheyenne, and Arapaho warriors who died protecting their families and defending their people's way of life against soldiers under the command of Lieutenant Colonel George A. Custer. The Indian memorial was dedicated in 2003, 122 years after the unveiling of the monument to the soldiers of the Seventh Cavalry, which stands nearby. *Photo by Sharon A. Small.*

ing committee mainly responded to outside pressures and interest groups to move issues such as the establishment of the National Museum of the American Indian and the designation of the Little Bighorn National Monument through Congress. In that regard, President Bush held firmly to the philosophy he developed as vice president: avoid taking on fixed responsibilities.[63] The next president took a different approach.

"I VOW TO HONOR AND RESPECT TRIBAL SOVEREIGNTY": PRESIDENT WILLIAM JEFFERSON CLINTON

American Indians remember President William Jefferson Clinton as a positive force in government-to-government relationships and the recognition of tribal sovereignty, and as a champion of tribal self-governance. Of all of the presidents since 1974, President Clinton's voice and direct participation in the development of the United States policy toward Native Americans were the clearest and most forthright. He rarely depended on his domestic counsel for advice.

Clinton was sworn in as the forty-second president of the United States on January 20, 1993, and took the oath of office for a second term on January 20, 1997. Clinton assumed an active role in Native American affairs from the time of his first inauguration to his last days in the White House. The first indication of his proactive approach was the appointment in August 1993 of Ada Deer (Menominee) to the post of assistant secretary for Indian affairs.

Recalling the Clinton administration's accomplishments in Indian affairs, Deer credited the president with reaffirming the government-to-government relationship with Native nations and settling a century-old boundary dispute with the Crow Tribe that restored tribal lands and provided compensation for lost coal reserves and revenue. Clinton also signed legislation that advanced tribal control of Indian education, placing fifty-two percent of Indian schools under the management of tribal councils or tribal boards of education.[64]

The most public display of President Clinton's inclusion of Native nations in the government-to-government process occurred in 1994, when he invited the leaders of all federally recognized tribes to meet with him at the White House, making it, incredibly, the first time since 1822 that tribal leaders had been invited to meet directly with a sitting president of the United States.[65] In his invitation, President Clinton declared, "I look forward to this historic meeting and to affirming our commitment to strengthening the nation-to-nation relationship we have with tribal governments."[66]

Of the 556 tribal leaders invited, some 322 attended the meeting. The Mashantucket Pequot—a tribe once thought to have been massacred into extinction by Puritan settlers but who now owned the Foxwoods Resort Casino in Connecticut, the largest casino in

"THAT'S PART OF WHAT IT TAKES TO GET A BILL THROUGH CONGRESS": ADA DEER AND THE STRUGGLE TO RESTORE THE MENOMINEE TRIBE OF WISCONSIN, 1970s

In 1992, when Ada Deer became the first woman to hold the office of assistant secretary for Indian affairs, she was already a veteran fighter for Native rights. In the early 1970s, Deer (Menominee) was one of the main leaders in the struggle to restore the Menominee Tribe of Wisconsin's federally recognized status after the government terminated its trust relationship with the tribe under legislation passed in 1953. A tireless crusader, Deer worked with grassroots organizations and lobbied the halls of Congress. "I talked to everyone I could," she recalled. "I held meetings with reporters, I held meetings with legislative aides. I went around to receptions. I smiled. I shook hands. I prepared bumper stickers and fact sheets and made it look like there were thousands of Indians screaming about termination. That's part of what it takes to get a bill through the Congress."

Deer's tenacity paid off in 1973, when President Nixon signed the Menominee Restoration Act. Afterward, Deer went on to serve on the American Indian Policy Review Commission as well as the board of directors of the Native American Rights Fund (NARF) from 1984 to 1990. When she became assistant secretary for Indian affairs two years later, Deer proclaimed that "the days of federal paternalism are over" and advocated a policy of "strong, effective tribal sovereignty" during her term in office. On her watch, some 223 Native Alaskan villages

Ada Deer, chairperson of the Menominee Restoration Committee, at a news conference in Shawano, Wisconsin, 1975. *©Bettmann/CORBIS.*

and 12 tribes achieved federal recognition, the number of tribes contracting for their own services increased to 180, and 130 Native tribes signed gaming agreements with 24 states. After resigning in 1997, Deer recalled that her main goal was to oversee the BIA's "transition from paternalistic landlord to true partner on a government-to-government basis with American Indian tribes."[67]

North America—sponsored the opening breakfast.[68] The meeting continued over a four-hour period, during which President Clinton took questions directly from the tribal leaders. The discussions included religious freedom, economic development, the reaffirmation of self-determination and tribal sovereignty, and the unique government-to-government relationship enshrined in the United States Constitution. In closing, President Clinton stated that "in every relationship between our people, our first principle must be to respect your

President Clinton listening to tribal drums played at the Pine Ridge Reservation in South Dakota, as Oglala Sioux Tribal president Harold Salway looks on, 1999.
The first sitting president to visit an Indian reservation since Franklin D. Roosevelt, Clinton came to Pine Ridge to speak about economic development—a topic of moment at the nation's second-largest reservation, where the unemployment rate reached 75 percent that year.

[Native American] rights to remain who you are and to live the way you wish to live. . . . I pledge to fulfill the trust obligations of the Federal Government. I vow to honor and respect tribal sovereignty based upon our unique historic relationship and to protect your right to fully exercise your faith as you wish."[69] Afterward, Clinton signed a presidential memorandum that stated that, "Each department and agency shall consult, to the greatest extent practicable and permitted by law, with tribal governments prior to taking actions that effect federally recognized tribal governments."[70]

One of the areas of concern that Native leaders raised during the 1994 White House meeting was the protection of and access to Indian sacred sites. Tribal leaders expressed their displeasure with the practice of allowing off-road vehicles, timber-harvesting trucks, and commercial development in or near Indian religious ceremonial sites. They also emphasized Native Americans' need for religious items such as eagle feathers, which are regulated under the Endangered Species Act but are central to Native ceremonies. Clinton heard what they were saying. On April 28, 1994, he signed a memorandum that supported the sanctity of Native American sacred sites, defined as "any specific, discrete, narrowly delineated location on federal land that is identified by an Indian tribe, or Indian individual . . . as sacred by virtue of its established religious significance to, or significance to, or ceremonial use by, an Indian religion."[71] He also issued an executive order that directed the heads of executive departments and agencies to expedite the distribution of eagles for Native American religious purposes, and sought to involve Native American tribes, organizations, and individuals in the distribution process.

President Clinton went on to sign numerous executive orders during his presidency that increased funding for the Indian Health Service and the Indian Head Start program, reduced class size in BIA-funded schools, modernized schools on Indian reservations, ensured that tribal colleges and universities were more fully recognized as accredited institutions, and provided internet service to remote Indian schools, libraries, rural health clinics, and hospitals. During his administration, President Clinton's assistant secretary for Indian affairs, Kevin Gover (Pawnee/Comanche), issued a well-received apology to American Indians on behalf of the United

States government for the historical misconduct of the Bureau of Indian Affairs.

Perhaps the most enduring legacy of the Clinton presidency was the long-term effect of Public Law 103-413, which amended the Indian Self-Determination Act of 1976. The measure, signed on October 25, 1994, made tribal self-governance a permanent part of the American fabric and authorized up to fifty additional tribes per year to enter into self-governance agreements with the United States government.[72] A direct result of President Clinton's meeting with tribal leaders, the self-determination amendments fulfilled the president's promise to recognize Native nations on a government-to-government basis. Under the provisions of the law, Indian tribes could now administer, manage, and redesign programs, activities, and services previously managed by the BIA as well as administer funds based on tribal priorities. In this way, tribes were empowered to manage their own affairs to meet the individual needs of their communities.

There is no area where tribal self-governance has proven more beneficial than in the negotiation of tribal/state compacts for high-stakes gaming on Indian reservations. President Clinton's support for this economic stimulus has had a lasting impact. Today, gaming on Indian reservations exceeds $28 billion annually. Many Native nations are investing in housing, education, businesses, and reservation infrastructure on a scale that could have never occurred had it not been for President Clinton's strong support for nation-to-nation status and tribal self-governance. His presidency proved very positive for American Indian people.

"TRIBAL SOVEREIGNTY MEANS JUST THAT": PRESIDENT GEORGE W. BUSH

For Native Americans, George W. Bush brought a troubling legacy to the White House. As governor of Texas and a candidate for president, Bush opined that states' rights trumped tribal rights—anathema for Native Americans, who had worked tirelessly for generations to affirm the sovereignty of Indian nations and the legal and political relationship of their nations and the United States government. In particular, tribes viewed Governor Bush's campaign against construction of the Speaking Rock Casino in Texas as an unsettling omen.[73]

George W. Bush was sworn in as the forty-third president of the

United States on January 21, 2001. Native leaders were soon worried about Bush's appointment of Gale Norton as secretary of the interior and Neal McCaleb as assistant secretary for Indian affairs. Neither Norton nor McCaleb had legislative records that indicated that they would support tribal sovereignty or recognize tribal rights over states' rights.[74]

These initial concerns were somewhat mollified when Bush declared November 2001 as National American Indian Heritage Month.[75] In the declaration, Bush acknowledged the importance of Native people in the shaping of United States history, pluralism, and diversity, and recognized American Indians and Alaska Natives for their service in the armed forces and other endeavors that required bravery and sacrifice. The president concluded with a promise that his administration would "continue to work with tribal governments on a sovereign-to-sovereign basis to provide Native Americans with new economic and educational opportunities. . . . We will protect and honor tribal sovereignty and help to stimulate economic development in reservations communities. We will work with the American Indians and Alaska Natives to preserve their freedoms, as they practice their religion and culture."[76]

Part of this work involved reassuring Native people that the government-to-government relationship between the United States and Indian nations would remain sacrosanct. Although Bush reaffirmed the government-to-government relationship, he accomplished little else in American Indian policy during his first term of office.

During his reelection campaign in 2004, President Bush issued a memorandum to assuage fears that he had changed his mind about tribal sovereignty and government-to-government relations. The document, "Government-to-Government Relationship with Tribal Governments," stated that "the United States has a unique legal and political relationship with Indian tribes and a special relationship with Alaska Native entities as provided in the Constitution of the United States, treaties, and Federal statutes."[77] The Bush administration, the memorandum noted, was committed to working "with federally recognized tribal governments on a government-to-government basis," and strongly supported and respected "tribal sovereignty and self-determination for tribal governments in the United States." Said the president, "I take pride in acknowledging and reaffirming the existence and durability of our unique relationship and these abiding principles."[78]

The reference to supporting and respecting tribal sovereignty was most likely included to defuse criticism from Indian leaders who had been unsettled by Bush's remark in 2004 that "tribal sovereignty means just that, it's sovereignty. You're a—you've been given sovereignty, and you're viewed as a sovereign entity."[79] Tension arose over the president's use of the word "given." Native people have always viewed sovereignty as an inherent right. The United States may have moved consistently over the years to reduce Indian sovereignty, but the government had no ability to "give" or "grant" sovereignty. As Jacqueline Johnson (Tlingit), the executive director of the National Congress of American Indians, put it: "It's not something that was given to us . . . we've always had [it]."[80]

On April 30, 2004, President Bush gave hope to American Indian parents when he signed an executive order that built on the No Child Left Behind Act. Bush thanked tribal leaders who had helped to draft the order and expressed his administration's commitment to helping American Indian and Alaska Native children meet the standards set by the education act.[81] Unfortunately, many felt the outcome was far different. West Virginia representative Nick Rahall, chairman of the House Natural Resources Committee, blasted the Bush administration for failing to meet the "most basic needs of those in Indian Country" and for neglecting much-needed repairs and improvements at BIA-funded schools.[82]

The administration's handling of Indian health also came under critical scrutiny. President Bush's 2009 budget proposal included a reduction of $21 million in funding for the Indian Health Service.[83] Bush proposed a budget of zero for urban Indian health, in spite of the fact that sixty-seven percent of all Native Americans lived off- reservation. The Senate countered, passing an Indian health package that provided $35 billion dollars in government funding over ten years to improve disease screening and mental health programs. This funding would boost primary care for the federally funded Indian Health Service, prompt new construction and modernization of health clinics on reservations, and recruit more Indians into health care professions. The bill would also increase tribal access to Medicare and Medicaid.[84]

President George W. Bush presenting the Congressional Gold Medal of Honor to Navajo code talker John Brown, Jr., at the U.S. Capitol in 2001. Bush gave the medal, the highest honor bestowed by the U.S. government, to four of the five surviving code talkers, whose fluency in the Navajo language enabled U.S. troops during World War II to issue field dispatches in a "code" the Japanese could never break. *Photo by Mike Theiler.* © *gettyimages.*

Despite his relatively lackluster record of achievements on behalf of Native people, President Bush did publicly acknowledge a brave Native soldier who gave his life for his country. At a ceremony at the White House on March 3, 2008, the president presented the Congressional Medal of Honor to the family of the late Army Master Sergeant Woodrow Keeble for his heroism during the Korean War. The first Lakota Indian to receive this honor, Keeble gave his life to save fellow soldiers during an October 1951 campaign to capture a mountain stronghold protecting a major enemy supply depot in Kumsong, North Korea. The operation, designated "Nomad-Polar," was the last major United Nations offensive during the Korean War. The Lakota warrior was also posthumously awarded four Purple Hearts for wounds sustained in battle, as well as the Bronze Star for his heroism on Guadalcanal during World War II.[85]

In his comments, President Bush apologized for the long-overdue presentation of the award, and stated that Sergeant Keeble's "act of heroism saved many American lives and earned him a permanent

HONORING GOVERNMENT-TO-GOVERNMENT RELATIONS:
BARACK OBAMA VISITS CROW COUNTRY, 2008

Six months before his historic election to the presidency, Senator Barack Obama courted American Indian voters in his bid to win the Democratic primaries in Montana and South Dakota.

Obama, who campaigned on the theme of "change," launched an energetic Native outreach effort that included visits to Indian reservations and discussions with tribal councils. His interest in Native concerns and voters helped him garner widespread support in Indian Country, including endorsements from more than 100 tribal leaders as well as prominent Native publications such as *Indian Country Today*.

At the Crow Reservation, Obama told a crowd of approximately 3,000 tribal members that his Indian policy would honor "the unique government-to-government relationship between tribes and the federal government," as well as uphold the government's treaty obligations, which he described as "paramount law." He also promised to appoint a White House senior advisor on Indian issues, to hold an annual summit meeting with tribal leaders in Washington, D.C., and to bring "quality affordable health care and world-class education to reservations across America."

Obama also thanked his Crow "parents," Hartford and Mary Black Eagle, for sponsoring his adoption into the Crow Nation. "I like my new name, Barack Black Eagle," he declared. "That is a good name. And since now I'm a member of the family, you know I won't break my promises to my own brothers and my own sisters." ⚊

Then Democratic presidential hopeful Senator Barack Obama greeting tribal members at a political rally at the Crow Reservation in Montana in 2008. *AP Photo/Chris Carlson.*

place in his fellow soldiers' hearts. When Woody was through, six-teen enemy soldiers were dead, the hill was taken, and the Allies had won the day."[86] Russell Hawkins, Woodrow Keeble's stepson, accepted the award on his behalf almost six decades after his gallant actions and twenty-six years after his death.

LOOKING FORWARD

It is impossible to predict how future presidents and Native nations will interact as we move farther into the twenty-first century. Will Native leaders continue to press for greater recognition of tribal sovereignty and shore up the gains that have been won since the 1970s? Will future occupants of the Oval Office continue to respect the government-to-government relationship that Native nations and the federal government have reestablished and reaffirmed during the past four decades? No one knows. But one thing is certain: Native nations have fought for and achieved recognition in our time, and they will not easily surrender their place at the table. Indian leaders have fought to retain their tribal sovereignty, and future leaders will maintain their nation's innate sovereignty regardless of who lives at 1600 Pennsylvania Avenue. The voices of Native leaders are strong and articulate, and, as Indian nations grow stronger and more self-sustaining, it will behoove future American presidents to reckon with them. "Presidents that think they can get along without advice on Indian affairs will find out that they have made a serious mistake," observed Phileo Nash, the commissioner of Indian affairs under Presidents Kennedy and Johnson. "Presidents of the United States, for a long time, have been tested by where they stand on Indian affairs. . . . I believe every president of the United States knows that."[87] Every Native American leader knows the hard-fought battles that their people have waged with American presidents and the United States government, and they are well seasoned to assert their sovereignty to protect their people, lands, and values.

ACKNOWLEDGMENTS

CLIFFORD E. TRAFZER would like to thank Chancellor Tim White, Dean Steve Cullenberg, and Melissa Conway of the University of California, Riverside; the reference, document, and special collections librarians at the Rivera Library, University of California, Riverside; the editorial staff of the National Museum of the American Indian, especially Mark Hirsch; and Lee Ann, Louise, Tess, Hayley, and Tara, who gave me time to work.

MATTHEW SAKIESTEWA GILBERT would like to thank Frederick Hoxie, Swanlund Professor of History; Robert Warrior, director of American Indian Studies; and Antoinette Burton, professor of history at the University of Illinois, Urbana-Champaign.

DUANE CHAMPAGNE would like to thank Amy Ware, a graduate student in American Studies at the University of Texas, Austin, for sharing her research on Will Rogers and President Roosevelt.

THE SMITHSONIAN NATIONAL MUSEUM OF THE AMERICAN INDIAN (NMAI) would like to thank Mrs. Philip E. Nuttle for her generous support of the museum's Research Unit in general and this project in particular; Dr. Helen Maynor Scheirbeck (Lumbee), former senior advisor for Museum Programs and Scholarly Research at the NMAI, for encouraging us to focus on American presidents and Native leaders; Frederick E. Hoxie, Swanlund Professor of History at the University of Illinois, Urbana-Champaign; K. Tsianina Lomawaima (Creek), professor of American Indian studies at the University of Arizona; David Wilkins (Lumbee), professor of American Indian Studies at the University of Minnesota; the late Dr. John

Mohawk (Seneca) for participating in an all-day discussion in 2006 that helped to frame the topic; Ceni Myles, former manager of Seminars and Symposia at the NMAI, for organizing and contributing to that discussion; Clifford E. Trafzer, for being a steadfast friend to the Museum; the authors, for agreeing to participate in this project, particularly Robert W. Venables and Troy Johnson, who came aboard in the eleventh hour; Jose Barreiro, for reading and commenting on earlier drafts of the manuscript; and Bruce Nichols and Stephanie Meyers, of HarperCollins Publishers, for their encouragement and assistance in bringing the manuscript to press.

ENDNOTES

INTRODUCTION

1. U.S. Forest Service, Black Hills National Forest Service, January 23, 2004, at www.fs.fed.us/r2/blackhills; Keystone Area Historical Society, Keystone Characters, at www.keystonechamber.com/kahs/characters.html.

2. Today, modern Native nations use the term *tribal sovereignty* to explain their place in the world and their relationship to other nations, including the United States. Each tribe has supremacy in its own affairs based on the spiritual, political, and economic gifts of creation. Each Native nation is preeminent in its own affairs, because each has its own rules, laws, boundaries, and responsibilities. For American Indian people, authority rests with the tribe or nation, not outsiders or newcomers who have their own ways and their own sovereignty. Supreme power rests with the tribe, not just in political matters, but in all matters. In the past, each Native nation enjoyed its own cultural, political, economic, and religious sovereignty, determining for itself the boundaries of communal actions and societal rules. Each nation was dominant in determining its own course of action, subordinate only to creative forces that had put them on earth. In this way, each Native nation was superior unto itself with independent authority to act and live in accordance with its own laws. Each tribe had dominion over its own affairs and lands, and was master of its own destiny. Thus, each nation had "supreme controlling power in communities," found within their own homelands and among their own people. See *The Compact Edition of the Oxford University Dictionary* (Oxford, England: Oxford University Press, 1987), 490.

3. Clifford E. Trafzer, *As Long as the Grass Shall Grow and Rivers Flow: A History of Native Americans* (Fort Worth, Texas: Harcourt, 2000), 252–54; Peter Nabokov, *Where the Lightning Strikes: The Lives of American Indian Sacred Places* (New York: Viking, 2006), 207; Clyde Milner II, "America, Only More So," in Clyde Milner II, Carol O'Connor, and Martha Sandweiss, eds., *The Oxford History of the American West* (New York: Oxford University Press, 1994), 4–5; Tony Perrottet, "Mount Rushmore," *Smithsonian* Vol. 23, no. 2 (May 2006), 81.

4. Peter Nabokov, *A Forest of Time: American Indian Ways of History* (Cambridge: Cambridge University Press, 2002), 126–49.

5. Clifford E. Trafzer and Richard D. Scheuerman, *Renegade Tribe: The Palouse Indians and the Invasion of the Inland Pacific Northwest* (Pullman, Washington: Washington State University Press, 1986), 104–10.

6. Contemporary American Indian leaders, including Monica Mayer, Wayne Nicken, Lori Alvord, Dee Ann DeRoin, Pauline Murillo, Dan Calac, and Jeff Henderson, have knowledge of traditional Native medicine as well as Western medicine.

7. Alden T. Vaughan, *Transatlantic Encounters: American Indians in Britain, 1500–1776* (Cambridge: Cambridge University Press, 2006), xii, 113–30; Stephen Cook, "The Art and Material Culture of the Four Indian King Paintings," *Crosspaths* Vol. 5, no. 3 (Fall 2002), 12.

8. Clifford E. Trafzer, *The People of San Manuel* (Patton, California: San Manuel Band of Mission Indians, 2002), 64–69; Trafzer and Scheuerman, *Renegade Tribe*, 23–25.

9. Paivi Hoikkala, "Traditions and Transformations: American Indian Women in Historical Perspective," in Philip Weeks, ed., *They Made Us Many Promises* (Wheeling, Illinois: Harlan Davidson, 2002), 269–90; Rebecca Kugel and Lucy Eldersveld Murphy, eds., *Native Women's History in Eastern North America* (Lincoln, Nebraska: University of Nebraska Press, 2007), xiii-xxii.

10. Oren Lyons made these statements during a lecture at the Tribal Science Conference at the Quinault Indian Reservation in 2006.

11. Herman J. Viola, *Diplomats in Buckskins: A History of Indian Delegations in Washington City* (Norman, Oklahoma: University of Oklahoma Press, 1995), 94, 104–6.

12. Katharine C. Turner, *Red Man Calling on the Great White Father* (Norman: University of Oklahoma Press, 1951), 10.

13. Gerald McMaster and Clifford Trafzer, eds., *Native Universe: Voices of Indian America* (Washington, D.C.: National Geographic Books, 2004), 144–47; Wilcomb E. Washburn, ed., *Handbook of North American Indians*, Vol. 4: History of Indian–White Relations (Washington, D.C.: Smithsonian Institution, 1988), 189.

14. Turner, *Red Man Calling,* 10.

15. Ibid.

16. Ibid.

17. Turner, Ibid., 22.

18. Ibid.

19. Ibid., 10.

20. Francis Paul Prucha, *American Indian Treaties: The History of a Political Anomaly* (Berkeley, California: University of California Press, 1994), 224; Jack Campisi, "Meaning in the Reverse: Indian Peace Medals," *Cross Paths* Vol. 6, Issue 4 (Winter 2003–4), at http://www.pequotmuseum.org/Home/CrossPaths/CrossPathsWinter20034/MeaningintheReverseIndianPeaceMedals.htm; Vine Deloria, Jr., "Promises Made, Promises Broken," in McMaster and Trafzer, eds., *Native Universe,* 149.

21. "Treaties," in Frederick E. Hoxie, ed., *Encyclopedia of North American Indians: Native American History, Culture, and Life from Paleo-Indians to the Present* (Boston: Houghton Mifflin Company, 1996), 643–46; Prucha, ibid., 1.

22. Francis Paul Prucha, *The Great Father: The United States Government and the American*

Indians (Lincoln, Nebraska: University of Nebraska Press, 1986), 21.

23. Ibid., 21–22.

24. Herman J. Viola, *Diplomats in Buckskins: A History of Indian Delegations in Washington City* (Norman, Oklahoma: University of Oklahoma Press, 1995), 94, 104–6.

25. Peter M. Whiteley, "Bartering Pahos with the President," *Ethnohistory*, Vol. 51, no. 2 (Spring 2004), 359–414.

26. Ibid., 94.

27. Jefferson to Congress, January 18, 1803, in Gunther Barth, ed., *The Lewis and Clark Expedition* (Boston, Massachusetts: Bedford Books, 1998), 15–16; Prucha, *Great Father*, 50.

28. Prucha, *Great Father*, 51.

29. Reginald Horsman, "American Indian Policy in the Old Northwest," *The William and Mary Quarterly*, 3rd Series, vol. 18, no. 1 (January 1961), 48.

30. Anthony F. C. Wallace, *Jefferson and the Indians: The Tragic Fate of the First Americans* (Cambridge, Massachusetts: Harvard University Press, 1999), vii-viii.

31. Trafzer, *As Long as the Grass Shall Grow*, 142–45.

32. Michael D. Green, *The Politics of Indian Removal* (Lincoln, Nebraska: University of Nebraska Press, 1982), 156.

33. Ibid.

34. Ibid., 157, 159–60.

35. Trafzer, *As Long as the Grass Shall Grow*, 153–54.

36. Philip Weeks, *Farewell My Nation* (Wheeling, Illinois: Harlan Davidson, 1990), 86, 88.

37. Viola, *Diplomats in Buckskins*, 100–101.

38. Weeks, *Farewell My Nation*, 95; Duane Champagne, ed., *The Native North American Almanac: A Reference Work on Native North Americans in the United States and Canada* (Detroit, Michigan: Gale Research, 1994), 44.

39. Viola, *Diplomats in Buckskins*, 108.

40. Ibid, 109.

41. Trafzer and Scheuerman, *Renegade Tribe*, 133–34.

42. Ibid.

43. Ibid.

44. Trafzer, *As Long as the Grass Shall Grow*, 317, 328, 339, 418.

45. President Theodore Roosevelt, "First Annual Message to the Senate and House of Representatives," December 3, 1901, in John T. Woolley and Gerhard Peters, *The American Presidency Project* (Santa Barbara, California: University of California), at http://www.presidency.ucsb.edu/ws/?pid=29542.

46. Viola, *Diplomats in Buckskins*, 112.

47. Trafzer, *As Long as the Grass Shall Grow*, 400–2; Champagne, ed., *The Native North American Almanac*, 859.

CHAPTER I: NATIVE NATIONS AND THE NEW NATION, 1776–1820

1. President George Washington to Marquis de Lafayette, August 11, 1790, in John C. Fitzpatrick, ed., *The Writings of George Washington*, Vol. 31 (Washington, D.C., G.P.O., 1939), 87.

2. Joseph Brant to the Reverend Samuel Kirkland, March 8, 1791, in Charles M. Johnston, ed., *The Valley of the Six Nations: A Collection of Documents on the Indian Lands*

of the Grand River (Toronto: University of Toronto Press, 1964), 269.

3. The term "whites" was used by the Euro-Americans during the colonial period and the period discussed in this chapter, and thus the term seems appropriate.

4. Cadwallader Colden, *The History of the Five Indian Nations Depending Upon the Province of New-York in America* (1727 and 1747; Ithaca, New York: Cornell University Press, 1958).

5. The nineteenth-century English term "The Enlightenment" is from the eighteenth-century German word *Aufklärung* and is reflected in the eighteenth-century French phrase *siècle des lumières*. Peter Gay, *The Enlightenment: The Rise of Modern Paganism* (New York: Vintage, 1966), 21. In another book, Gay noted that "other countries had the thing, but not the word. The English did not import it from Germany until the nineteenth century." Peter Gay, ed., *The Enlightenment: A Comprehensive Anthology* (New York: Simon and Schuster, 1973), 13.

6. Robert F. Berkhofer, Jr., *The White Man's Indian* (1978; New York: Random House, 1979), 37–49. *cf.* Robert W. Venables, "American Indian Influences on the America of the Founding Fathers," in Oren Lyons and John Mohawk, eds., *Exiled in the Land of the Free* (Santa Fe, New Mexico: Clear Light Publishing, 1992), 73–124.

7. Paul A. W. Wallace, *Indians in Pennsylvania* (1961; Harrisburg, Pennsylvania: The Pennsylvania Historical and Museum Commission, 1968), 171.

8. Conrad Weiser, *Journal*, September 3, 1754, reprinted in Paul A. W. Wallace, *Conrad Weiser, 1696–1760: Friend of Colonist and Mohawk* (1945; Lewisburg, Pennsylvania: Wennawoods Publishing, 1996), 367; Timothy Pickering, handwritten notes, no date [1794], *The Microfilm Edition of the Timothy Pickering Papers* (Boston: Massachusetts Historical Society, 1966), 69 reels, Reel 59, 331–32. This is also quoted in Wilbur R. Jacobs, *Wilderness Politics and Indian Gifts: The Northern Colonial Frontier, 1748–1763* (Lincoln, Nebraska: University of Nebraska Press, 1950), 135 and 91 fn. 5. Tanacharisson's observation was recorded by Conrad Weiser, an interpreter and Pennsylvania agent active in Indian affairs. Conrad's observations appeared in London in 1759 in a publication entitled *Enquiry into the Causes of the Alienation of the Delaware and Shawnese Indians from the British Interest.* Then, during George Washington's second administration, Timothy Pickering copied this quote by hand. Pickering was gathering information to help him understand why Indians mistrusted whites, and meticulously assembled the background materials he needed as Washington's chief negotiator with the Iroquois Confederacy at the Treaty of Canandaigua in 1794 and then as Washington's secretary of war. See Timothy Pickering, handwritten notes, no date [ca. 1793–95], *The Microfilm Edition of the Timothy Pickering Papers,* 69 reels, Reel 59, 331–31A; and Timothy Pickering, "Papers to be carried to the Indian Treaty" [December 17, 1793], *The Microfilm Edition of the Timothy Pickering Papers.* 69 reels, Reel 59, 107–9.

9. Washington's secretary of war Henry Knox and Timothy Pickering, his chief negotiator with the Iroquois Confederacy at the Treaty of Canandaigua (1794) and later his secretary of war, played a major role in establishing American diplomacy with Native nations. See Francis Paul Prucha, *American Indian Treaties: The History of a Political Anomaly* (Berkeley, California: University of California Press, 1994), 65, 94–96.

10. Thomas Jefferson, *Notes on the State of Virginia, 1782,* in Merrill D. Peterson, ed., *Thomas Jefferson: Writings* (New York: The Library of America, 1984), 189.

11. Ibid.

12. Reginald Horsman, *Expansion and American Indian Policy, 1783–1812,* with a new preface by the author (1967; Norman, Oklahoma: University of Oklahoma Press, 1992), viii–ix and *passim.*

13. Colin G. Calloway, *The American Revolution in Indian Country* (New York: Cambridge University Press, 1995), 26–31.

14. Randolph C. Downes, *Council Fires on the Upper Ohio* (Pittsburgh, Pennsylvania: University of Pittsburgh Press, 1940), 157, 180–81.

15. David H. Corkran, *The Creek Frontier, 1540–1783* (Norman, Oklahoma: University of Oklahoma Press, 1967), 288.

16. Calloway, *The American Revolution in Indian Country*, 24; Corkran, 288–308.

17. Tese Mico, Council with the Creek Indians, September 7, 1775, in the Sir Henry Clinton Papers. The William L. Clements Library, University of Michigan, Ann Arbor, Michigan.

18. *The Declaration of Independence,* in Henry Steele Commager, ed., *Documents of American History* (9th ed.; Englewood Cliffs, New Jersey: Prentice-Hall, 1973), 101–2. The phrase "merciless Indian Savages" conveniently ignored how the English colonists triumphed in their wars with the French, in part through alliances with American Indians.

19. Paul Lawrence Stevens, "His Majesty's 'Savage' Allies: British Policy and the Northern Indians During the Revolutionary War. The Carleton Years, 1774–1778" (Ph.D. dissertation, State University of New York at Buffalo, 1984), 1, 233; Gavin K. Watt, *Rebellion in the Mohawk Valley: The St. Leger Expedition of 1777* (Toronto: The Dundurn Group, 2002), 122, 159, 177, 193, 195; and Barbara Graymont, *The Iroquois in the American Revolution* (Syracuse, New York: Syracuse University Press, 1972), 132–35.

20. Glenn F. Williams, *Year of the Hangman: George Washington's Campaign Against the Iroquois* (Yardley, Pennsylvania: Westholme, 2005), 206–9.

21. George Washington to John Sullivan, May 31, 1779, in Flick, *Sullivan-Clinton Campaign,* 90–91. An electronic version is available at http://etext.virginia.edu/toc/modeng/public/WasFi15.html.

22. Colonel Mason Bolton to Frederick Haldimand, October 2, 1779, in Haldimand Papers, B.100: 286; and Graymont, *Iroquois in the American Revolution*, 192–222.

23. Chief Irving Powless, Jr., "Treaty Making," in G. Peter Jemison and Anna M. Schein, eds., *Treaty of Canandaigua 1794* (Santa Fe, New Mexico: Clear Light Publishers, 2000), 28.

24. Conde de Aranda (Pedro Pablo Abarca y Bolea), "Memoir" August 3 and August 19–30, 1782 [translated from the Spanish by the editors]; Gouverneur Morris to John Jay, August 6, 1782, in Richard B. Morris, ed., *John Jay: The Winning of the Peace: Unpublished Papers* (New York: Harper & Row, 1980), 270–83. During the negotiations that led to the treaty, the Spanish negotiator, the Conde de Aranda, pointed out to one of the American negotiators, John Jay, that the lands "beyond the principal line of the boundaries of the Colonies [established by the British government between 1768 and 1771], was Indian land, to which both parties [i.e., the Americans and their allies on the one hand and the British on the other] had equal rights, or equally unjust claims" (p. 272). *cf.* Richard B. Morris, *The Peacemakers: The Great Powers and American Independence* (New York: Harper & Row, 1965), 321–23, 462–63.

25. George Washington to François Jean, Comte de Chastellux, October 12, 1783, in Fitzpatrick, ed., *The Writings of George Washington,* at http://memory.loc.gov/ammem.

26. Assembly of the State of New York, *Report of the Special Committee to Investigate the Indian Problem of the State of New York, Appointed by the Assembly of 1888* (Albany, New York: The Troy Press Company, 1889), 234–367.

27. Laurence M. Hauptman, *Conspiracy of Interests: Iroquois Dispossession and the Rise of New York State* (Syracuse, New York: Syracuse University Press, 1999), 214.

28. William Leete Stone, *The Life of Joseph Brant—Thayendanegea: Including the Border Wars of the American Revolution* (2 vols.; New York: Alexander V. Blake, 1838), II, 266.

29. Randolph C. Downes, *Council Fires on the Upper Ohio* (Pittsburgh, Pennsylvania: University of Pittsburgh Press, 1940), 300. *cf.* Isabel Thompson Kelsay, *Joseph Brant, 1743–1807: Man of Two Worlds* (Syracuse, New York: Syracuse University Press, 1984), 403.

30. Walter Lowrie and Matthew St. Clair Clarke, eds., *American State Papers. Indian Affairs.* Volume 4 of *Documents, Legislative and Executive, of the Congress of the United States* (Washington, D.C.: Gales and Seaton, 1832), 9.

31. Continental Congress, *Journals of the Continental Congress, 1774–1789* (Vol. 25; Washington, D.C.: Government Printing Office, 1922), 682–83.

32. The war was actually a continuation of the fighting begun in 1774, during Lord Dunmore's War. Robert S. Allen, *His Majesty's Indian Allies: British Indian Policy in the Defense of Canada, 1774–1815* (Toronto: Dundurn Press, 1992), 64–71.

33. Ibid., 64–72; Downes, *Council Fires on the Upper Ohio,* 294–321.

34. President George Washington, Seventh Annual Address, December, 8, 1795, in Fitzpatrick, ed., *The Writings of George Washington,* Vol. 34, 391.

35. "An Act to Regulate Trade and Intercourse with the Indian Tribes," July 22, 1790, in Wilcomb E. Washburn, ed., *The American Indian and the United States: A Documentary History* (4 vols.; Westport, Connecticut: Greenwood Press, 1973), III, 2151–53.

36. "An Act to Regulate Trade and Intercourse with the Indian Tribes," March 1, 1793, *The Avalon Project at Yale Law School,* at http://www.yale.edu/lawweb/avalon/statutes/native/na025.html; Felix Cohen, *Handbook of Federal Indian Law,* with a new foreword and other new material by Robert L. Bennett and Frederick M. Hart (1942; Albuquerque, New Mexico: University of New Mexico Press, 1972), 70; Jack Campisi, "The Oneida Treaty Period, 1783–1838," in Jack Campisi and Laurence M. Hauptman, eds., *The Oneida Indian Experience: Two Perspectives* (Syracuse, New York: Syracuse University Press, 1988), 58–59; and Francis Paul Prucha, *The Great Father: The United States Government and the American Indians* (2 vols.; Lincoln, Nebraska: University of Nebraska Press, 1984), I, 91–93. *cf.* Vine Deloria, Jr., and David E. Wilkins, *Tribes, Treaties, and Constitutional Tribulations* (Austin, Texas: University of Texas Press, 1999), 16.

37. James Thomas Flexner, *George Washington* (4 vols.; Boston, Massachusetts: Little Brown, 1965–72), III, 262–65; Horsman, *Expansion and American Indian Policy,* 66–72. *cf.* John Caughey, *McGillivray of the Creeks* (Norman, Oklahoma: University of Oklahoma Press, 1938).

38. Wiley Sword, *President Washington's Indian War: The Struggle for the Old Northwest, 1790–1795* (Norman, Oklahoma: University of Oklahoma Press, 1985), 100–116, 130–38.

39. The speech of Cornplanter, Half-Town, and the Great-Tree, Chiefs and Councillors of the Seneca Nation, to the Great Councillor of the Thirteen Fires, December 1, 1790, in *American State Papers, Class II, Indian Affairs,* Vol 4, 1832. *American State Papers. Documents, Legislative and Executive, of the Congress of the United States* (Washington, D.C.: Gales and Seaton, 1832), 140.

40. Ibid., 140–42.

41. The reply of the President of the United States to the speech of Cornplanter, Half-Town, and Great-Tree, Chiefs and Councillors of the Seneca Nation of Indians, December 29, 1790, in ibid., 142–43.

42. Sword, *President Washington's Indian War,* 171–201.

43. Harvey Lewis Carter, *The Life and Times of Little Turtle: First Sagamore of the Wabash* (Urbana and Chicago, Illinois: University of Illinois Press, 1987), 4–7, 229; Stewart Rafert, *The Miami Indians of Indiana: A Persistent People, 1654–1994* (Indiana Historical Society, 1996), 62; Clifford Trafzer, *As Long as the Grass Shall Grow and the Rivers Flow: A History of Native Americans* (Fort Worth: Harcourt College Publishers, 2000), 113.

44. George Washington, *Diary,* October 4, 1784, in Donald Jackson and Dorothy Twohig, eds., *The Papers of George Washington* (Charlottesville, Virginia: University Press of Virginia, 1978), IV, 66, at http://memory.loc.gov/ammem.

45. Sword, *President Washington's Indian War,* 204.

46. Francis Paul Prucha, *The Sword of the Republic: The United States Army on the Frontier, 1783–1846* (Bloomington, Indiana: Indiana University Press, 1969), 27–28.

47. Sword, *President Washington's Indian War,* 204; and T. Harry Williams, *The History of*

American Wars from Colonial Times to World War I (New York: Knopf, 1985), 87.

48. George Washington to François Jean, Comte de Chastellux, October 12, 1783, in Fitzpatrick, ed., *The Writings of George Washington,* at http://memory.loc.gov/ammem.

49. Timothy Pickering to the Reverend John Clarke, October 1, 1793, *The Microfilm Edition of the Timothy Pickering Papers,* 69 reels, Reel 35, 177.

50. Thomas Jefferson, quoted in Richard G. Miller, "The Federal City, 1783–1800," in Russell F. Weigley, ed., *Philadelphia: A 300-Year History* (New York: W. W. Norton, 1982), 182.

51. John L. Cotter, Daniel G. Roberts, and Michael Parrington, *The Buried Past: An Archaeological History of Philadelphia* (Philadelphia, Pennsylvania: University of Pennsylvania Press, 1993), 53.

52. Despite this, the epidemic struck Iroquois Country farther to the east, where Indians lived in closer proximity to white settlements. At Onondaga, the capital of the Iroquois Confederacy (in what is now central New York), most Onondagas had taken ill. Timothy Pickering to Rebecca Pickering, September 25, 1794, *The Microfilm Edition of the Timothy Pickering Papers,* 69 reels, Reel 1, 214.

53. Sword, *President Washington's Indian War,* 276–78.

54. Williams, *The History of American Wars,* 87.

55. William Leete Stone, *The Life of Joseph Brant—Thayendanegea: Including the Border Wars of the American Revolution* (2 vols.; New York: Alexander V. Blake, 1838), II, 377 n.*

and 397; Sword, *President Washington's Indian War,* 269; and Bert Anson, *The Miami Indians* (Norman, Oklahoma: University of Oklahoma Press, 1970), 129. *cf.* Dale Van Every, *Ark of Empire: The American Frontier, 1784–1803* (1963; New York: Mentor Books, 1964), 323.

56. John Sugden, *Tecumseh: A Life* (New York: Henry Holt, 1997), 88; Sugden, *Blue Jacket: Warrior of the Shawnees* (Lincoln, Nebraska: University of Nebraska Press, 2000), 175–80; Sword, *President Washington's Indian War,* 299–311; and Anson, *The Miami Indians,* 127–30.

57. Sword, *President Washington's Indian War,* 299–306.

58. Sugden, *Blue Jacket,* 175–80; Sword, *President Washington's Indian War,* 299–311; Anson, *The Miami Indians,* 127–30.

59. Mercy Otis Warren, *History of the Rise, Progress, and Termination of the American Revolution, Interspersed with Biographical, Political, and Moral Observations,* edited and annotated by Lester H. Cohen (reprint of the three-volume, 1805 edition in two volumes; Indianapolis, Indiana: Liberty Fund, 1994), II, 634. *cf.* 579, 667, and 669; Kate Davies, *Catharine Macaulay & Mercy Otis Warren: The Revolutionary Atlantic and the Politics of Gender* (New York: Oxford University Press, 2005), 2, 7, 287.

60. "Queshawksey, or George Washington" is listed on page 44, first column, in "A treaty of peace between the United States of America and the Tribes of Indians, called the Wyandots, Delawares, Shawanoes [sic], Ottawas, Chipewas [sic], Potawatimes [sic], Miamis, Eel-river, Weea's, Kickapoos,

Piankashaws, and Kaskaskias" in Charles J. Kappler, ed., *Indian Treaties, 1778–1883* (reprint of 1904 ed.; New York: Interland Publishing, 1972), 39–45; and Charles C. Royce, *Indian Land Cessions in the United States . . . Extract from the Eighteenth Annual Report of the Bureau of American Ethnology* (reprint 1900; New York: Arno Press, 1971), "Indiana," Plate CXXVI [map] and 654–56.

61. Samuel Flagg Bemis, *Jay's Treaty: A Study in Commerce and Diplomacy* (rev. ed.; New Haven, Connecticut: Yale University Press, 1962), 347, 360–62, and 360 n9.

62. John Mohawk, "The Canandaigua Treaty in Historical Perspective" in Jemison and Schein, eds., *Treaty of Canandaigua 1794,* 57–58.

63. Treaty of Canandaigua, November 11, 1794, in Kappler, ed., *Indian Treaties, 1778–1883,* 35.

64. Treaty of Canandaigua, November 11, 1794, in ibid., 37; Robert W. Venables, "Some Observations on the Treaty of Canandaigua" in Jemison and Schein, eds., *Treaty of Canandaigua 1794,* 90–92.

65. Timothy Pickering to Henry Knox, October 15, 1794, and Captain Joseph Brant, November 20, 1794, in *The Microfilm Edition of the Timothy Pickering Papers,* 69 reels, Reel 60, 205, and Reel 62, 108.

66. Kelsay, *Joseph Brant,* 576.

67. Despite Brant's actions, the Mohawk Nation remained a sovereign presence in New York, along the St. Lawrence, at Akwesasne, and in Ontario and Quebec, Canada. Kelsay, *Joseph Brant, 1743–1807,* 576–78; Treaty with the Mohawk, March 29, 1797, in Kappler, ed., *Indian Treaties, 1778–1883,* 50–51.

68. John Adams, First Annual Message, *The Adams Papers* (New Haven, Connecticut: The Avalon Project Web Site, 1998), at http://www.yale.edu/lawweb/avalon.

69. William G. McLoughlin, *Cherokee Renascence in the New Republic* (Princeton, New Jersey: Princeton University Press, 1986), 47.

70. John Adams, "Talk of the President of the United States to his beloved chiefs, warriors, and children, of the Cherokee nation," August 27, 1798, in *American State Papers, Class II, Indian Affairs,* 1832, Vol. 4, of *American State Papers. Documents, Legislative and Executive, of the Congress of the United States* (Washington, D.C.: Gales and Seaton, 1832), 640–41.

71. "Articles of a Treaty between the United States of America, and the Cherokee Indians," October 2, 1798, in Kappler, ed., *Indian Treaties, 1778–1883,* 51–55.

72. Sugden, *Tecumseh,* 105–6; Horsman, *Expansion and American Indian Policy,* 145, 166.

73. Wallace, *Jefferson and the Indians,* 248.

74. Thomas Jefferson to William Henry Harrison, February 27, 1803, in *The Writings of Thomas Jefferson,* Andrew A. Lipscomb and Albert Ellery Bergh, eds. (20 vols.; Washington, D.C.: Thomas Jefferson Memorial Association, 1903), X, 370.

75. Thomas Jefferson to William Henry Harrison, February 27, 1803, in ibid., X, 370–71.

76. Sherene Baugher and Robert W. Venables, "Indians within New York State: Separate Nations, Not Just Ethnic Americans," in Thomas A. Hirschl and Tim B. Heaton, eds., *New York State in the 21st Century* (Westport, Connecticut: Praeger, 1999), 79, 89–90.

77. Arthur C. Parker, "The Code of Handsome Lake, the Seneca Prophet [1913]," in William N. Fenton, ed., *Parker on the Iroquois* (three "books" in one edition; Syracuse, New York: Syracuse University Press, 1968), Book Two, 38; Robert W. Venables, "Iroquois Environments and 'We the People of the United States,'" in Christopher Vecsey and Robert W. Venables, eds., *American Indian Environments: Ecological Issues in Native American History* (Syracuse, New York: Syracuse University Press, 1980), 108–9; and Robert W. Venables, "Some Observations on the Treaty of Canandaigua," in Jemison and Schein, eds., *Treaty of Canandaigua 1794,* 96. While the *Gai wiio* is often called "The Code of Handsome Lake" or "The Handsome Lake Religion," those who follow the principles of these teachings believe that the Creator's messages were and are no more the personal thoughts of Handsome Lake than the Ten Commandments were the personal thoughts of Moses.

78. Francis Paul Prucha, "American Indian Policy in the Twentieth Century," *The Western Historical Quarterly* Vol. 15, no. 1 (January, 1984), 15; Alan Brinkley, *The Unfinished Nation: A Concise History of the American People* (New York: McGraw-Hill, Inc., 1993), 188–89.

79. Arthur C. Parker, "The Code of Handsome Lake, the Seneca Prophet," in Fenton, ed., *Parker on the Iroquois,* 9–13, 66. This passage, together with the entire code, is still a part of Iroquois religious life. For example, the passage quoted in the text was recited at Onondaga on June 12, 1980.

80. Thomas Jefferson to Handsome Lake, November 3, 1802, in Wallace, *The Death and Rebirth of the Seneca,* 270–71.

81. Robert W. Venables, "Iroquois Environments and 'We the People of the United States,'" in Vecsey and Venables, eds., *American Indian Environments,* 108.

82. Tecumseh's call for pan-Indian unity had been proposed by the Shawnee Nation as early as 1746. Corkran, *The Creek Frontier,* 118.

83. R. David Edmunds, *The Shawnee Prophet* (Lincoln, Nebraska: University of Nebraska Press, 1983), 54–56.

84. Thomas Jefferson, address to the Wyandots, Ottawas, Chippewas, Potawatomies, and Shawnees, January 10, 1809, in *The Writings of Thomas Jefferson,* Lipscomb and Bergh, eds., XVI.

85. The speech of the principal chiefs and warriors of the Wyandots, delivered on the 30th day of September, 1809, in *American State Papers, Class II, Indian Affairs,* 1832, Vol. 4 of *American State Papers. Documents, Legislative and Executive, of the Congress of the United States* (Washington, D.C.: Gales and Seaton, 1832), 796.

86. Colin G. Calloway, *The Shawnees and the War for America* (New York: Viking, 2007), 156–57; R. David Edmunds, "Tecumseh," in Frederick E. Hoxie, ed., *Encyclopedia of North American Indians: Native American History, Culture, and Life from Paleo-Indians to the Present* (Boston: Houghton Mifflin, 1996), 621; Alvin M. Josephy, Jr., *The Patriot Chiefs: A Chronicle of American Indian Leadership* (New York: Viking, 1961), 155–56.

87. Sugden, *Tecumseh,* 226–36.

88. John Sugden, *Tecumseh's Last Stand* (Norman, Oklahoma: University of Oklahoma Press, 1985), 125–35; and Allen, *His Majesty's Indian Allies,* 144–46.

89. McLoughlin, *Cherokee Renascence,* 191–94; and Gregory Evans Dowd, *A Spirited Resistance: The North American Indian Struggle for Unity, 1745–1815* (Baltimore, Maryland: Johns Hopkins University Press, 1992), 185–88.

90. James Mooney, *Myths of the Cherokees and Sacred Formulas of the Cherokees* (reprint in one volume of, respectively, the 1900 and 1891 editions; Nashville, Tennessee.: Charles and Randy Elder, Booksellers-Publishers, 1982), 89–97; and Joel W. Martin, *Sacred Revolt: The Muskogees' Struggle for a New World* (Boston, Massachusetts: Beacon Press, 1991), 156–68.

91. *Articles of agreement and capitulation,* August 9, 1814, in Kappler, ed., *Indian Treaties, 1778–1883,* 107–10; McLoughlin, *Cherokee Renascence,* 194–95.

92. Rufus King, Speech in the United States Senate, 1815 [ca. February 15], in Charles R. King, ed., *The Life and Correspondence of Rufus King,* 6 vols. (New York: G. Putnam's Sons, 1894–1900), V, 551, 553.

93. Article IX, Treaty of Ghent (1814), in Charles W. Eliot, ed. *American Historical Documents, 1000–1904* (New York: F. Collier & Son, 1910), 263. Interestingly, Rufus King objected to this clause, believing that Great Britain had no right to insert a clause that might interfere with negotiations between Indian nations and the United States government.

94. See Henry Clay to John Gunter, June 6, 1831, in James F. Hopkins and Mary W. M. Hargreaves, eds., *The Papers of Henry Clay* (11 vols, Lexington, Kentucky: University of Kentucky Press, 1959–92), VIII, 358.

95. Robert Ernst, *Rufus King, American Federalist* (Chapel Hill, North Carolina: University of North Carolina Press, 1968), 351–52.

96. McLoughlin, *Cherokee Renascence,* 221.

97. "Articles of a treaty concluded, at the Cherokee Agency, within the Cherokee nation," July 8, 1817, in Kappler, ed., *Indian Treaties, 1778–1883,* 140–44.

98. An excellent book covering the complicated politics of the Buffalo Creek Reservation and the Erie Canal's impact on all Iroquois lands in Hauptman, *Conspiracy of Interests,* 101–18, 137, and passim.

99. Treaty of Big Tree, September 15, 1797, in Kappler, ed., *Indian Treaties, 1778–1883,* 1027–30.

100. Onondaga would again become the official capital in 1847. Elizabeth Tooker, "The League of the Iroquois: Its History, Politics, and Ritual" in Bruce Trigger, ed., *Handbook of North American Indians,* Vol. 15, Northeast (Washington, D.C.: Smithsonian Institution, 1978), 436.

101. Red Jacket, speech at Buffalo Creek, July 9, 1819, in Charles M. Snyder, ed., *Red and White on the New York Frontier . . . the Papers of Erastus Granger, Indian Agent, 1807–1819* (Harrison, New York: Harbor Hill Books, 1978), 93–95. *cf.* John C. Calhoun to Jasper Parrish, May 14, 1818, in Reginald Horsman, "The Origins of Oneida Removal to Wisconsin, 1815–1822," in Laurence M. Hauptman and L. Gordon McLester III, eds., *The Oneida Journey from New York to*

Wisconsin, 1784–1860 (Madison, Wisconsin: University of Wisconsin Press, 1999), 58.

102. Red Jacket, speech at Buffalo Creek, July 9, 1819, in Snyder, ed., *Red and White,* 93–95.

CHAPTER II: NATIVE NATIONS IN AN AGE OF WESTERN EXPANSION, 1820–80

1. Michael Paul Rogin, *Fathers & Children: Andrew Jackson and the Subjugation of the American Indian* (New Brunswick, New Jersey: Transaction Publishers, 1995), 180.

2. Herman Viola, *Diplomats in Buckskins: A History of Indian Delegations in Washington City* (Bluffton, South Carolina: Rivilo Books, 1995), 97; Colin Calloway, ed., *Our Hearts Fell to the Ground: Plains Indian Views of How the West Was Lost* (Boston, Massachusetts: Bedford Books/St. Martin's Press, 1996), 56–59.

3. Robert J. Miller, *Native America, Discovered and Conquered: Thomas Jefferson, Lewis & Clark and Manifest Destiny* (Westport, Connecticut: Praeger, 2006), 8–12.

4. Miller, *Native America, Discovered and Conquered,* 8–12.

5. John Coward, *The Newspaper Indian: Native American Identity in the Press, 1820–90* (Urbana, Illinois: University of Illinois Press, 2006); Rogin, *Fathers & Children,* 122.

6. President John Quincy Adams, Fourth Annual Message, December 2, 1828, John T. Woolley and Gerhard Peters, *The American Presidency Project* (Santa Barbara, California: University of California), at http://www.presidency.ucsb.edu/ws/?pid=29470.

7. James Mooney, *Myths of the Cherokees and Sacred Formulas of the Cherokees* (reprint in one volume of, respectively, the 1900 and 1891 editions (Nashville, Tennessee: Charles and Randy Elder, Booksellers-Publishers, 1982), 108–10; Grant Foreman, *Sequoyah* (Norman, Oklahoma: University of Oklahoma Press, 1938), 3–31; and William G. McLoughlin, *Cherokee Renascence in the New Republic* (Princeton, New Jersey: Princeton University Press, 1986), 350–54; Raymond D. Fogelson, "Sequoyah," in Frederick E. Hoxie, ed., *Encyclopedia of North American Indians* (Boston, Massachusetts: Houghton Mifflin, 1996), 580–82.

8. Charles Francis Adams, *Memoirs of John Quincy Adams,* Vol. 6 (Philadelphia, Pennsylvania: J. B. Lippincott, 1864), 271–72.

9. Mary Young, "Indian Removal and Land Allotment: The Civilized Tribes and Jacksonian Justice," *The American Historical Review,* Vol. 64, no. 1 (October 1958), 31; Alan Brinkley, *The Unfinished Nation: A Concise History of the American People* (New York: McGraw Hill, 1993), 218.

10. Lynn Hudson Parsons, "A Perpetual Harrow Upon My Feelings: John Quincy Adams and the American Indian," *New England Quarterly,* Vol. 46, no. 3 (September 1973), 374–76.

11. Rogin, *Fathers & Children,* 183, 185, 187–88, 191.

12. Massachusetts Congressman Edward Everett called the Indian Removal bill "the greatest question that ever came before Congress, short of the question of peace and war." Rogin, *Fathers & Children,* 206.

13. Ibid., 215.

14. President Andrew Jackson. Message to Congress, December 1830, quoted in Young, "Indian Removal and Land Allotment," 31.

15. James Atkins Shackford, *David Crockett: The Man and the Legend* (reprint ed., Westport, Connecticut: Greenwood Press,1981), 116–17; M. J. Heale, "The Role of the Frontier in Jacksonian Politics: David Crockett and the Myth of the Self-Made Man," *The Western Historical Quarterly*, Vol. 4, no. 4 (October, 1973), 406–9, 414, 417; Stanley Folmsbee and Anna Grace Catron, "David Crockett, Congressman," *East Tennessee Historical Society Publications* 29 (1957), 62–4; Gales & Seaton's, *Register of Debates in Congress*, March 30, 1830, 717; March 25, 1830, 1133, March 26, 1830, 1135; John Ross to David Crockett, January 13, 1831, in Gary E. Moulton, ed., *The Papers of Chief John Ross*, Vol. 1, 1807–39 (Norman, Oklahoma: University of Oklahoma Press, 1985), 210–12; Walter Blair, *Davy Crockett: Legendary Frontier Hero* (Springfield, Illinois, Lincoln-Herndon Press, Inc., 1986), 181–87.

16. Thomas L. McKinney, U.S. Commissioner of Indian Affairs, cited in Gary E. Moulton, *John Ross, Cherokee Chief* (Decatur, Georgia: University of Georgia Press, 1978), 1–2, 31.

17. Francis Paul Prucha, *American Indian Treaties: The History of a Political Anomaly* (Berkeley, California: University of California Press, 1994), 166-67.

18. Rogin, *Fathers & Children*, 214.

19. Ibid., 26–7.

20. Principal Chief John Ross, "To the Senate and House of Representatives," Red Clay Council Ground, Cherokee Nation, September 28, 1836, at http://historymatters.gmu.edu/d/6598.

21. Compiled by Chadwick "Corntassel" Smith, "Forced Removal," *Cherokee Nation History Course* (Tahlequah, Oklahoma: Cherokee Nation, 2000), Section 6–2 and 6–6; Russell Thornton, "Cherokee Population Losses During the Trail of Tears: A New Perspective and a New Estimate," *Ethnohistory*, Vol. 31, no. 4 (1984), 292.

22. Theda Perdue and Michael D. Green, *The Cherokee Removal: A Brief History with Documents*, 2nd ed. (Boston, Massachusetts: Bedford/St. Martins, 2005), 89–90, 167; Grant Foreman, *Indian Removal: The Emigration of the Five Civilized Tribes of Indians* (Norman, Oklahoma: University of Oklahoma Press, 1974), 34–38.

23. Perry A. Armstrong, *The Sacs and the Black Hawk War* (Springfield, Illinois: H. W. Rocker, 1887), 90–91; Ma-Ka-Tai-Me-She-Kia-Kiak, *Black Hawk: An Autobiography*, Donald Jackson, ed. (Urbana, Illinois: University of Illinois Press, 1955), 61–62.

24. Ma-Ka-Tai-Me-She-Kia-Kiak, *Black Hawk,* 154–56.

25. Alvin M. Josephy, Jr., *The Patriot Chiefs: A Chronicle of American Indian Resistance* (New York: Penguin, 1993), 211–53; Armstrong, *The Sacs and the Black Hawk War,* 472; Ma-Ka-Tai-Me-She-Kia-Kiak, 129–30; James Lewis, *The Black Hawk War of 1832,* at http://lincoln.lib.niu.edu/blackhawk/page2d.html.

26. Josephy, Jr., *The Patriot Chiefs* (New York: Penguin, 1993), 211–15; Viola, *Diplomats in Buckskins*, 34–35; Trafzer, *As Long as the Grass Shall Grow*, 140–42; James H. Merrell, "American Nations, Old and New: Reflections on Indians and the Early Republic," in

Frederick E. Hoxie, Ronald Hoffman, and Peter J. Albert, eds., *Native Americans and the Early Republic* (Charlottesville, Virginia: University Press of Virginia, 1999), 338.

27. Armstrong, *The Sacs and the Black Hawk War,* 504.

28. Josephy, Jr., *The Patriot Chiefs,* 191–95.

29. Ibid., 205.

30. Ibid., 208; *Daily Herald and Gazette* (Cleveland, Ohio), November 28, 1838.

31. "The Great Nation of Futurity," *The United States Democratic Review*, Vol. 6, no. 23, (1839), 428–30.

32. John T. Woolley and Gerhard Peters, *The American Presidency Project* (Santa Barbara, California: University of California), at http://www.presidency.ucsb.edu/ws/?pid=29480.

33. James M. McPherson, *Battle Cry of Freedom: The Civil War Era* (New York: Oxford University Press, 1988), 47.

34. Stephen Anzovin and Janet Podell, eds., *Speeches of the American Presidents*, 2nd ed. (H. W. Wilson, 2001), 154.

35. James Rawls, *Indians of California: The Changing Image* (Norman, Oklahoma: University of Oklahoma Press, 1984), 81, 116; McPherson, *Battle Cry of Freedom,* 64.

36. Clifford E. Trafzer and Joel R. Hyer, eds., *Exterminate Them! Written Accounts of the Murder, Rape, and Enslavement of Native Americans during the California Gold Rush* (East Lansing, Michigan: Michigan State University Press, 1999), 15, 18–19, 126.

37. William B. Secrest, *When the Great Spirit Died: The Destruction of the California Indians 1850–1860* (Sanger, California: Word Dancer Press, 2003), 93; Trafzer, *Exterminate Them!,* 22–23, 88; Theodore Hittell, *History of California, Vol. III* (San Francisco, California: N. J. Stone & Company, 1898), 840, 848, 851, 860.

38. Secrest, *When the Great Spirit Died,* 155.

39. Susan Hazen-Hammond, *Timelines of Native American History: Through the Centuries with Mother Earth and Father Sky* (New York: Berkley Publishing Group, 1997), 124; Francis Paul Prucha, *American Indian Treaties: The History of a Political Anomaly* (Berkeley, California: University of California Press, 1994), 243–46.

40. Paul Wallace Gates, *Fifty Million Acres: Conflicts Over Kansas Land Policy, 1854–1890* (Ithaca, New York: Cornell University Press, 1954), 6–8.

41. H. Craig Miner and William E. Unrau, *The End of Indian Kansas: A Cultural Revolution, 1854–1871* (Lawrence, Kansas: University Press of Kansas, 1990), 58; Gates, *Fifty Million Acres,* 3–4, 7.

42. Clifford E. Trafzer and Richard D. Scheuerman, *Renegade Tribe: The Palouse Indians and the Invasion of the Inland Pacific Northwest* (Pullman, Washington: Washington State University Press, 1986), 33, 40; Peter Nabokov, "Long Threads," in Alvin M. Josephy, Jr., ed., *The Native Americans: An Illustrated History* (Atlanta, Georgia: Turner Publishing, Inc., 1993), 315.

43. Robert M. Kvasnicka, "United States Treaties and Agreements," in Wilcomb Washburn, ed., *Handbook of North American Indians: History of Indian-White Relations*, Vol. 4 (Washington, D.C.: Smithsonian Institution, 1988), 200; Lt. Lawrence Kip, *Army Life on*

the Pacific: A Journal, at http://www.ccrh.org/comm/umatilla/primary/wallawal.htm; Clifford E. Trafzer, "The Legacy of the Walla Walla Council, 1855," *Oregon Historical Quarterly* Vol. 106, no. 3 (Fall 2005).

44. Trafzer and Scheuerman, *Renegade Tribe,* 51.

45. Ibid., 33, 40, 53; Nabokov, "Long Threads," in Josephy, Jr., ed., *The Native Americans,* 315.

46. Trafzer and Scheuerman, *Renegade Tribe*, 66.

47. Ibid., 68–69.

48. Ibid., 74.

49. Ibid., 71–74.

50. Annie Heloise Abel, *The American Indian and the End of the Confederacy 1863–1866* (Lincoln, Nebraska: University of Nebraska Press, 1993), reprinted from the original edition, *The American Indian Under Reconstruction* (Cleveland: Arthur H. Clark Company, 1925), 44.

51. David A. Nichols, *Lincoln and the Indians: Civil War Policy and Politics* (Columbia, Missouri: University of Missouri Press, 1978), 19, 21.

52. Ibid., 76; *Biographical Dictionary of the United States Congress, 1774–2005* (Washington, D.C.: Government Printing Office, 2005), 1779–80; Ralph K. Andrist, *The Long Death: The Last Days of the Plains Indian* (Norman, Oklahoma: University of Oklahoma Press, 1964), 29–30; http://www.mnhs.org/places/sites/arh/history.htm.

53. Nichols, *Lincoln and the Indians*, 76–77.

54. Ibid., 34–35; Andrist, *The Long Death*, 29–30.

55. Pope to Henry H. Sibley, 17 September 1862, quoted in Carol Chomsky, "The United States–Dakota War Trials: A Study in Military Injustice," *Stanford Law Review*, Vol. 43, no. 1

(November 1990), 22–23; Nichols, *Lincoln and the Indians*, 88.

56. Andrist, *The Long Death*, 61, 68.

57. Chomsky, "The United States–Dakota War Trials," 19, 22, 24, 28.

58. Ibid., 64; Nichols, *Lincoln and the Indians*, 98–103. One of the thirty-nine condemned men was pardoned. In the end, thirty-eight Dakotas went to the gallows in 1863.

59. Waziyatawin Angela Wilson, "Decolonizing the 1862 Death Marches," *American Indian Quarterly*, Vol. 28, nos. 1 & 2 (Winter/Spring 2004), 185.

60. Gary Clayton Anderson and Alan R. Woolworth, eds., *Through Dakota Eyes: Narrative Accounts of the Minnesota Indian War of 1862* (Minneapolis, Minnesota: Minnesota Historical Society Press, 1988), 1, 5–16, 228–29.

61. The Winnebago of Wisconsin recently changed their official name to the Hocak Nation (pronounced *Ho-chunk*).

62. Nichols, *Lincoln and the Indians*, 121–23; George Manypenny, *Our Indian Wards* (New York: Da Capo Press, 1974), 139–42.

63. Brenda Manuelito, "Manuelito," in Hoxie, ed., *Encyclopedia of North American Indians*, 356–57.

64. Nichols, *Lincoln and the Indians*, 165–66.

65. Ibid., 168.

66. Andrist, *The Long Death*, 74–77, 84.

67. Duane Schultz, *Month of the Freezing Moon: The Sand Creek Massacre, November 1864* (New York: St. Martin's Press, 1990), 1–2, 134; Andrist, *The Long Death*, 90.

68. Roy P. Basler, ed., *The Collected Work of Abraham Lincoln*, Vol. 6 (New Brunswick,

New Jersey: Rutgers University Press, 1953),
151–52.

69. Viola, *Diplomats in Buckskins,* 99.

70. President Abraham Lincoln, Third Annual
Message, December 8, 1863, John T. Woolley
and Gerhard Peters, *The American Presidency
Project* (Santa Barbara, California: University
of California), at http://www.presidency.ucsb.
edu/ws/?pid=29504.

71. Manypenny, *Our Indian Wards,* 158.

72. Nichols, *Lincoln and the Indians,* 141.

73. Ibid., 203–4.

74. Nabokov, "Long Threads," in Josephy, ed., *The
Native Americans, 316.*

75. Jean Edward Smith, *Grant* (New York: Simon
& Schuster, 2001), 522.

76. Colin Calloway, ed., *Our Hearts Fell to the
Ground: Plains Indian Views of How the West
Was Lost* (Boston: Bedford Books/St. Martin's
Press, 1996), 153–55; James C. Olson, "Red
Cloud," in Hoxie, ed., *Encyclopedia of North
American Indians,* 530–31; Katherine C.
Turner, *Red Men Calling on the Great White
Father* (Norman, Oklahoma: University of
Oklahoma Press, 1951), 120–21.

77. James C. Olson, *Red Cloud and the Sioux
Problem* (Lincoln, Nebraska: University of
Nebraska Press, 1965), 112–13.

CHAPTER III: DARK DAYS: AMERICAN PRESIDENTS AND NATIVE SOVEREIGNTY, 1880–1930

1. Dee Brown, *Bury My Heart at Wounded Knee:
An Indian History of the American West* (New
York: Bantam Books, Inc., 1970), 1,15.

2. Peter Nabokov, "Long Threads," in Alvin
Josephy, Jr., ed., *The Native Americans: An
Illustrated History* (Atlanta, Georgia: Turner
Publishing, Inc., 1993), 359.

3. Carolyn Gilman and Mary Jane Schneider, *The
Way to Independence: Memories of a Hidatsa
Indian Family, 1840–1920* (St. Paul, Minnesota:
Minnesota Historical Society, 1987), 158,
226–28, 232, 315; http://www.pbs.org/weta/
thewest/program/episodes/eight/tospeak.htm.

4. Herman Viola, *Diplomats in Buckskins: A
History of Indian Delegations in Washington
City* (Bluffton, South Carolina: Rivilo Books,
1995), 109; Catharine S. Fowler, "Sarah
Winnemucca," in Frederick E. Hoxie, ed.,
Encyclopedia of North American Indians
(Boston, Massachusetts: Houghton Mifflin,
1996), 684–85; http://www.aoc.gov/cc/art/nsh/
winnemucca.cfm.

5. *New York Times,* "For the Ponca Indians,"
December 13, 1879.

6. Nabokov, "Long Threads," in Josephy, ed., *The
Native Americans,* 359, 361.

7. Helen Hunt Jackson, *A Century of Dishonor:
The Classic Exposé of the Plight of the Native
Americans* (Mineola, New York: Dover
Publications, Inc., 2003).

8. Tom Holm, *The Great Confusion of Indian
Affairs: Native Americans and Whites in the
Progressive Era* (Austin, Texas: University of
Texas Press, 2005), 7.

9. John T. Woolley and Gerhard Peters, *The
American Presidency Project* (Santa Barbara,
California: University of California), at http://
www.presidency.ucsb.edu/ws/?pid=29522.

10. Nabokov, "Long Threads," in Josephy, ed., *The
Native Americans,* 368–69.

11. John J. Jenney, "The New Indian Law,"
Friends' Intelligencer, August 13, 1887, 524.

12. Clifford E. Trafzer, *As Long as the Grass Shall Grow and Rivers Flow: A History of Native Americans* (New York: Harcourt College Publishers, 2000), 330.

13. *Los Angeles Times*, "Washington Notes," October 14, 1888.

14. *New York Times*, "Indian Orators Heard," October 16, 1888.

15. Ibid.

16. *New York Times*, "The Sioux Reservation," October 18, 1888.

17. *Los Angeles Times*, "Washington Notes," October 21, 1888.

18. Stephen Cornell, *The Return of the Native: American Indian Political Resurgence* (New York: Oxford University Press, 1988), 62.

19. Alvin M. Josephy, Jr., *500 Nations: An Illustrated History of North American Indians* (New York: Alfred A. Knopf, Inc., 1994), 440, 441.

20. *New York Times*, "Col. Forsyth Exonerated," February 13, 1891.

21. Viola, *Diplomats in Buckskins:*, 92.

22. Quoted in William T. Hagen, *Roosevelt and Six Friends of the Indians* (Norman, Oklahoma: University of Oklahoma Press, 2002), 16–17.

23. Andrew Jackson, quoted in Trafzer, *As Long as the Grass Shall Grow,* 5.

24. Nabokov, "Long Threads," in Josephy, ed., *The Native Americans,* 368–69.

25. John T. Woolley and Gerhard Peters, *The American Presidency Project* (Santa Barbara, California: University of California), at http://www.presidency.ucsb.edu/ws/?pid=25826.

26. Ibid., at http://www.presidency.ucsb.edu/ws/?pid=29530.

27. *New York Times,* "The President to the Indians," May 15, 1895.

28. *Chicago Daily Tribune*, "Creek Treaty Signed," September 30, 1897.

29. Ibid.

30. David Wallace Adams, *Education for Extinction: American Indians and the Boarding School Experience, 1875–1928* (Lawrence, Kansas: University Press of Kansas, 1997), 97; Trafzer, *As Long as the Grass Shall Grow,* 288; "Carlisle Indian Industrial School," in Hoxie, ed., *Encyclopedia of North American Indians,* 101.

31. Robert W. Larson, *Red Cloud: Warrior Statesman of the Lakota Sioux* (Norman, Oklahoma: University of Oklahoma Press, 1999), 227.

32. George E. Hyde, *Spotted Tail's Folk: A History of the Brulé Sioux* (Norman, Oklahoma: University of Oklahoma Press, 1997), 318.

33. Ibid.

34. Ibid., 228.

35. *New York Times*, "Dissatisfied with Spotted Tail," July 21, 1880.

36. *New York Times*, "President Hayes' Tour," October 4, 1880.

37. Peter M. Whiteley, *Deliberate Acts: Changing Hopi Culture Through the Oraibi Split* (Tucson, Arizona: The University of Arizona Press, 1988), 42.

38. John D. Loftin, *Religion and Hopi Life in the Twentieth Century* (Indianapolis, Indiana: Indiana University Press, 1991), 72.

39. Leigh J. Kuwanwisiwma, "Hopi Face a New Millennium: 'Let Us Not Be Afraid,'" in *Thirst for Survival* (Second Mesa, Arizona: The Hopi Tribe and Ascend Media, 2005), 13.

40. Donald Eugene Miller, "The Limits of Schooling by Imposition: The Hopi Indians of Arizona" (Ph.D. thesis, University of Tennessee, Knoxville, 1987), 84; Kuwanwisiwma, "Hopi Face a New Millennium," 13.

41. Thomas Donaldson, *Moqui Pueblo Indians of Arizona* (Washington, D.C.: United States Census Printing Office, 1890), 56.

42. Ibid.

43. Bernard L. Fontana, "Historical Foundations," in Thomas Weaver, ed., *Indians of Arizona: A Contemporary Perspective* (Tucson, Arizona: University of Arizona Press, 1979), 36.

44. Interview with Lee Wayne Lomayestewa Shungopavi, Hopi Reservation, Arizona, March 23, 2006.

45. Ibid.

46. This interpretation was passed down to me by elders on the Hopi Reservation, in February 2004.

47. Harry C. James, *Pages from Hopi History* (Tucson, Arizona: University of Arizona Press, 1974), 138–39.

48. *New York Times*, "Indians at the Inaugural," February 3, 1905.

49. *Washington Post*, "Why Indians Are Sad," March 9, 1905.

50. *New York Times*, March 5, 1905; *Washington Post*, March 5, 1905; Herman Viola, *Diplomats in Buckskins*, 111–12.

51. One year earlier, the group of Sioux Indians had told Roosevelt that they would vote for him in the upcoming election, to which Roosevelt replied that he would give them a "square deal." When the Sioux returned to Yankton, they gathered some momentum for the presidential election and "swung the whole Indian vote to President Roosevelt."

52. *Geronimo's Story of His Life*, edited by S. M. Barrett (New York: Duffield & Co., 1906), 213–16; Arnold Krupat, ed., *Native American Autobiography: An Anthology* (Madison, Wisconsin: University of Wisconsin Press, 1994), 203–5; James Riding In, "Geronimo," in Hoxie, ed., *Encyclopedia of North American Indians*, 220–23.

53. Frederick E. Hoxie, "The Reservation Period, 1880–1960," in Bruce G. Trigger and Wilcomb Washburn, eds., *The Cambridge History of the Native Peoples of the Americas*, Vol. 1, North America, Part 2 (Cambridge, Massachusetts: Cambridge University Press, 1996), 220–21.

54. *Washington Post*, "Hear Indians' Plea," February 17, 1911.

55. Ibid.

56. Ibid.

57. A Hopi chief named Yukeoma, from the northeastern Arizona village of Hotevilla, did visit President Taft in 1911. See Katharine C. Turner, *Red Man Calling on the Great White Father* (Norman, Oklahoma: University of Oklahoma Press, 1951), 194–214.

58. *Washington Post*, "Wilson to the Indian," May 25, 1913; Alan Trachtenberg, *Shades of Hiawatha: Staging Indians, Making Americans, 1880–1930* (New York: Hill & Wang, 2005), 268–70.

59. *Washington Post*, "Real Indians Here to Aid Their Race," May 8, 1921.

60. Frederick E. Hoxie, *Talking Back to Civilization: Indian Voices from the Progressive Era* (Boston/New York: Bedford/St. Martins, 2001), 123–24, 133–38; Hoxie, *Parading*

Through History: The Making of the Crow Nation in America, 1805–1935 (Cambridge: Cambridge University Press, 1997), 264; Frederick E. Hoxie and Tim Bernardis, "Robert Yellowtail," in R. David Edmunds, ed., *The New Warriors: Native American Leaders Since 1900* (Lincoln, Nebraska: University of Nebraska Press, 2001), 64.

61. Albert Hurtado, Peter Iverson, and Thomas Paterson, eds., *Major Problems in American Indian History: Documents and Essays*, 2nd ed. (Boston: Houghton Mifflin Company, 2000), 383.

62. Frederick E. Hoxie, *Parading Through History*, 344–48.

CHAPTER IV: FROM FULL CITIZENSHIP TO SELF-DETERMINATION, 1930–1975

1. Lewis Meriam (technical director), *The Problem of Indian Administration* (Baltimore, Maryland: Johns Hopkins Press, 1928).

2. http://www.nps.gov/heho/historyculture/herbert-hoover.htm; "The Herbert Hoover Story," http://www.nps.gov/heho/forteachers/curriculummaterials.htm; Herbert Hoover, *The Memoirs of Herbert Hoover: The Cabinet and the Presidency 1920–1933* (New York: Macmillan, 1952), 317.

3. Hoover, *Memoirs*, 318.

4. Ibid. See also http://en.citizendium.org/wiki/Herbert_Hoover.

5. Hoover, *Memoirs*, 318. Herbert Hoover, *Public Papers of the Presidents of the United States 1930* (Washington, D.C.: U.S. Government Printing Office, 1976), 6; David Burner, "Herbert Hoover," at www.presidentprofiles.com/Grant-Eisenhower/Hoover-Herbert.html.

6. Hoover, *Memoirs*, 317; Hoover, *Papers, 1930*, 3, 6; Kenneth R. Philp, "Herbert Hoover's New Era: A False Dawn for the American Indians, 1929–1932," *Rocky Mountain Social Science Journal* 9 (April 1972), 53–60.

7. Hoover, *Memoirs*, 317.

8. Ibid; Hoover, *Public Papers of the Presidents of the United States, 1931* (Washington, D.C.: U.S. Government Printing Office, 1976), 58, 88, 99. Hoover vetoed legislation that compensated Indian nations for lost lands, arguing that land-claims bills were raids on the federal treasury. He also believed that present-day values should not be applied to Indian land-claims because the increased value of land was due to the work and investments of non-Indians. Ultimately, Hoover urged Congress to pass a comprehensive act enabling adjudication and settlement of Indian land claims. Congress passed such legislation in 1934, but Roosevelt vetoed the measure, preferring to fund programs for Indian communities as compensation for past wrongs. In 1946, President Harry S. Truman signed into law the Indian Claims Commission Act, which followed the philosophy and views of Hoover rather than Roosevelt. See Kenneth R. Philp, *Termination Revisited: American Indians on the Trail to Self-Determination, 1933–1953* (Lincoln, Nebraska: University of Nebraska Press, 1999), 19; John Fahey, *Saving the Reservation: Joe Garry and the Battle to Be Indian* (Seattle, Washington: University of Washington Press, 2001), 16.

9. Hoover, *Papers, 1931*, 88.

10. http://www.nps.gov/heho/forteachers/index.htm; www.answers.com/topic/charles-curtis;

William E. Unrau, *Mixed-Bloods and Tribal Dissolution: Charles Curtis and the Quest for Indian Identity* (Lawrence, Kansas: University Press of Kansas, 1989), 163–66.

11. Garrick Bailey and Roberta Glenn Bailey, "Will Rogers," in Frederick E. Hoxie, ed., *Encyclopedia of North American Indians* (Boston, Massachusetts: Houghton Mifflin, 1996), 555–57; "Welcome to the Writings of Will Rogers," Will Rogers Memorial Museum, http://www.willrogers.com/papers/intro.html; "Will Rogers' Biography," Official Site of Will Rogers, http://www.cmgww.com/historic/rogers/index.php.

12. Steven K. Gragert, *Will Rogers' Weekly Articles: The Hoover Years, 1931–33* (Stillwater, Oklahoma: Oklahoma State University Press, 1982), 65.

13. Will Rogers, *Radio Broadcasts of Will Rogers* (Stillwater, Oklahoma: Oklahoma State University Press, 1983), 66–67. I am indebted to Amy Ware for the "Bacon, Beans, and Limousines" information as well as the analysis in her forthcoming dissertation: "The Cherokee Kid: Will Rogers and the Tribal Genealogies of American Indian Celebrity" (unpublished doctoral dissertation, University of Texas, Austin, draft).

14. Gragert, ed., The *Hoover Years*, 214, 220.

15. Will Rogers, "Letter to Franklin D. Roosevelt Dated 1931," *Franklin D. Roosevelt Papers as Governor of New York*, "Rogers, Will" File, Franklin Delano Roosevelt Library, Hyde Park, New York; H. C. McSpadden, "Letter to Will Rogers from H. C., McSpadden, dated July 9, 1931," in *Franklin D. Roosevelt Papers as Governor of New York*, "Rogers,

Will" File, Franklin Delano Roosevelt Library, Hyde Park, New York. Warm Springs, Georgia, had an ancient history. Creek and other Indians believed the mineral waters had powers capable of treating serious injuries or illnesses. For Indians, a location that has healing powers is a sacred place. After European settlers moved into Georgia, they, too, discovered the waters and many availed themselves of treatment. By the early 1830s, a health resort was built by American settlers. In 1927, Roosevelt thought so highly of the place that he established the Georgia Warm Springs Foundation, a hospital for polio patients. The Roosevelt Warm Springs Institute for Rehabilitation became internationally known for working with a variety of disabilities.

16. Franklin D. Roosevelt, "Letter to Will Rogers," April 3, 1931, *Franklin D. Roosevelt Papers as Governor of New York*, "Rogers, Will" File, Franklin Delano Roosevelt Library, Hyde Park, New York.

17. Will Rogers, "Telegram to Governor Roosevelt," November 25, 1932, *Franklin D. Roosevelt Papers as Governor of New York*, "Rogers, Will" File, Franklin Delano Roosevelt Library, Hyde Park, New York.

18. Steven K. Gragert, *Will Rogers' Weekly Articles: The Roosevelt Years, 1933–35*, Vol. 6 (Stillwater, Oklahoma: Oklahoma State University Press, 1982), 6.

19. Bryan Sterling and Frances N. Sterling, *Will Rogers' World* (New York: M. Evans & Co, 1989), 172.

20. Samuel I. Rosenman (compiler), *The Public Papers and Addresses of Franklin D. Roosevelt,*

Vol. 2, The Year of Crisis (New York: Random House, 1938), 63.

21. See Kenneth R. Philp, *John Collier's Crusade for Indian Reform, 1920–1954* (Tucson, Arizona: University of Arizona Press, 1977).

22. Samuel I. Rosenman (compiler), "The Presidential Statement Endorsing the Wheeler-Howard Bill to Aid the Indians," *The Public Papers and Addresses of Franklin D. Roosevelt*, Vol. 3, The Advances of Recovery and Reform (New York: Random House, 1938), 202–3.

23. Rosenman, "Wheeler-Howard Bill," 203.

24. Roosevelt to Wickard, March 20, 1942, in John Collier, *From Every Zenith: A Memoir* (Denver, Colorado: Sage Books, 1963), 292–93; Vine Deloria, Jr. and David E. Wilkins, *Tribes, Treaties, and Constitutional Tribulations* (Austin, Texas: University of Texas Press, 2000), 36.

25. Quoted in Frederick E. Hoxie, "The Reservation Period, 1880–1960," in Bruce G. Trigger and Wilcomb E. Washburn, eds., *The Cambridge History of the Native Peoples of the Americas*, Vol. 1, North America, Part 2 (Cambridge, Massachusetts: Cambridge University Press, 1996), 229.

26. Ibid., 230.

27. Hoover, *Memoirs*, 318.

28. Ralph Keyes, *The Wit & Wisdom of Harry Truman: A Treasury of Quotations, Anecdotes, and Observations* (New York: Gramercy Books, 1995), 49.

29. Keyes, *Wit & Wisdom*, 104.

30. Dean J. Kotlowski, "Burying Sergeant Rice: Racial Justice and Native American Rights," *Journal of American Studies* 38 (August 2004), 199–225.

31. Cesar Ayala and Jennifer McCormick, "Felicita 'La Prieta' Mendez (1916–1998) and the End of Latino School Segregation in California," *Centro Journal* XX (Fall 2007), 19; Paul Rosier, "'They Are Ancestral Homelands': Race, Place, and Politics in Cold War Native America, 1945–1961," *Journal of American History* 92 (March 2006), 1300–26.

32. Philp, *Termination*, xii; Donald McCoy, *The Presidency of Harry S. Truman* (Lawrence, Kansas: The University Press of Kansas, 1984), 296; Hoover, *Memoirs*, 318; Richard S. Kirkendall, ed., *The Harry S. Truman Encyclopedia* (Boston, Massachusetts: G. K. Hall & Co, 1989), 47, 172.

33. Harry S. Truman, *Public Papers of the Presidents of the United States* (Washington, D.C.: U.S. Government Printing Office, 1962), 414–15.

34. William Pemberton, "Truman and the Hoover Commission," *Whistle Stop: The Newsletter of the Harry S. Truman Library Institute*, Vol. 19, no. 3 (1991), at http://www.trumanlibrary.org/hoover/commission.htm; Charles Wilkinson, *Blood Struggle: The Rise of Modern Indian Nations* (New York: W. W. Norton & Co., 2005), 64; Alvin M. Josephy, Jr., "Modern America and the Indian," in Frederick E. Hoxie and Peter Iverson, eds., *Indians in American History: An Introduction*, 2nd ed. (Wheeling, Illinois: Harlan Davidson, Inc., 1998), 206.

35. Kirkendall, *Encyclopedia*, 47, 172.

36. McCoy, *Presidency*, 106, 168, 296.

37. I paraphrase the story from Carlo D'Este, *Eisenhower: A Soldier's Life* (New York: Holt, 2003), 67–68; Alexander M. "Babe" Weyand,

"The Athletic Cadet Eisenhower," *Assembly* (Spring, 1968), Association of Graduates, United States Military Academy (USMA); Lars Anderson, *Carlisle vs. Army: Jim Thorpe, Dwight Eisenhower, Pop Warner, and the Forgotten Story of Football's Greatest Battle* (New York: Random House, 2007), 261, 285–92; www.nps.gov/eise/historyculture/index.htm.

38. Dwight D. Eisenhower, *Public Papers of the Presidents of the United States, 1953* (Washington, D.C.: U.S. Government Printing Office, 1960), 582.

39. Hoxie, "The Reservation Period, 1880–1960," 241.

40. Eisenhower, *Papers, 1953,* 564–65.

41. See Edward Charles Valandra, *Not Without Our Consent: Lakota Resistance to Termination, 1950–59* (Urbana, Illinois: University of Illinois, 2006); Charles Wilkinson, *Blood Struggle,* 19.

42. Dwight D. Eisenhower, *Public Papers of the Presidents of the United States, 1954* (Washington, D.C.: U.S. Government Printing Office, 1960), 582.

43. Wilkins, *Struggle,* 57–86; Fahey, *Battle,* 41; Hoxie, "The Reservation Period, 1880–1960," 241.

44. Fahey, *Reservation,* 19, 25; Richard Drinnon, *Keeper of the Concentration Camps: Dillon S. Myer and American Racism* (Berkeley, California: University of California Press, 1987); Clayton R. Koppes, "From New Deal to Termination: Liberalism and Indian Policy, 1933–1953," *Pacific Historical Review* 46 (November 1977), 543–66; Kathleen A. Dahl, "The Battle Over Termination on the Colville Indian Reservation," *American Indian Culture and Research Journal,* 18 (Winter 1994), 29–53.

45. Sasha Torres, *Living Color: Race and Television in the United States* (Durham, North Carolina: Duke University Press, 1998), 43; Thomas Cowager, " 'The Crossroads of Destiny': The NCAI's Landmark Struggle to Thwart Coercive Termination," *American Indian Culture and Research Journal* 20 (Fall 1996), 215–16; Rosier, "Cold War," 1300–26.

46. John Fahey, "Joseph Garry," in Hoxie, ed., *Encyclopedia of North American Indians,* 215–16.

47. Wilkins, *Struggle,* 178–82.

48. Joan Abalon, "The American Indian Chicago Conference," *Journal of American Education,* Vol 1, no. 2 (January 1962), 17–23; Nancy Lurie, "American Indian Chicago Conference," *Current Anthropology,* Vol. 2, no. 5 (1961), 478–500. A number of University of Chicago students and associates helped organize the Indian Chicago Conference, including Dr. Nancy Lurie, who acted as assistant coordinator, and anthropologists Joan Abalon, Albert Warhaftig, and Robert K. Thomas.

49. Vine Deloria, Jr., "Bob Thomas as Colleague," in *A Good Cherokee, A Good Anthropologist: Papers in Honor of Robert K. Thomas* (Los Angeles, California: UCLA American Indian Studies Center, 1998), 28; Albert Warhaftig, "Looking Back to Tahlequah: Robert K. Thomas' Role Among the Oklahoma Cherokee, 1963–1967," in ibid., 96–97. Helen Peterson paid a price for her participation in the Indian Chicago Conference. Some

tribal leaders thought the meeting was too socialistic, and Peterson lost her position as executive director in the next NCAI election.

50. Thomas Clarkin, *Federal Indian Policy in the Kennedy and Johnson Administrations, 1961–1969* (Albuquerque, New Mexico: University of New Mexico Press, 2001), 17–20.

51. Nancy Oestreich Lurie, "Sol Tax and Tribal Sovereignty," *Human Organization* (Spring 1999), 4; http://findarticles.com/p/articles/mi_qa3800/is_199904/ai_n8842482/pg_4.

52. *American Indian Conference*, University of Chicago, June 13–20, 1961, 5–6; http://www.digitalhistory.uh.edu/native_voices/voices_diplay.cfm?id=98.

53. Clarkin, *Kennedy and Johnson*, 17–20.

54. Lurie, "Tribal Sovereignty," 7; http://findarticles.com/p/articles/mi_qa3800/is_199904/ai_n8842482/pg_4.

55. Christine Bolt, *American Indian Policy: Case Studies of the Campaign to Assimilate the American Indians* (London: Unwin Hyman, 1987), 206; Lurie, "Tribal Sovereignty," 7; http://findarticles.com/p/articles/mi_qa3800/is_199904/ai_n8842482/pg_4.

56. John F. Kennedy, *Public Papers of the Presidents of the United States, 1962* (Washington, D.C.: U.S. Government Printing Office, 1963), 619.

57. Kennedy, *Papers*, 619.

58. Quoted in Frank Friedel and Hugh Sidey, *The Presidents of the United States of America* (London: Scala Publishers, 2006), 74.

59. Lyndon B. Johnson, *Public Papers of the Presidents of the United States, 1963–64.* (Washington, D.C: U.S. Government Printing Office, 1965), 149.

60. Alvin M. Josephy, Jr., "Bob Burnette," in Hoxie, ed., *Encyclopedia of North American Indians*, 88–90.

61. Deloria, "Colleague," 27–29.

62. Lyndon B. Johnson, "Remarks at the Swearing in of Robert L. Bennett as Commissioner of Indian Affairs," April 27, 1966, in John T. Wooley & Gehard Peters, *The American Presidency Project* (Santa Barbara, California: University of California at Santa Barbara), at http://www.presidency.ucsb.edu/ws/?pid=27563.

63. Wilcomb Washburn, "The Native American Renaissance, 1960 to 1995," in Trigger and Washburn, eds., *Cambridge History of the Native Peoples of the Americas,* Vol. 1, North America, Part 2 (Cambridge, England: Cambridge University Press, 1996), 430.

64. Helen Maynor Scheirbeck, "Status of Eastern Tribes." Paper presented at the American Indian Nations: Yesterday, Today, and Tomorrow Conference, Great Falls, Montana, July 2–4, 2005.

65. Kevin Washburn, "Tribal Self-Determination at the Crossroads," *Connecticut Law Review* 38 (May 2006), 777–96; Duane Champagne, "Organizational Change and Conflict: A Case Study of the Bureau of Indian Affairs," *American Indian Culture and Research Journal* 7 (Summer,1983), 3–28; Wilkins, *Struggle*, 189–99.

66. Lyndon B. Johnson, *Public Papers of the Presidents of the United States, 1968–69* (Washington, D.C.: U.S. Government Printing Office, 1970), 335.

67. Ibid., 337.

68. Ibid., 344.

69. Emma R. Gross, "Setting the Agenda for American Indian Policy Development, 1968–1980," in Jennie Joe, ed., *American Indian Policy and Cultural Values: Conflict and Accommodation* (Los Angeles, California: UCLA American Indian Studies Center, 1987), 56–57.

70. Jerry Reynolds, "Rating the Presidents: Richard M. Nixon," *Indian Country Today,* March 2, 2004.

71. Richard Nixon, *The Memoirs of Richard Nixon* (New York: Touchstone, 1978), 19–20; Richard Nixon, Letter to Wallace "Chief" Newman, March 17, 1980, La Casa Pacifica, San Clemente, California, reproduced in *The Chief: A Tribute to Wallace J. Newman* (Whittier, California: Office of Development, Whittier College, 1980), 5; Gross, "Agenda," 56–57.

72. Mel Rich, "Wallace J. Newman: A Brief Account of His Life," in *The Chief,* 13–15, 19–21. Newman returned to coach the Whittier baseball team from 1957 to 1964.

73. "Wallace J. Newman: A Retrospective," in ibid., 23.

74. Ibid., 24.

75. Ibid. In 1948, Coach Newman was in trouble with Whittier fans because he continued to play antiquated offensive football formations rather than moving to the then-popular T formation. More important, three consecutive defeats against archrival Occidental College had encouraged many Whittier fans to call for Newman's resignation. Ray Canton, a former Whittier football player, solicited support for Newman from United States congressman Richard Nixon, a former Whittier substitute tackle, and a member of the Whittier College Board of Trustees. "No one is going to fire Chief Newman," Nixon replied. Nixon's support for Newman inspired the team, which defeated Occidental 54–6 on their home field in Eagle Rock, California, the following season. Whittier again defeated Occidental in the 1950 football season, Newman's last as coach before retiring. In all, Whittier won 18 out of 20 games after Nixon spoke out in defense of Newman and captured the next two conference championships. See Ray Canton, "The Chief: Stand Up and Be Counted," in ibid., 51–52.

76. Amanda Keil, "The Peaceful People and the First Nations: A Brief History of Friends and Native Americans" (New York: American Friends Service Committee, 2001), 5–6; Nixon, *Memoir,* 8–20. Even today, many local Quaker communities organize efforts to preserve Native rights and share spiritual teachings and principles with Native communities.

77. Reynolds, "Nixon," 1.

78. Ibid.; Troy R. Johnson, *The Occupation of Alcatraz Island: Indian Self-Determination & the Rise of Indian Activism* (Urbana, Illinois: University of Illinois Press, 1996).

79. Richard Nixon, *Public Papers of the Presidents of the United States, 1970* (Washington, D.C.: U.S. Government Printing Office, 1971), 565.

80. Nixon, *Papers, 1970,* 565–66.

81. Ibid., 566.

82. Troy Johnson, *Red Power: The Native American Civil Rights Movement* (New York: Chelsea House Publications, 2007).

83. Peter Nabokov, *Where the Lightning Strikes: The Lives of American Indian Sacred Places*

(New York: Viking, 2006), 73–81; Leonard Garment, *Crazy Rhythm: From Brooklyn and Jazz to Nixon's White House, Watergate, and Beyond* (New York: Da Capo, 2001), 226; Duane Champagne, *Native America: Portrait of the Peoples* (Detroit, Michigan: Visible Ink, 1994), 147.

84. Nixon, *Papers, 1970,* 567–73.

85. Nixon, *Papers, 1970,* 575.

CHAPTER V: THE ERA OF SELF-DETERMINATION: 1975–TODAY

1. Bob Green, *Fraternity: A Journey in Search of Five Presidents* (New York: Crown, 2004), 32.

2. Ibid., 88–89.

3. Ibid., 89. Garment resigned from the Ford administration in December 1974, leaving Bradley Patterson, Jr., as President Ford's Native American specialist.

4. Bradley H. Patterson, Jr., Remarks at Senate Indian Affairs Briefing, "The Enduring Validity of Indian Self-Determination," U.S. Committee on Indian Affairs, Briefing Booklet, January 11, 1999, at http://www.senate.gov/~scia/106brfs/selfd.htm.

5. Author phone interview with Bradley Patterson, Jr., Washington D.C., March 1993.

6. John T. Woolley and Gerhard Peters, *The American Presidency Project* [online], Santa Barbara, California: University of California (hosted), Gerhard Peters (database). http://www.presidency.ucsb.edu/ws/?pid=4518 (cited henceforth as *The American Presidency Project*).

7. U.S. Congress, *Treaty with the Sioux—Brulé, Oglala, Miniconjou, Yanktonai, Hunkpapa, Blackfeet, Cuthead, Two Kettle, Sans Arcs,* *and Santee and Arapaho, 1868* (Treaty of Fort Laramie, 1868). Ratified February 16, 1868; proclaimed February 24, 1868.

8. *Sioux Tribe v. United States*, 316 U.S. 317 (1942), at http://laws.findlaw.com/us/316/317.html.

9. Ibid.

10. *The American Presidency Project*: President Gerald R Ford. "Statement on Signing Indian Claims Commission Appropriations Legislation," October 29, 1974, at http://www.presidency.ucsb.edu/ws/index.php?pid=4518&st=indian+claims+commission&st1=.

11. Bradley Patterson, *The Ring of Power: The White House Staff and Its Expanding Role in Government* (New York: Basic Books, 1998), 224–25.

12. Canada, Department of Indian Affairs, *Annual Report*, 1885.

13. Dean J. Kotlowski, "Alcatraz, Wounded Knee, and Beyond: The Nixon and Ford Administrations Respond," *The Pacific Historical Review*, Vol. 72, no. 2 (May 2003), 223.

14. Ibid.

15. *The American Presidency Project*: President Gerald R. Ford. "Statement on Signing the Indian Self-Determination and Education Assistance Act," January 4, 1975, at http://www.presidency.ucsb.edu/ws/index.php?pid=4739&st=&st1=.

16. George Castile, *Taking Charge: Native American Self-Determination and Federal Indian Policy, 1975–1993* (Tucson, Arizona: University of Arizona Press, 2006), 17.

17. Ibid., 18.

18. Ibid., 20.

19. Patterson, *The Ring of Power,* 131–32. Hamilton Jordan, former chief of staff for President Carter, felt that the administration gave cabinet officers too much latitude in selecting appointees, resulting in an administration staffed by people who did not share or necessarily understand the direction and actions that the administration wanted to take on specific issues such as Indian affairs. See ibid., 132.

20. Castile, *Taking Charge,* 27–33.

21. U.S. Senate Committee on Indian Affairs, *History of the Committee on Indian Affairs,* at http://Indian.senate.gov/cominfo.htm.

22. *The American Presidency Project:* President Jimmy Carter. State of the Union Message, January 19, 1978, at http://www.presidency.ucsb.edu/ws/index.php?pid=30856.

23. *The American Presidency Project:* President Jimmy Carter. "Maine Indian Claims Settlement Act of 1980," House Resolution 7919, at http://www.presidency.ucsb.edu/ws/index.php?pid=45264. It is interesting to note that Matthews, the speechwriter, also served on the President's Reorganization Project, which distanced the president from direct handling of Indian issues.

24. The change was not a presidential initiative but the result of an ongoing legislative process, slowly making its way through two previous presidencies. The move was not supported by influential Indian groups, such as the National Congress of American Indians (NCAI), which viewed it as a precursor to the abolition of the Bureau of Indian Affairs.

25. Quoted in Lane Ambrose, Sr., *Return of the Buffalo: The Story Behind America's Indian Gaming Explosion* (Westport, Connecticut: Greenwood Publishing Group, 1995), 13–14.

26. *The American Presidency Project:* President Jimmy Carter. Deloria to Carter, Washington, D.C., April 13, 1978, at http://www.presidency.ucsb.edu/ws/index.php?month=&year=1978.

27. *The American Presidency Project:* President Jimmy Carter. Harris to Carter, Washington, D. C., April 6, 1978, at http://www.presidency.ucsb.edu/ws/index.php?month=&year=1978. Carter's domestic affairs advisor Stuart Eizenstat informed Kathy Fletcher, assistant director of the White House domestic policy staff, that the administration had decided not to make a formal presidential Indian policy statement. See, ibid., Eizenstat to Fletcher, Washington, D.C., April 21, 1978, at http://www.presidency.ucsb.edu/ws/index.php?month=&year=1978.

28. *The American Presidency Project:* President Jimmy Carter. State of the Union Message, January 19, 1979, at http://www.presidency.ucsb.edu/ws/index.php?pid=32657.

29. Charles Wilkinson, *Blood Struggle: The Rise of Modern Indian Nations* (New York: W. W. Norton & Co., 2005), 220–30; Duane Champagne, *Native America: Portrait of the Peoples* (Detroit, Michigan: Visible Ink, 1994), 67–69; Dean J. Kotlowski, "Alcatraz, Wounded Knee, and Beyond: The Nixon and Ford Administrations Respond to Native American Protest," *Pacific Historical Review* 72, no. 2 (May 2003), 224.

30. Castile, *Taking Charge,* 106–07.

31. *The American Presidency Project:* President Jimmy Carter. "American Indian Religious

Freedom—Statement on Signing S.J. Res. 102 Into Law," August 12, 1978, at http://www.presidency.ucsb.edu/ws/index.php?pid=31173&st=american+indian+religious+freedom&st1.

32. *Lyng v. Northwest Indian Cemetery Protective Association*, 485 U.S. 439 (1988), at http://laws.findlaw.com/us/485/439.html.

33. Cecil Andrus interview with President James Earl Carter, quoted in Green, *Fraternity*, 104.

34. *Winters v. United States*, 207 U.S. 564 (1908), at http://laws.findlaw.com/us/207/564.html.

35. *The American Presidency Project:* President Jimmy Carter. Harris to Carter, Washington, D.C., October 1978, at http://www.presidency.ucsb.edu/ws/index.php?month=&year=1978.

36. *New York Times,* "Moscow Summit: Remarks on 'Humoring' Indians Brings Protests from Tribal Leaders," May 19, 1988.

37. Ibid.

38. *New York Times,* "Indian Hike to Reagan Ranch," August 22, 1988.

39. Brad Agnew, "Wilma Mankiller," in R. David Edmunds, ed., *The New Warriors: Native American Leaders Since 1900* (Lincoln, Nebraska: University of Nebraska Press, 2001), 211–12, 219–21, 226–29.

40. *Public Papers of President Ronald W. Reagan,* Ronald Reagan Presidential Library. "Statement by Assistant to the President for Press Relations Fitzwater on the President's Meeting with American Indian Leaders," December 12, 1988, at http://www.reagan.utexas.edu/archives/speeches/1988/121288a.htm.

41. Reagan began his efforts to recognize government-to-government relations by shifting the White House liaison to Native Americans from the Office of Public Liaison to the Office of International Relations. Reagan also appointed an American Indian representative to the Advisory Commission on Intergovernmental Relations. According to Assistant Interior Secretary Kenneth L. Smith (Warm Springs Wascoe), the philosophical thrust of the president's Indian message was based on the president's campaign pledges along with the administration's overall goal for the nation.

42. Samuel R. Cook, "Ronald Reagan's Indian Policy in Retrospect: Economic Crisis and Political Irony," *Policy Studies Journal*, Vol. 24 (1996).

43. Ibid.

44. Peter Iverson, "Peter MacDonald," in R. David Edmunds, *American Indian Leaders: Studies in Diversity* (Lincoln, Nebraska: University of Nebraska Press, 1980), 223–32, 235–39; Mark N. Trahant, "The 1970s: New Leaders for Indian Country," in Frederick E. Hoxie and Peter Iverson, eds., *Indians in American History: An Introduction,* 2nd ed. (Wheeling, Illinois: Harlan Davidson, Inc., 1998), 246–49; Wilcomb E. Washburn, "The Native American Renaissance, 1960–1995," in Bruce G. Trigger and Wilcomb E. Washburn, eds., *The Cambridge History of the Native Peoples of the Americas,* Vol. 1, North America, Part 2 (Cambridge, Massachusetts: Cambridge University Press, 1996), 410; "MacDonald Applies for City Job," *Gallup Independent* (web edition), August 6, 2005, at http://www.gallupindependent.com/2005/august/080605macdonald.html; "Navajo Leader Faces Fraud Suit in Arizona Court,"

New York Times, January 28, 1990, at http://query.nytimes.com/gst/fullpage.html?res=9C0CE2DE153AF93BA15752C0A96695826; Joan Hoff, "Re-evaluating Richard Nixon: His Domestic Achievements," The Nixon Era Center, Mountain State University, at http://www.nixonera.com/library/domestic.asp#note14.

45. Ibid.

46. LaDonna Harris, *A Comanche Life* (Lincoln, Nebraska: University of Nebraska Press, 2000), 133.

47. Ibid.

48. *Public Papers of President Ronald W. Reagan.* Ronald Reagan Presidential Library. "Statement on Indian Policy," January 24, 1983, at http://www.reagan.utexas.edu/archives/speeches/1983/12483b.htm.

49. Castile, *Taking Charge,* 47.

50. Ibid., 34–35.

51. Ibid., 65–66.

52. *Public Papers of President Ronald W. Reagan,* 1986–1988, Ronald Reagan Presidential Library. "Presidential Proclamations, Executive Orders, and Statements," at http://www.reagan.utexas.edu/search/speeches/speech_srch.html.

53. Castile, *Taking Charge,* 62–66, 73–76, 98–99.

54. Bradley H. Patterson, Jr., *The White House Staff* (Washington, D.C: Brookings Institution Press, 2000), 302.

55. Herbert S. Parmet, *George Bush: The Life of a Lone Star Yankee* (New Brunswick, New Jersey: Transaction Publishers, 2000), 104.

56. Gary C. Anderson, "LaDonna Harris," in R. David Edmunds, ed., *The New Warriors: Native American Leaders Since 1900* (Lincoln,

Nebraska: University of Nebraska Press, 2001), 123–27, 137–140.

57. *Public Papers of the Presidents:* George H. W. Bush. Office of the Federal Register, at http://www.gpoaccess.gov/pubpapers/search.html.

58. Public Law 101–477, *Native American Languages Act of 1990,* October 30, 1990.

59. *Public Papers of the Presidents:* George H. W. Bush. Office of the Federal Register, Weekly Press Document, March 2, 1992, at http://www.gpoaccess.gov/pubpapers/search.html, 384.

60. Bob Reece, "The Story of the Indian Memorial." Friends of the Little Bighorn Battlefield, at http://www.friendslittlebighorn.com/Indian%20Memorial.htm.

61. "Chronology of Little Big Horn Battlefield," at http://www.sisterwolf.com/sculpture/history.html.

62. *Public Papers of the Presidents:* George H. W. Bush. 1992: 1023, 1161, 1193, 1471–73, 1478, at http://frwebgate4.access.gpo.gov/cgi-bin/waisgate.cgi?WAISdocID=801232267242+2+0+0&WAISaction=retrieve.

63. Patterson, *The White House Staff,* 302.

64. United States Department of the Interior, Department of Interior Press Release, January 9, 1997.

65. White House Press Release, March 23, 1994. The invitation was intended to convey the respect Clinton held for Native Americans, a respect he had begun to show prior to his presidency. As a presidential nominee, Clinton made a determined effort to include Native Americans in his presidential campaign, and worked with sixty Native American delegates who

attended the 1992 Democratic National Convention. Kevin Gover (Comanche-Pawnee) was among those who led an energetic registration drive that resulted in President Clinton receiving approximately sixty percent of the Indian vote. In return for the Native American vote, and to assuage Native fears that he would cut the budget for the Indian Health Service, President Clinton invited the leaders of the 556 federally recognized tribes to meet with him at the White House.

66. *Public Papers of the Presidents:* William J. Clinton. "Statement Announcing a Meeting with Native American Leaders," March 23, 1994, 541, at http://frwebgate4.access.gpo.gov/cgi-bin/waisgate.cgi?WAISdocID=801806269762+9+0+0&WAISaction=retrieve.

67. Clara Sue Kidwell, "Ada Deer/Menominee," in Edmunds, ed., *The New Warriors*, 249–57; Hoxie, "The Reservation Period," in Trigger and Washburn, eds., *The Cambridge History of the Native Peoples of the Americas*, 233.

68. *Public Papers of the Presidents:* William J. Clinton. "Remarks to Native American and Native Alaska Tribal Leaders," April 29, 1994, at http://frwebgate.access.gpo.gov/cgi-bin/getpage.cgi?dbname=1994_public_papers_vol1_misc&page=800&position=all. Other tribal leaders in attendance included Richard "Skip" Hayward (Pequot); Peterson Zah (chairman, Navajo Nation); Larry Nuckolls (Absentee Shawnee Tribe); Ferrell Secakuku (chairman, Hopi Nation); Truman Carter (Sac and Fox Nations); and Richard Malonovich (Agua Caliente Band of Cahuilla Indians).

69. Ibid.

70. United States Department of Housing and Urban Development, Tribal Consultation Chronology. Washington, D.C., April 29, 1994. The memorandum was formalized and reissued as an Executive Order on May 14, 1998, and again on November 6, 2000.

71. Government Services Agency, Washington, D.C., Administrative Memorandum 1072.1. "General Services Administration Policy toward American Indians," April 1994. The memorandum stated that the Government Services Administration "will accommodate, to the extent practicable and consistent with security, and operational requirements, Indian tribal access to sacred sites and off-reservation treaty fishing, hunting, and gathering sites located on land or property managed by the Government Services Administration. The GSA will develop Indian tribal specific protocols to protect, to the maximum extent practicable and consistent with the Freedom of Information Act, Privacy Act, National Historic Preservation Act, Archeological Resources Protection Act, and other applicable law Indian tribal information regarding protected Indian tribal trust resources that has been disclosed to, or collected by, GSA."

72. Prior to the Passage of Public Law 103–413, only thirty tribes had self-governance status. As of the date of this publication, more than 300 tribes now enjoy that autonomy. Public Law 103–413, Self-Determination Act Amendments, Title I and Self-Governance Permanent Authorization, Title II were the culmination of nearly two years of congressional hearings that brought together various past attempts to address the economic future of Native nations. These

included S550, the Tribal Self-Governance Demonstration Technical Amendments Bill of April 1993; JR 3508, the Tribal Self-Governance Act of 1994; S1618, the Tribal Self-Governance Act of 1993; HR 4842, the Indian Self-Determination Act Amendments of October 1994; Title I–ISD, the Contract Reform Act of 1994; and Title II, the Tribal Self-Governance Act of 1994.

73. David E. Wilkins, *American Indian Politics and the American Political System* (Lanham, Maryland: Rowman & Littlefield Publishers, Inc., 2002), 85, 102. Bush contended that the casino violated the state's anti-gambling laws. The Tigua Tribe's slot machines were similar to the Texas-run lottery games that used computers to randomly generate numbers for players, much like gaming machines in use in other state casinos.

74. Valerie Tailman, "Native Nations and the Politics of 2000," *Native Americas*, Vol. 17, no. 3 (2001), 27.

75. *Kaiser Daily Health Report*, at http://www.kaisernetwork.org.

76. United States Department of the Interior. Office of the Assistant Secretary-Indian Affairs. Office of Public Affairs, November 2001. Presidents Nixon, Reagan, George H. W. Bush, and Clinton had all designated November of each year as National American Indian Heritage Month.

77. *Public Papers of the Presidents*: George W. Bush. November 23, 2004.

78. The White House, Washington, D.C. "Memorandum for the Heads of Executive Departments and Agencies," September 23, 2004.

79. *Seattle Post-Intelligencer Reporter*, "Bush's Comment on Tribal Sovereignty Creates a Buzz," August 13, 2004.

80. Ibid.

81. White House Press Release, Washington, D.C. "President Signs Indian Education Executive Order," April 30, 2004.

82. United States Committee on Natural Resources, Washington, D.C. "Bush Budget Fails Indian Country Yet Again," February 5, 2008.

83. Office of Management and Budget, Washington, D.C. *Budget of the United States Government 2009*, February 4, 2008.

84. United States Committee on Natural Resources, "Bush Budget Fails Indian Country Yet Again." Senate Indian Affairs Committee Chair Byron Dorgan stated that, in 2008, he would ask for an additional $1 billion in Indian Health Service funding when the Senate considers President Bush's budget proposal.

85. White House Press Release, Washington, D.C. "President Bush Attends Medal of Honor Ceremony for Woodrow Wilson Keeble," March 3, 2008.

86. United States Department of Defense. American Forces Press Service News Release, March 3, 2008.

87. Quoted in Kenneth R. Philp, ed., *Indian Self-Rule: First-Hand Accounts of Indian-White Relationships from Roosevelt to Reagan* (Logan, Utah: Utah State University Press, 1995), 92.

FURTHER READING

Brinkley, Alan and Davis Dyer, eds., *The American Presidency*. New York: Houghton Mifflin, 2004.

Calloway, Colin. *The Shawnees and the War for America*. New York: Penguin, 2008.

Deloria, Vine, Jr., and David E. Wilkins. *Tribes, Treaties, and Constitutional Tribulations*. Austin, Texas: University of Texas Press, 2000.

Edmunds, David R., ed. *The New Warriors: Native American Leaders Since 1900*. Lincoln, Nebraska: University of Nebraska Press, 2001.

———. *Tecumseh and the Quest for Indian Leadership*. 2nd ed., New York: Pearson Longman, 2006.

Fixico, Donald L. *Termination and Relocation: Federal Indian Policy, 1945–1960*. Albuquerque, New Mexico: University of New Mexico Press, 1990.

Gould, Lewis L. *The Modern American Presidency*. Lawrence, Kansas: University of Kansas Press, 2004.

Hoxie, Frederick E. *A Final Promise: The Campaign to Assimilate the Indians, 1880–1920*. Lincoln, Nebraska: University of Nebraska Press, 2001.

———, ed., *Encyclopedia of North American Indians: Native American History, Culture, and Life From Paleo-Indians to the Present*. Boston, Massachusetts: Houghton Mifflin Co., 1996.

Prucha, Francis Paul. *American Indian Treaties: The History of a Political Anomaly*. Berkeley, California: University of California Press, 1994.

Richter, Daniel K. *Facing East from Indian Country: A Native History of Early America*. Cambridge, Massachusetts: Harvard University Press, 2003.

Viola, Herman J. *Diplomats in Buckskins: A History of Indian Delegations in Washington City*. Bluffton, South Carolina: Rivilo Books, 1995.

Wallace, Anthony F. C. *Jefferson and the Indians: The Tragic Fate of the First Americans*. Cambridge, Massachusetts: Harvard University Press, 1999.

Wilkins, David E., and K. Tsianina Lomawaima. *Uneven Ground: American Indian Sovereignty and Federal Law*. Norman, Oklahoma: University of Oklahoma Press, 2002.

Wilkinson, Charles. *Blood Struggle: The Rise of Modern Indian Nations*. New York: W. W. Norton & Co., 2005.

INDEX

CONTRIBUTORS

CLIFFORD E. TRAFZER (of Wyandot ancestry) is the Rupert Costo Chair of American Indian Affairs and professor of history at the University of California, Riverside. He is the author of numerous books and articles, including (with Gerald McMaster) *Native Universe: Voices of Indian America* (2004), and *As Long as the Grass Shall Grow and Rivers Flow: A History of Native Americans* (2000).

ROBERT W. VENABLES taught in the American Indian Program and Cultural Landscapes Program at Cornell University from 1988 until his retirement in 2007. His many publications include the two-volume *American Indian History: Five Centuries of Conflict and Coexistence* (2004).

DONNA AKERS (Choctaw) is an associate professor of history and ethnic studies at the University of Nebraska, Lincoln. She is the author of *Living in the Land of Death: The Choctaw People, 1830–1860* (2004).

MATTHEW SAKIESTEWA GILBERT (Hopi) is from the village of Upper Moencopi, in northeastern Arizona. He is an assistant professor of American Indian studies and history at the University of Illinois, Urbana-Champaign, and is currently completing a book entitled *Education Beyond the Mesas: Hopi Student Involvement at Sherman Institute, 1902–1929*.

DUANE CHAMPAGNE (Turtle Mountain Band of Chippewa, North Dakota) is a professor of sociology and American Indian studies at the University of California, Los Angeles. He is the author and/or editor of more than 125 publications, including, most recently, *Social Change and Cultural Continuity Among Native Nations* (2007).

TROY JOHNSON is the chair of American Indian studies at California State University, Long Beach. He is the author of numerous books and articles on Native American history, including *The Occupation of Alcatraz Island: Indian Self-Determination and the Rise of Indian Activism* (1996).

MARK G. HIRSCH, author and editor of the sidebars for *American Indians/American Presidents,* is a historian and writer at the National Museum of the American Indian. Coauthor of *The American Presidency: A Glorious Burden* (Smithsonian Institution Press, 2000) and a regular contributor to *American Indian* magazine, he has edited numerous books on American and Native American history.